C0-AQX-862

Computer Mediated Communication and the Online Classroom

Volume Two: Higher Education

Edited by

Marie Collins
Pennsylvania State University
Zane L. Berge
Georgetown University

HAMPTON PRESS, INC.
CRESSKILL, NEW JERSEY

Printed in the United States of America

Library of Congress Cataloging-in-Publication Data

Computer mediated communication and the online classroom / edited by
Zane L. Berge and Mauri P. Collins.
p. cm.
Includes bibliographical references (p.) and index.
Contents: v. 1. An overview and prerspectives -- v. 2. Higher education -- v. 3. Distance learning.
ISBN 1-881303-10-1 (v. 2). -- ISBN 1-881303-11-X (pbk. : v. 2)
1. Educational technology. 2. Computer-asisted instruction. 3. Distance education. 4. Interactive media. I. Berge, Zane L. II. Collins, Mauri P.
LB1028.3.C6396 1995
371.3'078--dc20

94-23868
CIP

Hampton Press, Inc.
23 Broadway
Cresskill, NJ 07626

CONTENTS

Preface v
About the Contributors ix

Introduction: Computer-Mediated Communications and the Online Classroom in Higher Education
Mauri Collins and Zane Berge 1

1. **Designing Computer-Mediated Conferencing into Instruction**
Robert Nalley 11

2. **The Network-Based Writing Classroom: The ENFI Idea**
Michael Day and Trent Batson 25

3. **Patterns of Social Interaction and Learning to Write: Some Effects of Network Technologies**
Karen Hartman, Christine M. Neuwirth, Sara Kiesler, Lee Sproull, Cynthia Cochran, Michael Palmquist, and David Zubrow 47

4. **Computers and Urban Commuters in an Introductory Literature Class**
Helen Schwartz 79

5. **Collaborative Investigation Online: Eighteenth-Century Literature Moves to the Computer Lab**
Russell A. Hunt 93

6. **NEOs and the Development of the Electronic Classroom at MIT**
Edward Barrett 111

7. **Computer-Mediated Communications Applications in Selected Psychology and Political Science Courses**
Cecilia G. Manrique and Harry W. Gardiner 123

8. Computer-Mediated Teacher Induction
Ted J. Singletary and Holly Anderson 137

9. Computer-Mediated Communication in Medical Education
Karen E. Bruce 153

10. Online Training for Online Information Retrieval Systems
Gail S. Thomas 167

11. Networks and Networking
Mauri Collins 179

Glossary 191
Author Index 203
Subject Index 207

Preface

Editing the books in this series has been a new experience for us. We "met" online via the Internet while Mauri Collins was living in Las Vegas, NV, and Zane Berge in Springfield, VA. Collins was among the first 100 subscribers to IPCT-L (for which we thank Patty Crossett for her inspiration). Berge set up the LISTSERV discussion group, "Interpersonal Computing and Technology" (IPCT-L@GUVM), at Georgetown University in February 1992. We did not meet face-to-face until shortly before the first editorial board meeting in Pennsylvania, where the final selections from among the proposals were made. Since then we have spent countless hours together online, reading, editing, discussing, revising, and writing.

In Spring 1992 a debate was raging on IPCT-L, sparked by one contributor who asked how access to and use of computer-mediated communication in and out of the classroom could be justified to administration. As the contributor pointed out, CMC consumes computing time and resources, the connection to regional and national networks is expensive, and in these days of budget constraints and restraints, it is becoming increasingly necessary to justify such expenses to administrators.

Our discussion centered on the value to students, staff, and faculty of open access to the Internet from educational institutions. The Internet is an open communication channel that allows for free and open expressions in ways that are sometimes vulgar and profane and, at first glance, may not appear to contribute anything to the academic process. The contributor pointed out that this kind of discourse was not something that could be pointed to during the budgetary process as adequate reason to continue to pay the connection and usage charges that allow faculty and students free access to both internal and external resources.

Many members of the list responded to this challenge and pointed to benefits they had realized, both in terms of classroom accomplishment and personal and scholarly growth—their free access to many and diverse resources including local, national and international libraries and databases; and the colleagues they had "met" via CMC and with whom they subsequently collaborated—all attributed to their access to networked computers.

Another contributor, Dr. Gerald Phillips, Emeritus Professor of Speech Communication at the Pennsylvania State University, suggested that, although administrators might be unable or reluctant to follow our networked discussion, they do understand documentation and that list members should get together and write a grant to research the scholarly uses of electronic mail with Berge and Collins (the IPCT-L moderators) as leaders in this effort. He also mentioned in the same message that a book might even emerge from this effort.

After some extended discussion, we (Berge, Collins, and Phillips) decided that, although a research project might be beyond our scope, a book on computer-mediated communication would be feasible. Very early on, we settled on *Computer-Mediated Communication and the Online Classroom* as the title and determined that the desired content was to be examples of the uses of CMC in teaching and learning, written in such a way as to provide exemplars for those who are searching for ways to integrate CMC into their own classrooms and to justify continued support of network access to administrators. We contacted Hampton Press with our idea, and they expressed sufficient interest to ask us to submit a book proposal.

A call for chapters, distributed only through IPCT-L and a number of other electronic discussion group lists, brought us 93 chapter proposals via electronic mail. These were forwarded, again via electronic mail, for blind review, and then reviewed once more by our editorial board at their first face-to-face meeting in June 1992. Thirty-five of these proposals were finally accepted (with three subsequently dropping out) and notices sent.

To ease the distribution of common materials (e.g., the table of contents, instructions to authors, etc.), the editors set up a private listserv discussion group and subscribed all the authors and co-authors, the editors, and the editorial board. This allowed rapid dissemination of information and gave the authors and the editors a forum for discussion, suggestions, and questions. However, chapters were not posted for general critique to the list, although some authors did share drafts with one another. Only the two chapters considered critical to the content of the other chapters were posted. These were Santoro's introductory chapter on computer-mediated communications, and Sudweeks, Collins, and December's chapter on internetworking resources. We posted these chapters so that the other authors could reference them, instead of re-explaining, for example, some of the basic file retrieval tools.

The initial "Instructions to Authors" detailed a time line for drafts and revisions, with all drafts being sent and returned via electronic mail. Through all subsequent revisions, the drafts were edited online using an evolving set of "copy-editing symbols" and returned to the authors. It was not until the final revisions had been accepted that the authors sent in hardcopy and disks.

It became evident that the book, as originally planned, would run in excess of 500 pages. After some discussions and a look at the "natural breaks" in the subject areas, we proposed to the publisher that there be three books, not one. After some deliberation, the one book did become three with the series title: *CMC and the Online Classroom*. The three volumes are "CMC and the Online Classroom: An Overview and Perspectives," "CMC and the Online Classroom: Higher Education," and "CMC and the Online Classroom: Distance Learning."

Toward the end of the process, we asked the authors if they had been involved in any similar publishing efforts, in which all text, up to the final hard copy, was handled via electronic mail, and what their reactions were to the process. Reactions were mixed. Some of those who replied were evidently pleased with the system we had developed, the access the listserv provided to the other authors, and the speed at which their queries were responded to. One chapter was written by authors residing in Australia, Singapore, and the United States, who collaborated using electronic mail, and the Sudweeks's chapter made the round trip from the eastern United States to Sydney, Australia no less than six times on one particular day. Several authors remarked on how different and harsh it felt to see the editor's comments, in capital letters, on the screen, even though they were used to editorial commentary on paper.

The most consistent request for a change in process was for a more comprehensive table of contents, and for chapters be made available online for general discussion. We decided not to do this because, with the number of authors involved, we felt it would be very time consuming for all concerned. Many of the authors commented that the amount and speed of information and feedback flow helped them significantly in drafting their chapters; they could ask questions and get help from the editors or other authors in a most timely manner.

Among the editors, publisher, authors, or potential authors, there were over 1,200 email messages, exchanges of drafts, or postings in relation to this set of books, in the first year or the project (with hundreds more since then). This figure excludes the information exchanged privately among authors and some "broadcast" announcements to the 50+ authors, editors, and publisher. Without question, that amount of information and feedback could not have been exchanged via traditional mail in that time frame. One author noted that our process allowed us to exchange a quantity of information that otherwise would have been too time consuming using other communication channels. He continued by saying that he did not take as much advantage of the potential as he might have and concluded that we have come a long way down the line in bringing the editing process online, "but it seems to me . . . that there's a long road out there yet." We agree.

This set of volumes is perhaps the first to be electronically coordinated and edited online from start to finish. The concept was suggested, conceptualized, announced, accepted, drafted, edited, redrafted several times, and made ready for delivery to the publisher online. Was all the work worth it? It certainly was from the perspective of the authors and editors. In the final analysis, however, how well we have travelled this road is to be answered by our readers.

Dr. Gerald Phillips, Emeritus Professor of Speech Communication, Penn State University and book editor for Hampton Press, deserves a great deal of the credit (and none of the blame) for this book. He instigated the initial discussions on IPCT-L, suggested the book, put the editor's names together in the same sentence for the first time, and provided us with invaluable encouragement, guidance, and advice. Gerry Santoro has been an inexhaustible source of technical information, and Brad Erlwein assisted in the original selection of the manuscripts. Mark Evangelistia has patiently helped us set up and keep the Listserv lists functioning. Both the Academic Computer Center at Georgetown University and the Center for Academic Computing at Penn State University have been generous with their computer resources. Michael Day served as our "editor's editor," and we thank him for his stylistic and substantive revisions to this Preface, the glossary and the introduction to each of the books.

Above and beyond all, we thank Nancy Biggs Berge for her patience, tolerance, and hospitality, and for living with the time demands involved in our editing three books in one year (to say nothing of three issues of the IPCT Journal, two conference presentations, two book chapters, and three articles). We dedicate this book, with love and gratitude, to all our children: Jenna and Mark Berge, Doug Collins, Kim and Mike Snyder, Sarah and Simon Waghorn, Krys and Hozz Hosmer, and Jay, Ben, Norah, and Joshua Strebel.

Z.L.B.
M.P.C.

September 1994

About the Contributors

Holly Anderson is an Associate Professor at Boise State University where she teaches graduate and undergraduate methods and foundations courses.
handerson@claven.idbsu.edu

Edward Barrett is Senior Lecturer in the Program in Writing and Humanistic Studies at Massachusetts Institute of Technology and Director of MIT's Undergraduate Technical Writing Cooperative.
ebarrett@Athena.MIT.EDU

Trent Batson is the Director of the Alliance for Computers and Writing, and of the ENFI Project, Gallaudet University, Washington DC.
TWBATSON@GALLUA.GALLAUDET.EDU

Zane Berge is Director of the Center for Teaching and Technology and Assistant Director for Training Service, Academic Computer Center, Georgetown University, Washington, DC.
berge@guvax.georgetown.edu

Marie (Mauri) Collins is a doctoral student in Instructional Systems at the Pennsylvania State University, University Park, PA and is Instructional Television Program assistant at WPSX-TV.
mauri@cac.psu.edu

Michael Day is Assistant Professor of English at South Dakota School of Mines and Technology in Rapid City, SD.
mday@silver.sdsmt.edu

Harry Gardiner is Professor of Psychology at the University of Wisconsin-La Crosse and teaches courses in cross-cultural psychology.
gardiner@uwlax.edu

Russell Hunt is Professor of English, and Learning and Teaching Development Officer, at St. Thomas University, Fredericton, New Brunswick.
HUNT%UNB.CA@UNBMVS1.csd.unb.ca

Sara Keisler is a Professor at Carnegie Mellon University studying gruop and organizational aspects of computing and computer-based communication technologies.

Department at the University of Wisconsin - La Crosse.
MANRIQUE@UWLAX.EDU

Robert Nalley is an Assistant Professor of Education at the University of Maine at Fort Kent, MA, specializing in Instructional Technology and Science Education.
rnalley@maine.bitnet

Helen Schwartz teaches an introductory literature class at Indiana University-Purdue University at Indianapolis (IUPUI).
hschwart@indycms.bitnet

Ted J. Singletary is Associate Professor of Teacher Education at Boise State University, Boise, Idaho, teaching science and mathematics curriculum and instruction courses.
tsingletary@claven.idbsu.edu

Gail S. Thomas developed courses in introductory and advanced online information retrieval systems and networking classes. She now teaches these classes for the Media Studies Program, New School for Social Research.
GTHOMAS@UNISON.CINCINNATI.OH.US

David Zubrow is a member of the Technical Staff at the Software Engineering Institute, Carnegie Mellon University, Pittsburgh, PA.
dz@SEI.CMU.EDU

Introduction

Volume Two: Computer-Mediated Communication and the Online Classroom in Higher Education

Mauri P. Collins
Pennsylvania State University
Zane L. Berge
Georgetown University

In the first volume in this series, *Computer-Mediated Communication and the Online Classroom: Overview and Perspectives,* we noted that the term computer-mediated communication (CMC) was used to encompass the merging of computers and telecommunications technologies to support teaching and learning. We surveyed the range of educational users of CMC from several different perspectives.

Gerald M. Santoro delineated the terminology and processes of CMC and described typical functions and users; Jill H. Ellsworth followed up with a introduction to the uses of CMC in the classroom.

James N. Shimabukuro described the growth of educational computer conferencing using a "generational model" and explored a future scenario that depicts the use of a fourth generation network in which students and instructors from international locations meet together in a single, virtual classroom.

Joseph Kinner and Norman Coombs outlined the problems and opportunities of adaptive computing and provided vignettes of hearing and deaf students interacting in the same virtual classroom. Ann Pemberton and Robert Zenhausern extended the use of CMC in the classroom to provide a delivery system for rehabilitation to educationally impaired adolescents, teaching them basic computer literacy, motivational reading, writing and thinking activities, and an introduction to the world. Their chapter concluded with a list of resources specific to the needs of those involved in special education.

Linda S. Fowler and Daniel D. Wheeler presented the results of a survey of teachers using CMC in Kindergarten-Grade 12. They reported results that included an increase in student's cultural understanding, and they also noted a need for extensive institutional support for teachers if the use of CMC is to become widespread.

Katy Silberger examined the changes in the traditional role and services offered by libraries in higher education as they face the technological opportunities inherent in the use of new electronic information formats, particularly electronic journals and monographs and electronic publishing networks.

George D. Baldwin's chapter focuses on the implicit conflict between Native American cultural values and beliefs and the use of English language-based CMC. The chapter concludes with a list of Native American bulletin boards and discussion groups. Alexander McAuley's chapter in the third volume of this series gives another perspective on the use of CMC by Native Americans.

John J. Saraille and Thomas A. Gentry's "Fractal Factory" is based on their contention that the study of fractals provides a rich insight into the natural world and will provide the lay person with some basics towards understanding the theoretical basis of fractal compression being used in the digital transmission of video signals.

In outlining the subject of scholarly communication using CMC, Raleigh C. Muns's chapter delineated among the various network conferencing systems. Michael Szabo discussed the history of in-class computer conferencing by providing an historical overview of "Plato," one of the most powerful systems for the computer-assisted instruction.

The first book in this series concluded with Fay Sudweeks, Mauri Collins and John December's introduction to the many facets of networks, networking, and the Internet. The authors provided specific instructions for using the most common Internet navigational tools and information to assist prospective "internauts" in locating further information and resources.

Considered together, the chapters in this volume revolve around the questions: "What do we know about teaching and learning?" and "How can educators and learners use CMC productively as we move into the 21st century?" *Computer-Mediated Communication and the Online Classroom in Higher Education,* the second in this 3-volume series, focuses on several themes relating to both in-class and distance learning. These themes include accommodation of different learning styles and the empowerment of learners, regardless of physical challenges or social/cultural differences. Further, learners may now use the same tools and methods that professionals use; at the same time, pioneer educators using CMC are taking an interdisciplinary, project-oriented approach to teaching and learning—all of which creates authentic practice.

We find that CMC is changing instructional methods in several ways, including: (a) generating improved technological tools that allow classes to use a fuller range of interactive methodologies, and (b) encouraging teachers and administrators to pay more attention to the instructional design of courses. Both of these factors can improve the quantity, quality, and patterns of communication in the skills students practice during learning—a change that requires, in many cases, both teachers and students to learn different roles.

Educators often categorize the use of instructional CMC in three ways: for conferencing, informatics, and computer-assisted instruction (CAI). Computer conferencing provides e-mail, interactive messaging, and small and large group discussion. Informatics (repositories or maintainers of organized information) include library online public access catalogs (OPACs), interactive access to remote databases, program/data archive sites (e.g., archives of files for pictures, sound, text, movies), campus-wide information systems (CWIS), wide-area information systems (WAIS), and information managers, such as Gopher and Veronica.

In CAI, the computer is used to structure and manage both the presentation of information and the possible responses available to the human user. Uses of computer conferencing, informatics, and CAI include:

- mentoring, such as advising and guiding students
- project-based instruction, either within the classroom or in projects involving community, national, or international problem solving
- guest lecturing, which promotes interaction between students and persons in the larger community

- didactic teaching, that is, supplying course content, posting assignments, or other information germane to course work
- retrieval of information from online information archives, such as OPACs, ERIC, and commercial databases
- course management, for example, advising, delivery of course content, evaluation, collecting and returning assignments
- public conferencing, such as discussion lists using mainframe Listserv software
- interactive chat, used to brainstorm with teachers or peers and to maintain social relationships
- personal networking and professional growth and such activities as finding persons with similar interests on scholarly discussion lists
- facilitating collaboration
- individual and group presentations
- peer review of writing, or projects involving peer learning, groups/peer tutorial sessions, and peer counseling
- practice and experience using emerging technologies that may be intrinsically useful in today's society
- computer-based instruction, such as tutorials, simulations, and drills.

As the authors in this volume discuss the various methods, it becomes clear that there are many benefits to using CMC, but there are also some limitations that must be recognized. As the reader moves through these chapters, it will become apparent that one of the greatest benefits of CMC is its ability to liberate instruction from the constraints of time and distance. The convenience of access from home, school, or office permits many students and instructors to better meet travel, job, and family responsibilities. Educators and trainers, especially those involved in distance learning, have been searching for the "Holy Grail" of instruction for a long time—to be able to teach and have students learn anything, anytime, anywhere. To a large degree, CMC now can fulfill two thirds of this desire.

CMC promotes self-discipline and requires students to take more responsibility for their own learning. Using CMC, instructors can vary a course's instructional design to include everything from structured projects to open projects in which students are free to work on "messy"—but authentic—problem solving. On the other hand, because students must manage their own learning, this newfound independence may be a hindrance to those students who need more structure.

No one can deny that we have entered an information age in

which power comes to those who have information and know how to access it. If we consider which factors of CMC will be most important to education in the information age, it seems that our goals should be to develop self-motivated learners and help people learn to find and share information. If designed well, CMC applications can be used effectively to facilitate collaboration among students as peers, teachers as learners and facilitators, and guests or experts from outside the classroom.

One of the more important aspects of CMC use in instruction is that it is text-based. Facility in writing is essential across the entire curriculum, and with the present technology one cannot communicate on a computer network without writing. Just as important, if used effectively, CMC encourages and motivates students to become involved in authentic projects and to write for a real audience of their peers or persons in the larger world community, instead of merely composing assignments for the teacher. At the same time, we must recognize that not all students can express themselves well in writing, and, even for those who can, the act of writing and using online text-based applications can be a time-consuming struggle.

In this regard, there is an emerging body of literature, added to by several authors in this volume, who speak from their own experiences concerning the empowerment of persons with disabilities, physical impairment, disfigurement, or speech impediments, which hinder their equal participation in face-to-face encounters. CMC promotes an equalization of users. Because CMC is, at present, primarily text-only, the consequent reduction in social cues leads to a protective ignorance surrounding a person's social roles, rank, and status. Further, it is impossible to know if another person took several hours to draft a one screen response, or several minutes. Responses are judged by the ideas and thoughts conveyed, more so than by who is doing the writing. As a result, the lack of social cues and the asynchronous nature of the medium affords those with physical limitations or personal reticence the possibility of participating fully and equally in communicative activities within a mainstream environment. However, researchers realize that when social context cues are minimized nonreticent personalities can be encouraged to become overly zealous in their responses, or to become publicly inflammatory and aggressive on a personal level in ways that generally do not occur in other media. Second, it has been noted that some students prefer the social aspects of the classroom and are unsettled by the lack of face-to-face interaction in CMC, or the lack of a (sometimes) charismatic lecturer during presentation.

Another potential benefit of CMC is in promoting multicultural awareness. With the demographic make-up of many countries changing so rapidly, it is becoming increasingly important to develop communication skills for a culturally diverse community and world. Still, although CMC enhances some of these valuable skills for the 21st century, we must remember that because the bulk of CMC is conducted in English and in the written rather than in the spoken word, it may perpetuate some cultural hegemonies.

Many authors recognize CMC's capability, under certain circumstances, to reduce the sense of isolation sometimes felt by students and teachers. However, still others believe that the lack of social cues and face-to-face interaction increases the sense of isolation for persons using this medium to teach and learn. They point out that CMC may interfere with face-to-face relationships or be addictive.

However, as the chapters in this volume make clear, we cannot deny its value as a teaching tool. We simply need to remember that responsible use of CMC means using it in addition to other media, not as a replacement. As educators, our job is to provide options to fit a variety of learning styles, and it is in this regard that CMC can help the most. There are technical benefits to using CMC, such as the ease of circulating and archiving files and documents (e.g., teacher messages, student work, assignments).

On the other hand, the learning curve, with regard to learning the system and the technical "how tos" of the computer and telecommunications, can be steep. The cost of buying and supporting systems or accessing other networks is a significant "overhead" item in schools and colleges today, as is the cost and inconvenience of upgrading, repairing, or replacing hardware. Further, computer systems are not 100% reliable, a fact that adds to inconvenience and wasted time. With so many systems to learn and sources to tap, information overload has become a problem as some users struggle with the lack of criteria to help them to decide what to keep and what to discard from the swiftly flowing stream of incoming information.

All these factors—the idea that teachers, information designers, and instructional developers can use CMC to promote collaboration, cooperation, the sharing of ideas, and as an equalizing medium—means that the roles of students and teachers will change. No longer perceived as the sole experts and information providers, teachers become facilitators and guides. Conversely, students are no longer passive learners, attempting to mimic what they see and hear from the expert teacher. They become participants, collaborators in the creation of knowledge and meaning. Yet we must attempt not to reproduce or augment the problems associated with the gap between technology "haves" and "have nots" when we design CMC and computer conferencing applications and curricula. Every software, networking, or curriculum innovation reflects, to some degree, the unarticulated assumptions about the world view of the culture that created it. We must be aware of this fact and strive to create and use CMC innovations that allow for multiplicity, for change, for difference.

In response to increased pressure on universities and instructors to provide instructional delivery systems that go beyond the traditional "chalk-and-talk" form of lecture, computer-mediated conferencing has emerged as a tool for instructional communication not bound by prescribed meeting times or by geographic proximity. Successful integration of CMC into the curriculum, however, depends on one's ability to design and use CMC applications that meet course goals, delivery goals, or both. As part of course planning, we must address issues such as course goals, hardware availability, and student readiness. Large expenditures on CMC for the classroom will not help unless teachers understand how the technology helps fulfill the goals of the course. To this end, the chapters in this volume provide examples and practical advice.

In Chapter 1, Robert Nalley describes the instructional design process that led to the incorporation of CMC into two existing courses and offers practical guidance in instructional design to those who would consider CMC as an instructional tool.

Michael Day's and Trent Batson's chapter (Chapter 2) demonstrates how a particular application of CMC, Electronic Networks For Interaction (ENFI), is being used to change the social dynamics of the writing classroom. ENFI is not a specific software package but rather an electronic implementation of the concept that writing can actually be taught in a computer lab with a network supporting real-time CMC. Because ENFI allows teachers and students to explore, collaborate, and expand on ideas in class in writing, and allows them to see each other in the process of developing ideas, writing to and for each other and not just to "the teacher," ENFI supplements and expands on the activities teachers can use to help students meaningfully participate in a discourse community and improve their writing.

The study conducted by Karen Hartman, Sara Kiesler, Lee Sproull and their colleagues (Chapter 3) examines the effects of using network technologies in learning to write on teacher-student and student-student interactions. In a writing course emphasizing multiple drafts and collaboration, two sections used traditional modes of communication (face-to-face, paper, phone); and two other sections, in addition to using traditional modes, also used various electronic modes (electronic mail, bulletin boards, etc.). The patterns of social interaction were measured twice: six weeks into the semester and again at the end of the semester. Results indicate that teachers in the networked sections interacted more with their students than teachers in the regular sections. Whereas teachers in the regular sections marginally increased their use of traditional communication over time, teachers in the networked sections substantially increased their use of electronic communication over time without significantly decreasing their use of traditional modes of teacher-student communication. In addition, they found that teachers communicated more electronically with less able students than with more able students and that less able students communicated more electronically with other students.

In Chapter 4, Helen J. Schwartz uses experiences gained in an introductory literature class over the course of five semesters to explore the evolutionary process of answering the questions: "How and why should technology be used in a particular discipline?" and "How does it serve urban commuters in particular?" Nontraditional urban commuter students used computers in class and out to discuss course work as a supplement to face-to-face classes. Experience with five different configurations of pedagogical methods are described, including the use of a computer program developed by Schwartz for use in her classes. These helped shape procedures in a distance-education course, with subsequent replanning. Her current conclusions are presented, but she feels that teachers who learn from them must also evolve and discover their own answers.

Dramatic changes in theories of language and literacy learning have been underway for some time and have taken into account ideas of pragmatic coherence, authenticity in interpersonal dialogue, and situational constraints on communication. Only recently, however, have there been consequences for classroom practice at the postsecondary level. In the fifth chapter, Russell A. Hunt describes one set of strategies, called "Collaborative Investigation," for embedding written language in social situations in educational contexts. This strategy has been used in recent years in a wide range of disciplines and for students ranging from freshmen to those in graduate school. More specifically, it describes one way in which computer network technology has been utilized to address the logistic and practical difficulties posed by such uses of writing and reading and to facilitate treating language in authentically dialogic ways. A class collaboratively investigating 18th-century English literature used electronic mail for communication between student and teacher and between students, an electronic bulletin board for "class discussions" and decision making, and a dedicated common directory for creating, sharing, and editing research reports on various aspects of the subject and for producing a "class book"—a desktop-published result of the work of the course, of which each student got a copy.

Edward Barrett's chapter (Chapter 6) describes the Networked Educational Online System (NEOS) that was developed by writing faculty with support from Project Athena at MIT. NEOS does not model presumed cognitive states in students; rather it models the interactions among all members of a writing class. NEOS supports the creation, exchange, annotation, and display of text in real-class time, as well as out of class at numerous workstations throughout the fully distributed MIT network. Use of NEOS in the electronic classroom and out of class empowers students as peer reviewers and can significantly improve their writing skills. Barrett finds that many students prefer it to the traditional classroom for its ability to integrate theory and practice and for the greater interaction it supports among all class members and instructors.

In Chapter 7, Cecilia G. Manrique and Harry W. Gardiner describe some of the ways in which faculty members at the University of Wisconsin-La Crosse have employed electronic mail in fulfilling the institutional trilateral goals of bringing together computing, writing and an internationalized curriculum. Manrique and Gardiner include communication with students in foreign countries as components of Political Science and Cross-Cultural Psychology courses. Attention is given to some of the advantages and disadvantages of using electronic mail in specific courses, and they show where it has been successful as well as note some of the pitfalls that accompany such a nontraditional method of delivering education. Suggestions are made for incorporating electronic mail into a variety of courses through resources available to students and faculty in "netland."

Ted J. Singletary and Holly Anderson, in Chapter 8, describe the First-Year Teacher Network that was instituted by Boise State University to help ease the difficult induction process of new teachers entering the profession. Twenty-five first-year teachers in 10 southwestern Idaho counties communicated through an electronic bulletin board system on a wide range of classroom and emotional topics. The support program, now in its fourth year of operation, has been successful in providing neophytes with access to university expertise, online databases, and other services. The First-Year Teacher Network is perceived as a valuable source of peer support and as a way to reduce feelings of isolation.

Karen Bruce's discussion (Chapter 9) briefly elaborates on the importance of information technology in medicine, outlines the use of various types of CMC in that educational setting, and presents outcome data from a project implementing a 2-year longitudinal computer curriculum at East Carolina University School of Medicine. Bruce determined that the information explosion in medical practice and science had profoundly affected the information management needs of physicians and physicians-in-training. Over the last 60 years the structure and goals of medical education have remained essentially unchanged. The volume of medical knowledge, however, has grown exponentially. The sine qua non of a good medical education remains knowing all you need to know, not just knowing how to discriminate what you must know most of the time and where to find what you cannot possibly know all of the time. Current information technology, including computer-mediated communication (CMC), provides a number of tools to improve medical practitioners' management and utilization of this information. The value of information obtained via CMC continues to improve rapidly; however, as Bruce points out, the ability of physicians and physicians-in-training to use this technology has not kept pace.

Gail Thomas's chapter describes the development and presentation of two courses featuring online training for online information retrieval systems. Beginning and advanced courses use the Online Training and Practice (ONTAP) databases of Dialog Information Services, Inc., and the asynchronous computer conferencing capabilities of Unison's PARTI software to deliver skills training over the modem. Both beginning and advanced courses have been offered since 1989 for graduate academic credit through Connected Education, Inc., and the Media Studies Program, New School for Social Research, New York City, NY.

In the final chapter, Mauri Collins presents a brief introduction to the various wide area networks (BITnet, Internet, Fidonet, etc.), networking, and the use of Internet information retrieval tools. Common networking acronyms are defined and explained, and instructions for the use of the file transfer protocol (ftp) and the remote login protocol (Telnet) are given. The format for electronic mail addresses is decoded and explained. Listserv and Usenet discussion groups are introduced and differentiated and instructions are given for joining Listserv discussion groups. The chapter concludes with a short list of sources for further networking information.

Chapter
One

Designing Computer-Mediated Conferencing into Instruction

Robert Nalley
University of Maine at Fort Kent

In response to increased pressure on universities and instructors to provide instructional delivery systems that go beyond the traditional chalk-and-talk lecture, computer-mediated conferencing (CMC) is emerging as a tool for instructional communication that is not bound by prescribed meeting times or by geographic proximity (Hiltz, 1986; Hiltz & Meinke, 1989). Successful incorporation of CMC into a course, however, requires more than a simple decision to do so. The instructional method chosen must address an instructional problem and be designed into a course to solve the problem. This chapter describes the instructional design process that led to the incorporation of CMC into two existing courses.

In this chapter I review the instructional design process that led to the use of CMC in two courses: Foundations of Education and Computers for Educators. I describe the planning process and the subsequent day-to-day activities. In addition, this chapter offers practical guidance to those who would consider CMC as an instructional tool. Finally, I look back on the experience and make recommendations to those who would consider implementing CMC as part of a course.

Traditional classrooms are dominated by a lecture/recitation format. Instructors deliver prepared lectures representing their knowledge of the course material, and students prepare to imitate the instructor's knowledge-telling behavior on some form of examination. Face-to-face meetings between the instructor and the students are the norm. At best, discussion within such classrooms can be characterized as being between the instructor and the few students who are prepared and who have the opportunity to participate. Similarly, traditional university life is centered on those students who can devote a substantial amount of time to the campus and who can schedule group study and discussion sessions into their class schedules.

The opportunity to work and have discussions with other students is, possibly, as valuable an activity as class attendance itself. In part, this interaction is what is meant by a community of scholars. However, the process of creating a community of scholars among students depends on their freedom to gather with other students to work, to discuss, and to create meaning from their common needs and experiences (Selfe & Eilola, 1988). Students who have free access to their instructors and to each other, similarly, will have access to continued opportunities for intellectual growth. Because such an interaction has been part of a student's university life, a traditional university education has been weighted heavily in favor of those students who have both the financial and time resources required for class attendance and informal discussion. CMC has the potential to tip the balance toward those students who, in the past, have been otherwise disadvantaged or disconnected.

Successfully tipping the balance is another matter. Integrating CMC into a course depends on designing CMC into the instructional plan as a solution to either a course goal, a means to attain a goal, or both. Issues such as course goals, teaching strategy, hardware availability, and student readiness must be addressed as part of course planning. Successful integration of CMC into the course depends on the planning that occurs before CMC becomes part of a course. Success requires that students possess skills in the use of computer technology and that they see a need to communicate. Designing CMC into an instructional plan begins when the instructor takes the first step in preparation for instruction.

COMPUTER-MEDIATED COMMUNICATION (CMC)

CMC describes a broad field of communication practices that utilize computer technology. CMC encompasses uses of technologies that range from desktop computers to fax machines. The technology, however, is not the central issue in communication. No matter what the technology, an understanding of CMC is important because of the changes in communication practices that the use of technology brings about. Business people have discovered that CMC can significantly alter not only the quantity and quality of communication, but also the patterns of communication between people. This same discovery is taking place in education.

INSTRUCTIONAL DESIGN

Instructional design is the systematic planning of instruction to maximize learning. Based largely on the works of Gagné, Briggs and Wager (1992), and Romiszowski and de-Hass (1989), instructional design describes a set of procedures whereby instruction can be planned to increase the likelihood that the goals of instruction will be met and planned learning will occur. A number of models for designing instruction are available. Each model approaches the design process differently and emphasizes a different stage or outcome. The planning and execution of the project I am about to describe was based on the Dick and Cary model (1990). Dick and Cary divide the design process into roughly eight stages: (a) identification of instructional goals, (b) instructional analysis, (c) instructional resources, (d) learner characteristics, (e) performance objectives, (f) criteria for success, (g) instructional strategy, and (h) evaluation.

INSTRUCTIONAL GOAL IDENTIFICATION: SEEING A PROBLEM

Identifying instructional goals is the first step in planning instruction. Often equated with a needs assessment, identification and clarification of goals is vital to successful CMC implementation. A needs assessment, or clarification, need not be a formal, statistically correct effort. In most cases a sense of instructional needs or a few casual remarks by colleagues or students will be enough to convince one that a change in a course is needed. If course goals suggest that a new method of communication is necessary, CMC may provide a means. However, many modes of communication are available. A careful consideration of the problem and the possible communication solutions to the problem indicate whether CMC is an option.

What, then, is meant by communication? First of all, communication between people is more than the exchange of objective data. The data view of communication is closely tied to computer information. In contrast, human communication involves not only sending and receiving messages between people, but it also involves the act of meaning making by the people involved. Meaning making assumes a context within which the communication takes place and a goal that the communication attempts to serve. Communication, therefore, requires both a means for the exchange of information and a desire on the part of the people involved to create meaning from the experience.

The first need for improved communication in one of my courses became apparent in Foundations of Education, a class of 25 students, made up of freshmen and sophomores. Long before Spring 1992, the faculty of the University of Maine at Fort Kent had recognized that its student body was largely nontraditional. A majority of the students were off-campus, commuter students. Many of the them were married with families and held part-time or full-time jobs. Most were first-generation college students with no family history of higher education. Most importantly, other than the casual use of computers at the community high school, they had virtually no prior experience in the use of computers as a means for interpersonal communication. For the students in this course, their need to broaden their access to communication with each other was the problem to be solved. CMC was chosen as the solution.

Inclusion of CMC in a second course, Computers for Educators, arose from a distinctly different need. Computers for Educators, with an enrollment of 20 students, approached the use of a computer in the classroom as a teacher tool. The course was designed as a hands-on course for preservice teachers. As originally designed and taught, the course focused on classroom applications of word processing and spreadsheets. The computer as a potential communication tool for classroom teachers was not part of the course. Because the course presented the computer as a means for solving a number of information-handling problems, the computer as a communication device was an appropriate part of the course. The only need was to expand the content of the course to include CMC. CMC was clearly an appropriate activity for both courses, albeit for very different reasons and with very different goals.

Finally, for any course, if teachers are unable to make clear to their students the value of the CMC portion of the course, students will likely reject CMC as nothing more than technological game playing. And they will be right. Presenting CMC as an appropriate activity within an existing course structure is an important step.

INSTRUCTIONAL ANALYSIS: MAPPING THE ROUTE

The simple expectation that students will be able to discuss course material, whether in the classroom or via CMC, and that they will be able to manage computer technology with relative ease is not sufficient. An instructor must create a planned set of activities that have a reasonable chance for changing student behaviors. Delineating and sequencing that set of activities is instructional analysis.

Once again, the goal behaviors for the two classes were very different. The expectation for the Foundations class was an increased involvement in discussion. For Computers for Educators, the students were expected to demonstrate competence in the use of computers for telecommunication. What they discussed through CMC was a secondary issue. Consequently, the two courses required different instructional plans.

FURTHER ANALYSIS: RESOURCE ASSESSMENT

Having concluded that CMC was an appropriate means for solving an instructional problem for both courses, I immediately turned to our computer support staff. The University of Maine at Fort Kent, although small, supports an excellent computer facility. Two fully networked labs were available. The primary lab was housed on the ground floor of the largest classroom building. The lab had 25 stations with menu-driven applications software selections. In addition, each station had access to telecommunications software that made an automatic connection with the University of Maine central computer network. The connection from Fort Kent to the mainframe computer, over a distance of 250 miles, was through optical fiber.

For the students, connection was a matter of a menu selection and a short wait of less than 5 seconds. Although staff assistance was available, 15 minutes of each class session over a period of 3 weeks was devoted to computer training. The lab was less than 50 feet down a hallway from the classroom. Gaining access to the computers was not a problem . In addition, the lab had a regularly scheduled student assistant. During lab hours other than class time students could expect to find assistance in the lab. If considering CMC, some form of technical support is essential.

Part of that technical support came from the students. In addition, however, the proximity of a fully equipped lab with lab assistants in the same hallway as the classroom contributed greatly to my decision to attempt CMC. The students had easy access to both computers and technical assistance. Without such accessibility and support I would not have attempted CMC.

ENTRY BEHAVIORS: STARTING WHERE THE STUDENTS ARE

Having introduced the students to the advantages of CMC, their individual entry skills became important. For both courses it was necessary to assume that the students had no prior training in computer use. This assumption presented no problem for the Computers for Educators class. The course, as originally planned, was easily restructured to include a section concerning the technical aspects of using telecommunications in the classroom. In this case, the student's ability to meet the goals of the course was not dependent on prior knowledge or training. A 3-week block of class time was devoted to hands-on activities.

The Foundations course was not as easy to structure. Although the goals of the CMC activity were to provide a forum for extended discussion and to foster stronger group identification, the course structure, a traditional lecture, did not provide for computer training sessions. As a result, existing student computer skills became a critical barrier to the success of the project. As the course was composed mostly of nontraditional students, the Foundations class quickly responded to a suggestion of discussion beyond the regular class meeting with personal stories concerning work, family, and other reasons why they could not schedule additional meetings with other students. Although they tended to agree that further discussion would be useful, they were unable to describe a forum that would suit their varied schedules. It was at this point that I introduced CMC as a means to resolve the problem.

Their reactions to my description of CMC were varied. A few were excited and positive. They tended to have a history of prior computer use. Others were visibly anxious. The anxious students tended to have no experience with computers and saw technology as a threat to academic success. A large number of students objected to the idea that they should be required to use computers without formal training.

Student concerns about formal training need to be addressed. Whether the goal is to facilitate ongoing communication or to train students in the use of a communication technology, a plan for hands-on training is needed. The range of student computer-readiness skills will be one of the first major problems. Some students will be adept at computer use, whereas others will express a vocal aversion to computers. Offering training and support to the less able students is essential. Be aware of the computer-user culture that already exists. There is a culture of computer users and nonusers in most classes. It would be an unlikely class that had no veteran computer users.

Veteran student computer users may be the best training resource and the most adept at understanding the needs of novice users. Pairing students or creating cooperative work groups early in the course will help alleviate the stress experienced by novice users. Veteran computer users can be of great value if the teacher is personally responsible for training. If considering CMC without assistance for both technical advice and training, teachers should seriously consider whether a normal work load will stand the strain of increased responsibility.

PERFORMANCE OBJECTIVES: FRAMING THE TARGET

Performance objectives are usually written in a formal given-the-student-will form. Because writing objectives is a subject unto itself, it is not belabored here. For the purpose of discussing the two courses involved in this project, it is sufficient to say that clear, objective outcomes are essential as measures of success.

The course content and desired student outcome skills for the two courses were different. In the case of Foundations, the expected learning was a combination of verbal information and appropriate attitudes. The verbal information encompassed common ideas concerning education. I expected the students to be able to express opinions concerning such diverse topics as student and school rights, home schooling, instructional strategies, and so forth. In each case I expected them to express an opinion and to offer some evidence or philosophical view to support their opinions. Through their discussions I expected them to demonstrate some communicative competence concerning the broad subject of education in the United States. The communication was to take the form of comments posted in an e-mail distribution system.

I also expected to see a change in attitude concerning their sense of community with the other students in the class. My hope was that through increased discussion the students would become more familiar with each other and feel a greater connection with both the university and their peers.

The desired outcome for Computers for Educators was more easily defined. The goal was to have students demonstrate competence in the use of computers as a communications device. Competence meant the ability to exchange files and messages through a geographically distant computer. In practice, this meant that the students would be expected to create documents in a computer laboratory setting, to send files to a distant computer, and to retrieve files from a distant computer.

PERFORMANCE OBJECTIVES: OBSERVABLE BEHAVIORS

The performance objectives for both classes were reasonably simple and attainable. The Foundations students, as mentioned earlier, were required to make three postings per week. Each posting was to be a minimum of 25 lines (one screen). The posting was not judged on content or correctness. The goal was to increase involvement. I had made a decision early on that my judgment of their work would place a chill on their willingness to participate. Therefore, other than my prompting statements, I simply logged the messages by each student and read the postings to maintain a sense of their direction.

The Computers for Educators class had similar performance objectives. The students had a set of assignments each week requiring them to send short notes to me and occasionally to include information from other sources. The latter assignments required that they send the contents of a file stored on the system to me and that they upload and download other files. The final assignments required that they retrieve graphics from distant sites and share them with the class.

CRITERIA FOR SUCCESS: KNOWING SUCCESS WHEN YOU SEE IT

The goals in Foundations were both affective and cognitive. I expected to see a change in student attitudes toward communication with other students. I also expected to see more thoughtful discussion of the course materials at the end of the term. I chose to measure both outcomes through my judgment of short essay responses at the end of the term.

The goals for Computers for Educators were more procedural. I created a series of exercises that required the students to use the University of Maine system and Internet to send and receive files. Success was measured as their ability to present the materials described in the exercises. For example, each student was required to retrieve a graphics file and a graphics viewer from a distant computer and to display the graphic in class.

INSTRUCTION AND STRATEGY: FOUNDATIONS

Apart from the stages associated with designing instruction, Gagné et al. (1992) describe nine specific events as germane to instruction. The events are (generally) gaining attention, informing the learner of the objective, presenting the material to be learned, eliciting the performance, feedback, and enhancement. I discuss next only those parts related to gaining attention and eliciting the performance.

I first introduced the concept of CMC to my Foundations class as an instructional technique. The initial discussion centered on the need of students to express opinions, clarify ideas, and interact with other students. Through classroom discussions we formulated the problem as one of the barriers to this process. We discussed both geographic and time restraints.

I then presented the objectives. I described CMC and how it could give them an opportunity to become acquainted with each other outside of the classroom. I further explained what would be their obligations. Each student would be required to make three e-mail postings per week as a minimum. One posting would be a personal opinion concerning the material discussed in class that week. The remaining two postings would be discussions of comments made by others. In this way, each student had an opportunity to express an opinion to the group and to comment on the opinions of others.

I often prompted discussion (provided stimulus material) by making my own posting. Most of my prompts concerned issues relevant to public education. Each prompt included two or three ways to view a subject and asked for comment (elicited performance). Two subjects spurred discussion well past the week of the original prompt. The first discussion focused on law and rights. The course included a brief review of federal laws, state laws, and Supreme Court rulings that impact education. The discussion tended to be descriptions of situations they might see in the classroom. Questions such as whether a student's locker can be searched and under what conditions were typical. The second lengthy discussion concerned the sociology of public schools. A series of prompts relating to the social structure of schools and the behavior of students within that structure caused heated debate that spilled over into the classroom.

Each week, during the regular classroom session, I would recap my sense of the discussions and review procedural and technical problems. This was also a time for me to make positive comments about students' involvement and to ask for comments concerning subjects for discussion of interest to them.

INSTRUCTION AND STRATEGY: COMPUTERS FOR EDUCATORS

Computers for Educators, which had different goals, was planned with technical skill as the expected outcome. As with the Foundations class, I began by discussing the changing nature of instruction and instruction at a distance. Then, after a brief demonstration, I guided the class through their first log-on and entry into the e-mail system. Each of the twice weekly class meetings was devoted to specific procedural skills. We progressed from opening and reading mail to replying, initiating, and including other documents. The assignments most often required the individual student to post questions to me concerning the operation of the system. Using e-mail, we discussed e-mail, Telnet, file transfer protocols (FTP), and uploading and downloading documents. Because the overall goal was technical competence, the learning events were demonstration, individual practice, discussion, and then continued practice.

FORMATIVE EVALUATION

Be prepared to learn from experience. Students are different and courses are different. The first effort will probably not succeed in meeting original goals. Failure, however, is a matter of not learning from experience. Analyze the problems that occur and make changes. I found two problems dominated both courses: mastering the technology and self-expression.

Most of students found the technology initially to be intimidating. Although some had reasonably good computer skills, the logon-read-compose-send sequence held many opportunities for procedural errors. What might be seen by a veteran computer user as a problem to be solved with a keystroke can be seen by a novice as an hour or two of frustration. This was especially true of simple keystroke errors. For example, logging on was normally a matter of entering a personal identification code and a password in standard, labeled screen blanks. A mistype, however, would initiate a warning screen that was visually unlike the normal screen. In addition, the new logon screen required the student to enter the word "logon." This minor change in procedure was painfully difficult for some students.

Because it was not possible to describe the procedure for recovery from an accumulation of errors, small errors become insurmountable roadblocks. Discovering problems early on, I quickly created guides for the most common errors. I created handouts for logging on, for browsing mail files, for creating mail, and so on. Each handout described not only the normal procedure, but also common errors and recovery from them.

Even with support and guidance concerning errors, some students continued to be reluctant users. Reluctance to participate was a problem that had little to do with the technology. It is probably true that the same reluctance to speak in class will carry over to CMC. But, there is a difference. In CMC it is possible to prompt a student to comment without the larger group being aware of the personal exchange. After a prompt or two most students will respond. Having done so, the student can be easily drawn into the discussion. The skills that an instructor has in prompting discussion in the classroom are also useful in CMC.

I also found that the content of the discussions improved over time. Initially, some students wrote short comments that did little more than fulfill the stated assignment. Discussion in class, however, revealed that many of the students appreciated the time CMC allowed them to formulate their thoughts and to present them as clearly as possible. In the traditional classroom, time used for reflection and thought composition often results in a missed opportunity to speak.

The process of formative evaluation, therefore, allows one to measure success while involved in a project and to make adjustments. The uses of CMC should change and grow to fit one's personal circumstance. Even though one may implement CMC as a solution to one instructional problem, a person will find that new problems arise along with new opportunities. Change is difficult; so one should plan for debriefing sessions and for new procedures because planning is everything.

SUMMATIVE EVALUATION

In the end, the students were the best judges of whether the initial goals were reached. In the case of Foundations of Education, the students needed an opportunity to say whether they felt a closer connection to other members of the class and whether the increased discussion time helped them to understand the problems involved in public education. The change in attitude was most often made evident in casual or offhanded statements, both in class and online.

Many of the students said that they had originally been afraid of computers but had grown more comfortable with their use. I was also able to read messages posted by students to the group in which they said that they felt they knew each other better through the CMC activities than they did from face-to-face meetings in class. Two students openly admitted that, although they had exchanged messages for almost 10 weeks, they could not identify each other in class.

The final evaluations were in the form of a short essay and completed assignments. In both courses students were asked to describe their feelings concerning the use of CMC as a means for strengthening their understanding of the course material. In addition, the Foundations students were asked to write a second short essay describing their feelings about their sense of connectedness to the other students in the class. I make no claim that the results are as valid as a well-structured research project. Nonetheless, the students did tend to express that they felt better prepared to discuss the course material. Similarly, they tended to feel that the continued interaction outside of class had given them a means to know each other in a manner that would not have been possible otherwise. One student purchased a computer with a modem and completed many of the assignments from home.

I also needed a method for assessing the student skills in Computers for Educators. Success in this class was a simple matter of logging the messages from individual students. Success was very much performance based. Because most students were able to perform independently at the end of the term, I was able to say that discussing telecommunications with them using CMC was successful.

SUMMARY

Discussion that takes place in a CMC environment allows time for reflection. In a traditional classroom the flow of discussion is linear. Students take turns speaking, and the discussion moves ahead. In contrast, CMC opens the opportunity for discussion that can last for days. Many students will "lurk" in the background, reading and thinking. Only when they feel comfortable with their opinions will they insert themselves and post a comment. Furthermore, students will understand in different ways. This is true not only for the content of a course, but it will also be true for the use of the technology. Their knowledge of computer use and the ease of use they exhibit will depend on the personal history of each student.

At the outset, however, be realistic. Not every student will accept CMC as a supplement to face-to-face meetings, or as a means for creating group cohesion. Do not expect sweeping acceptance of CMC. CMC is not for everyone. Some students will continue to insist that the traditional, face-to-face lecture is the only effective method of instruction. Nonetheless, education has changed. If designed into a course, computer-mediated conferencing can be an effective tool for instruction both for university faculty and students.

REFERENCES

Dick, W., & Cary, L. (1990). *The systematic design of instruction* (3rd ed.). Glenview, IL: Scott, Foresman.

Gagné, R., Briggs, L., & Wager, W. (1992). *Principles of instructional design* (4th ed.). Orlando, FL: Harcourt Brace Jovanovich.

Hiltz, S. (1986). The "Virtual Classroom": Using computer-mediated communication for university teaching. *Journal of Communication, 14*(2), 95-104.

Hiltz, S., & Meinke, R. (1989). Teaching sociology in a virtual classroom. *Teaching Sociology, 17*(4), 431-446.

Romiszowski, A., & de-Haas, J. (1989). Computer mediated communication for instruction: Using e-mail as a seminar. *Educational Technology, 29*(10), 7-14.

Selfe, C., & Eilola, J. (1988). The tie that binds: Building discourse communities and group cohesion through computer-based conferences. *Collegiate Microcomputer, 6*(4), 339-348.

Chapter Two

The Network-Based Writing Classroom: The ENFI Idea

Michael Day
South Dakota School of Mines and Technology
Trent Batson
Gallaudet University

The use of computer-mediated communication (CMC) to teach writing holds great promise for a number of reasons. As is apparent from other chapters in this book, CMC means people communicating with other people. Most commonly, the form such communication takes is text—writing. People sit at computer terminals and write to each other. As the number of students sitting at terminals writing to each other increased over the last 10 years, many English teachers, who had heard far too many students say they hate to write, were intrigued. Students were being pulled away from their stereo systems, televisions and late-night parties to pound away on keyboards, spending long hours sending and receiving messages over various local and national networks.

Still, we know that a lifetime of casual chatter, either talk or "talk" in print, does not a speaker or a writer make. Therefore, we might suspect that all this chatter in writing on computer networks would not lead automatically to brilliant 500-word essays. Writing is really thinking: thinking through ideas and making them understandable to others through text. What students write on the networks in their free time are, of course, ideas, but in most cases the ideas are neither clearly expressed nor at the level of complexity we expect of college students in their academic writing. Further, learning the discourse of the networks is a skill, but not the same skill as developing a proposal in a business setting, writing a cover letter for a job, or analyzing an historical event.

But, shouldn't there be a way to take advantage of the growing interest in writing on computer networks among students? Isn't there some way we can expand on this interest to teach writing in college?

APPLICATIONS OF CMC TO TEACHING WRITING

First, we describe the kinds of problems writing teachers face in the traditional setting with which most are familiar; that is, the classroom in which the teacher succumbs to the environmental imperative and automatically assumes the role of the expert.

1. Demonstrating Writing

Teachers are supposed to be the experts in the classroom but often find it difficult to show students how they themselves write. Writing is simply too slow when using traditional display mechanisms such as the chalkboard or overhead projectors. Students are impatient at best, especially in a course they are most likely taking only because it's required, so they will not pay attention for long while the teacher writes on the chalkboard. These demonstrations would at best work only at the sentence level, in any case. Except for writing on the overhead or chalkboard, then, the only writing students see from their teacher is finished "perfect" writing in the form of handouts. The gap between their own writing and the perfect writing of their teacher, who is presumably their model for writing, may seem impossibly large.

2. Creating Realistic Writing Tasks

Students are typically asked to write as if they are experts, either about reading for class, about events, or about life situations. Yet, at their young age, most students are not experts. They may sense how great the gap is between the writing of experts and their own writing. Their attempts to sound authoritative, when they know almost nothing of the subject, usually result in the stilted English class essays with which, unfortunately, we are familiar.

3. Establishing a Meaningful Audience and Context for Students' Writing

Students tend to assume that their audience is the teacher, who usually knows far more about the subject than they do. This writing context is painfully artificial because the students feel they have very little they can actually say to the teacher that the teacher doesn't already know.

4. Encouraging Writing Practice

Teachers who have 30 to 50 students would be suicidal to require papers for every class session because students expect teachers to read and grade their papers. Yet, students should write as often as possible. Writing teachers want students to become adept at academic discourse, a complex and specialized form of discourse requiring extensive practice, yet the sheer numbers of students today overwhelm teachers and reduce the amount of teacher-monitored writing to a low level.

5. Creating Collaborative Opportunities

Many think of writing as a solitary activity, but some of the most productive writing comes out of group work. If teachers are to train students to write as writing is often done in the real world, they should train them to collaborate, at least in the idea-gathering and organizing stages of writing. Yet, in traditional classrooms, sharing of drafts or outlines or notes is awkward. Collaborative groups will typically work only in speech, which is a good way to develop ideas collaboratively, but this does not help in transferring those ideas to paper. We must remember that developing speaking skills is not the primary goal of the course.

6. The Time Lag Between Class Discussion and Student Writing

This lag is at least several hours, but most typically a day or two. Students will attend class on Monday, for example, and will be given a homework assignment. The next class is Wednesday, so the students, if they are typical, will carry out the assignment Tuesday night. This may be 36 hours after class discussion. By then, they may have forgotten the key ideas from the discussion or have lost interest.

7. Class Participation

Every teacher is familiar with the students who sit in the back like ghosts, rarely ever giving others in the class the benefit of their opinions and insights. Only the teacher knows, from what these students write in their essays, what others might have gained from their participation. These reticent students may be worried by their race, gender, or other physical characteristics, such as speech impediments, but frequently they do not participate, simply because they do not "think on their feet" as quickly as some of the other students.

* * * * *

There are other problems—too many others—but let's look at these seven. If teachers of skills other than writing, such as dance or art or music, were told that they could not demonstrate their skill to their students, that their students would practice—on average—40 minutes a week or so, and that this practice would occur out of their sight, these teachers would be excused for refusing to attempt to teach in such an impossible situation. But, because text generation is not like music or painting or dance—because it is hard to read at a distance of more than a couple of feet and slow to develop—writing teachers have had to adapt to exactly these impossible conditions. Perhaps this is why many of them hide behind the red marks they make on their students' papers. If they cannot actually teach them the skills necessary to be a good writer, they will just point out little errors. The impossibility of the task may also explain why so many frustrated writing teachers in college get out of teaching writing and into content courses as soon as they can.

But this chapter started with the hint of some relief for the writing teacher to be provided by CMC. Can CMC address the problems listed above? And, if so, how?

The ENFI Idea: A CMC Solution to Writing Class Dilemmas

One attempt to provide relief is the ENFI approach. ENFI means Electronic Networks for Interaction. The last word, Interaction, is the key to what ENFI actually does. Students meet in a writing classroom in which a local-area computer network has been set up, or the teacher brings her writing class to a networked lab. The server in the classroom or lab runs software that supports real-time group communication—the Interaction in ENFI. Teacher and students sit at stations on the network and write to each other—a group discussion in writing. Instead of the sound of voices in the room, one only hears keys clicking. Some people make side comments, and others occasionally laugh when a funny comment appears on the screen, but the locus of communication is really the screens, and everyone focuses on *writing*.

The teacher is fully a part of this communication in writing. Every comment that each person writes can be seen on all screens. At each station the screen shows scrolling comments from all participants; to create a comment of your own, you use a scratch-pad window, types a comment, then sends that comment to join the flow of comments coming from the group. Because everyone can write at once, a great deal of text is generated, and the computer program has to create a queue, based on the order in which the server receives the comments. The resulting stream of comments is not like a natural discussion, of course, but it may develop into three or four strands of separate topics. Although at first it may seem difficult to follow the separate strands or topics, classes typically get used to the nonlinear "flow" of the conversation rather quickly. Normally, the teacher does not control this "discussion," nor is he or she the filter through which all comments are made.

Addressing The Seven Problems

What follows are some suggestions about how this type of live, real-time group discussion in the writing class can help to ameliorate some of the problems of traditional writing classes. In all cases, we do not claim that ENFI itself provides benefits, or that the software and the environment it creates are value-free—indeed, as Kaplan (1991) notes, software and pedagogical innovations such as ENFI are but tools, and "no tool can be innocent, free of ideological constructions" (p. 27). However, we do believe that a capable teacher may be able to address the problems below more effectively in the ENFI environment than if he or she works exclusively in a traditional classroom.

1. Demonstrating Writing

Modeling text production and revision in a traditional classroom is difficult because the text is often hard to read and takes too long to generate by hand. Further, the lack of rhetorical context may make the demonstrated writing seem remote from the students' own needs and interests.

In an ENFI classroom, the teacher is fully a part of an ENFI discussion on the network (not as a traditional, controlling teacher but as a more equal participant), so the students can see the teacher producing writing-in-action; live writing, writing hot off the press, in the context of the discussion, and right on their screens. It may be encouraging for students to see their writing teacher engaged in the written discussion, writing not as the expert author of the perfectly written class handouts, but as one more participant in a written discussion. Further, the ENFI network environment is ideal for demonstrating revision. According to Spitzer, "the use of a network to show revision as it occurs may prove to be the most effective method of explaining and demonstrating the process" (1989, p. 63).

Leading a discussion in an ENFI setting is no picnic, of course, and most teachers accustomed to a traditional classroom are "at sea" initially. They may feel that they have lost control of the class, and many never do get their "sea legs." However, through a combination of oral discussion and writing on the network, a teacher can provide good examples of his or her writing, or any student's writing, for all students to see. By using an overhead projector with a liquid crystal computer output display, classes find it far easier to discuss writing that has just occurred in class than by the old method of racing out to the copy room and making 38 copies of a paper to distribute, breathlessly, to students.

Orchestrating demonstrations of writing is not a cinch: Training teachers to work in an ENFI environment is an ongoing task in the profession. Yet, once they get the idea, teachers begin to think of new ways to use an ENFI environment. Text production is no longer such a private struggle; it can now be shared more easily in a setting reminiscent of the old language labs.

2. Creating Realistic Writing Tasks

The main audience for student writers is usually their teacher, and because the teacher usually knows far more than the student about most topics, the writing context is too artificial to generate texts that show genuine concern for audience expectations.

For students, the appeal of getting on the Internet or campus network during their free time is the opportunity to meet and talk with other students, either on campus or at other campuses. This writing is fun because it's real communication with a purpose. Sometimes, writing in or for a writing class seems more like filling in a form than communication. The teacher says to write an essay, which means that the first sentence has to introduce the topic and state a theme, the second paragraph has to provide supporting evidence, and so on. Students know that they will be judged on how well they fill in this form. However, the difference between fun on the networks and tedium in the essay form does not have to be so marked.

The ENFI environment helps the class link the fun and sense of purpose in communicating to real people in real time on the network to the process of drafting classroom assignments. Students can brainstorm early stages of a writing assignment on the network, knowing that they are communicating these ideas to others for direct feedback. Because this "class discussion" is in writing, and because more students will have participated (because parallel production is possible), it will be easier for students to make the transfer to an individually produced rough draft from an ENFI discussion than from a teacher-led oral discussion. Students in a traditional writing class will have to rely on notes from class when they face the blank sheet of paper (or the blank screen) in their dorm rooms; those enrolled in an ENFI section will have access to a printout of the discussion, which will contain not only their preliminary ideas, but feedback from other students. Further, because they will likely have contributed more to the discussion than if they had been in an oral discussion (in which most students usually say very little), it is also more likely they will remember threads of the discussion.

Writing in an ENFI setting is more social and more directed than the isolated act we often associate with text production. More of the writing is actually communication for a purpose to a real and present audience (Spitzer, 1989, p. 65). Students do not have to rely on the teacher as the only audience for all writing. The ENFI setting better allows teachers to help students understand that writing actually has a purpose in life.

3. Establishing an Audience for Students' Writing

Although we have all done it, writing only to the teacher seems odd and contrived, so students may not develop sensitivity to the expectations of real and varied audiences.

One of the more complex cognitive challenges for young writers is to develop an internal sense of an audience for their writing. Ong (1975) contends that "the writer's audience is always a fiction" (p. 9); that is, that we have to use the imagination to anticipate the expectations of an audience. How does one imagine what an audience needs and wants to know? And how to adjust one's style, register, and tone appropriately? In other words, how does one shift from what composition specialists call "writer-based prose" to "reader-based prose"? In a traditional writing class, if the default audience for all writing is the teacher, students may not progress much toward developing reader-based prose because they practice with only one audience. On the other hand because ENFI provides an audience for student writing other than the teacher (the other students), and because that audience responds in real time or near real time, we believe ENFI helps students develop audience sensitivity (Hawisher,1992 p. 86; Spitzer, 1989, p. 59).

4. Encouraging Writing Practice

Students in a traditional classroom spend most of their time listening to the teacher or working in small groups in which they mostly talk; they don't spend much time writing in writing class.

In some ENFI classes, teacher and students may spend a full class period having a written discussion, both to develop ideas and to provide an opportunity for more practice in writing. The class might start with a question or comment (often provided by the instructor) and explore or expand on the issues it raises. The ongoing discussion generates *writing* instead of evanescent talk, but not the formalized (often stilted) writing found in student essays. On the classroom network, students often write in a discourse style closer to speech than to traditional academic writing, and sometimes this "conversational style" is carried over into individual assignments (Batson, 1988, p. 32; Bump 1990a, p. 56). This carry over effect shows that ENFI can provide a bridge between the speaking skills of students and their writing.

We do not claim that "conversational writing" is any better than traditional academic writing—each style develops from a distinct rhetorical context—but because it practically forces writers to include themselves and other discussants as subjects in their sentences, conversational writing may help them avoid some of the "institutional passive" fuzziness found in much of the stilted "academese" students often think of as good writing. That the direct, active style often finds its way into more formal written assignments demonstrates that ENFI can bridge the gap between classroom and individual writing.

Because it happens in writing, ENFI allows the conversational style to cross over into formal writing assignments when students choose to begin a paper by revising their comments from the transcript of class discussion. Teachers may encourage them to polish the style and elaborate on the content, but not necessarily to edit out the direct, active voice. Thus, the revised draft may more honestly reflect its grounding in the multivocal *controversia* of class discussion.

There is no automatic carry-over from network writing to the complex writing tasks in academia, but for many students the practice in writing can help reduce writing anxiety, make writing class more enjoyable, make the teacher seem more approachable, provide more knowledge about a subject for students, and provide models of other ways to say things in writing.

5. Creating Collaborative Opportunities

Collaborating in a traditional classroom is awkward because sharing text on paper is slow and tedious.

One of the most daunting experiences young students have is facing a blank sheet of paper or a blank computer screen, alone, with the task of writing an essay. Although collaborative writing has its own problems, it at least is a helpful alternative to solitary writing. When students work together in small groups on an assignment, they can share ideas. It is as if they are not complete writers in and of themselves but together can be. Some are good at generating ideas or finding sources, others at organizing the ideas, and still others at drafting or editing. Though the teacher is the expert, she or he cannot work with all the students individually on projects nor does he or she need to. Students can and do learn from each other as well.

Further, many instructors who use ENFI have noticed a synergistic process occurring when students collaborate to generate ideas in real-time written discussion (Bump 1990a, p. 55). That is, after one student contributes a partially formed idea, others may base comments on it, building a new hypothesis or train of thought not possible without the interaction.

The exploratory nature of ENFI makes it ideal for invention, for testing new ideas, and for capturing thoughts as they come into being—before the critical consciousness has a chance to kick in and censor the statement that might, with further consideration, have seemed too odd to utter. Because of the sheer pressure to enter into the conversation or not be heard, students must think on the fly, inventing at the edge of consciousness and possibility. In so doing they may stumble on truths and ideas they might have cast off in the highly reflective self-consciousness of the "solitary writer crafting sentences" scenario. If they permit these utterances to fly out, others may see in them ideas they had not foreseen, and build on them. In so doing, students actually *collaborate* to bring thought structures into being through writing.

The ENFI environment provides new avenues and support for collaboration because text generation is so easy and sharing text less a problem than in a traditional classroom. Collaboration is the default mode in an ENFI setting.

6. The Time Lag Between Class Discussion and Student Writing

So much time elapses between class discussion and the actual writing of homework assignments that interest in and understanding of the ideas under consideration may have faded.

Before computer labs, writing teachers had to mostly talk about writing while students listened. Occasionally students would join in, but, in general, they would write later. This is still the prevalent model in writing classes. For capable writers, talking about writing can be helpful because it helps conceptualize the task of writing in different contexts, but for the average student it is probably better to engage in more practice and less discussion.

Working in an ENFI environment, it is possible to complete parts of the writing process during class time, eliminating the time lag between invention and text production. With prompts from the teacher and comments from their peers, students capture and develop ideas in writing from the outset of the ENFI session. Class discussion, writing practice, and teacher feedback are not spread out over a week or more but can be telescoped into one class session.

7. Limited and Unequal Participation

Few students speak up in class discussion; considerations such as gender, race, and physical characteristics prevent some from participating equally or at all.

Instructors who use ENFI have noted that several of its features tend to draw students into the conversation. The fact that they have an audience other than the teacher empowers them to voice their own opinions with some conviction instead of sitting back and letting the teacher's wisdom wash over them. Students gain confidence in their ideas, and because they come to depend on each other for feedback, they can develop a strong sense of community in a limited time frame. Some teachers have even noted that students involved in ENFI participate more because they feel the same companionship and warmth that we associate with friendship from some of their peers (Hawisher, 1991, p. 87). The sense of investment in and belonging to a community of writers engaged in a common goal pervades and facilitates the interactions; that engagement is reflected not only in increased participation, but also in the level of personal involvement students put into their written comments through the use of personal pronouns and active verbs (Murray, 1991, p. 217).

Some of the preliminary research indicates that because ENFI eliminates many of the physical cues of face-to-face communication, it allows more and different types of students to participate (Bump 1990a, pp. 50-51, 55; Faigley, 1990, p. 8; Kiesler, Siegel, & McGuire, 1984, p. 1125). The more reticent students have time to compose responses, and the comments in general tend to be more frank but better thought out. Students tend to be less afraid about "speaking up" in class. On the computer, students have little recourse to body language or feelings of inferiority based on race, gender, and other hierarchies, especially when the participants are anonymous (Cooper & Selfe, 1990, p. 853; Hawisher, 1992, p. 88). But anonymity is a double-edged sword that can encourage "flaming" (rude comments), as we shall see later.

Unlike face-to-face discussion, in ENFI exchanges, everyone has access to the "floor" at the same time. Students can be working on comments at the same time and post them to the group almost simultaneously. Thus, no one is left out because he or she cannot get a word in edgewise.

ENFI and The Teacher

We have listed a number of typical writing class problems that ENFI can help address. However, there is no magic in a communication program, only in the teachers who use it. We are describing potential advantages; none of these accrue automatically. As always, the teacher is the critical factor. However, in our experience of observing ENFI over its lifetime (since 1984), it is clear that only a limited number of teachers who try to work in an ENFI environment succeed, or even feel comfortable. Whether this will change as more teachers themselves become involved with computers is pure speculation. Right now, ENFI is a presence on over a hundred campuses in the United States, but in no instance is ENFI the predominant writing class environment used on campus.

PSYCHOLOGICAL AND SOCIAL EFFECTS OF ENFI

Those of us working in an ENFI environment have noticed an interesting psychological aspect: Visitors to this kind of class do not disrupt a group discussion as they do in a traditional classroom. We would expect, in a traditional classroom, that if a visitor entered the room during a class discussion or lecture, all eyes would move to the visitor. If the students were working in small groups, a visitor would cause less disruption. However, regardless of whether an ENFI class is broken into small groups or is involved in a whole class discussion on the network, a visitor to the room does not cause disruption. In other words, psychologically, an ENFI environment is always a multiply centered environment. This is a by-product of the slight delay between a person's "utterance" and other people perceiving that utterance (by reading it on the screen). The "real time" here is not quite real time; it is delayed real time.

There is no "floor" for which people compete, or we might say that if there is a floor, everyone can share it. People are all engaging in a conversation of sorts, but each is working on different parts of the conversational stream, and each is working at a different pace. They share the same place physically but are in different time dimensions. The sense of private space is thus strengthened and enlarged.

ENFI, then, is not quite real-time conversation, but it is not quite electronic mail, either. Everyone actually breathes the same air, and, from time to time, they may all react to the same stimulus, either on screen or off. And, of course, people do talk to each other, even while they write to each other on the network. Existing in this never-never land of psychologically overlapping but separate time frames, physical closeness, and chronological distance, ENFI is a strange beast, indeed. We have had the experience of standing up in class and trying to start an oral discussion but having to wait while students finished responding to each other in writing. We seemed to be carrying on two conversations at the same time, even seeming to exist in two different places at once. After a semester of this, one's concept of writing (or even of reality) may never be the same. The multiple centers of invention and discourse help to destabilize monological, teacher-based sources of authority and encourage students to take an active role in the written production of knowledge from a variety of perspectives (Hawisher, 1992; Hawisher & Selfe, 1991; Kiesler, Siegel, & McGuire, 1984). Students can become authorities in localized centers of discourse.

Adopting a Network Persona

Within this unique psychological space, participants find themselves adopting voices and personae they may not recognize. This "increased role fluidity" seems to come with the territory. In the ENFI writing environment, one seems to be anonymous—or at least the "agent" writing on the screen, prompted by his or her fingers, is. This sense of anonymity (even when names are attached to all messages) leads to experimentation with one's usual voice. Students may "flame" (use rude, inflammatory language) against each other, unless strictly controlled by the teachers; or, more positively, they may experiment with different personae in their writing. A shy student may become more aggressive. Professor Jerome Bump at the University of Texas found one of his certified introvert students behaving like an extrovert (Bump divided his sections of a course on the basis of the Meyers-Briggs scale; Bump, 1990b). When he reported this at a conference, others in the audience recognized the conversion experience (from shy to outgoing—at least on the network) students can have in an ENFI environment.

Exploiting the Network-Persona Syndrome

Teachers can take advantage of the tendency to play act on the ENFI network by creating situational simulations. Instead of doing the usual "let's discuss the problems of urban America," a writing teacher can instead create an improvisational drama based on readings students do before class about a particular problem, for example, crime. They might be asked to act as members of a jury during the trial of a young first-time offender. On the network, they can act out their jury roles and explore the issue from the inside. They can move, imaginatively, into a drama about the problem; they are no longer in a classroom, but in the jury room. The drama works not only because of the network's psychological prompting to explore new personae, but because the interaction, as it is in writing, is slow enough for students to think of an appropriate line and masked enough to avoid the embarrassment of being "on stage."

Thus, CMC's ability to alter the social dimensions of a group can be turned to advantage. The very "playing around" and "flaming" phenomena noticed by many teachers who use CMC may well be the key advantages of CMC. Writing is, after all, an exercise in creating a persona or ethos that will inspire a desired reaction from a particular audience. The ENFI environment gives students a real audience and context for that persona.

The Challenge to the Teacher

Often, we believe, instructors new to ENFI struggle to make this environment work in the same way as their traditional class. They have faith that what they do in their traditional class somehow leads the students toward learning or improvement, so, regardless of whether they have evidence or not, the practices they have used in their traditional classrooms (like oral discussion and grading papers) seem sacrosanct. But, holding on to the traditional makes it hard to see the opportunities in an ENFI environment, or in other CMC environments. The fluidity of roles or personae in ENFI, along with the simulations that fluidity enables, is one of the great strengths of ENFI. Yet, when students adopt an alternate persona on the network, teachers may react negatively, thinking of it as frivolity. At best, they may tolerate it while trying to move ahead with a "serious" (teacher-led) discussion, as if a traditional discussion was necessarily the most appropriate or even productive activity in this environment.

Given that such a different psychological environment is created within the ENFI setting, and that different practices are therefore appropriate for reaching the goals of a course, how will teachers make this shift? As this discussion of ENFI may suggest, reconceiving one's own role in an ENFI classroom is not something one can achieve overnight, or after an single, introductory workshop.

We believe that if there are enough training opportunities, writing teachers at least have a fighting chance to make the adjustment. However, even with sufficient training, teachers are still surrounded by an entire profession, and the whole world, both of which seem to believe writing should be taught very much as it has always been taught, albeit with some gestures toward collaborative work and the writing process. It is hard to swim upstream.

SUMMARY

CMC, in the form of ENFI, offers unusual and challenging opportunities for the age-old profession of teaching others to write. Because ENFI significantly alters familiar social and psychological dimensions of the writing classroom, the positive effects mentioned here cannot always be achieved. Many teachers are therefore afraid to try ENFI, or, having tried it, retreat back to the traditional classroom. Yet, even as an undertaking limited in national scope, ENFI provides a new perspective on how people learn to write. Those who try it may never see their job the same way again. Here, as elsewhere in society, CMC continues to nibble away at the traditional way of doing things.

REFERENCES

Batson, T. (1988). The ENFI project: A networked classroom approach to writing instruction. *Academic Computing*, 2(5), 32-33, 55-56.

Bump, J. (1990a). Radical changes in class discussion using networked computers. *Computers and the Humanities*, *49*, 49-65.

Bump. J. (1990b, May). Presentation at the Computers and Writing Conference, Austin, TX.

Cooper, M., & Selfe, C.L. (1990). Computer conferences and learning: Authority, resistance, and internally persuasive discourse. *College English*, *52*, 847-869.

Faigley, L. (1990). Subverting the electronic network: Teaching writing using networked computers. In D. A. Daiker & M. Morenberg (Eds.), *The writing teacher as researcher: Essays in the theory and practice of class-based research* (pp. 290-311). Portsmouth, NH: Boynton/Cook.

Hawisher, G.E. (1992). Electronic meetings of the minds: Research, electronic conferences, and composition studies. In G.E. Hawisher & P. LeBlanc (Eds.), *Re-imagining computers and composition: Teaching and research in the virtual age* (pp. 81-101). Portsmouth, NH: Boynton/Cook.

Hawisher, G.E. & Selfe, C.L. (1991). The rhetoric of technology and the electronic writing class. *College Composition and Communication, 42,* 55-65.

Kaplan, N. (1991) Ideology, technology, and the future of writing instruction. In G.E. Hawisher & C.L. Selfe (Eds.), *Evolving perspectives on computers and composition studies: Questions for the 1990s* (pp. 11-42). Urbana, IL, and Houghton, MI: NCTE and Computers and Composition Press.

Kiesler, S., Siegel, J., & McGuire, T.W. (1984). Social psychological aspects of computer-mediated communication. *American Psychologist, 39,*1123-1134.

Murray, D. (1991). The composing process for computer conversation. *Written Communication, 8,* 35-55.

Ong, W. (1975). The writer's audience is always a fiction. *Publications of the Modern Language Association, 90,* 9-22.

Spitzer, M. (1989). Computer conferencing: An emerging technology. In G.E. Hawisher and C.L. Selfe (Eds.), *Critical perspectives on computers and composition instruction* (pp. 187-200). New York: Teachers College Press.

APPENDIX A: SOFTWARE THAT CREATES AN ENFI ENVIRONMENT

ENFI is an idea, not software. It is an environment or what might be called an alternative classroom, and it can be created by a number of different software solutions. The following are among those ENFI software solutions available now.

Aspects (Macintosh)

This is group-editing software that allows up to 12 users to share and edit files on a local network, or even across a wide-area network. Within the writing classroom, such a program might be useful for small group editing exercises and peer critiques. A convenient "chat box" window allows participants to have real-time written conversations as they edit. Thus, Aspects is ENFI software with the powerful bonus of supporting group editing.

Available from Group Logic, 1408 North Fillmore Street, Suite 10, Arlington, VA 22201; (800) 476-8781. Internet: grouplogic@Acx.com.

ClassWriter (Macintosh)

This software includes:

1. *The Electronic Dialectical Notebook,* a server-based conferencing program that allows the instructor to send a text along with an exercise to all the students' machines. The students are then electronically connected in pairs, and they complete the exercises and comment on each other's responses.
2. *Conversation,* a server-based ENFI tool that uses a local area network for conferencing. In Conversation, each message has its own window, accessible by double clicking on a menu that constantly updates as the conversation progresses. Conversation allows communication among diads or the entire group.

Available from Intellimation, Dept. 2HF, 130 Cremona Drive, P.O. Box 1530, Santa Barbara, CA 93116; (800) 346-8355.

Conference Writer (Macintosh)

Using its own word processing program and editor, Conference Writer allows writers to compose and share their writing with others in up to 12 groups.

Available from RDA/Mind Builders, 10 Boulevard Avenue, Greenlawn, NY 11740; (800) 654-8715.

Daedalus Integrated Writing Environment

This software is a bundle of five server-based writing tools, which contains:

1. *Write,* a basic word processor.
2. *Invent,* seven sets of heuristic prompt questions based on, among others, Aristotelian, Burkean, and tagmemic (Young, Becker, and Pike) rhetorical theories, to aid in the invention process.
3. *Respond,* a revision heuristic for responding to peers' drafts.
4. *Contact,* an electronic mail program for the composition classroom.

5. *Interchange*, a real-time conversation program that, like Conversation, uses simple networking capabilities to make text-based classroom discussion possible. Unlike Conversation, Interchange adds messages to a constantly scrolling field, which updates as soon as the participant clicks on the "send" button.

Available for Macintosh or DOS from The Daedalus Group, 1106 Clayton Lane, Suite 248W, Austin, TX 78723; (800) 879-2144. Internet: info@daedalus.com.

Forum (Macintosh)

Similar to Interchange, Forum sets up a discussion file or group of files on the server, to which participants may join and contribute. A convenient feature is the Forum Administration program, which can create and read detailed statistics of user activity.

Contact Robert Boston, 521 12th Street, Ames, IA 50010. Internet: boston@iastate.edu. BITnet: S2.RSB@ISUMVS.

OpenForum (Macintosh)

This software is a hypercard-based brainstorming tool that uses Appletalk to share idea windows. Each post is appended to the session record, to which all other connected participants can view and respond.

Available from MasterPlan, Inc., 6314 High Street, Haslett, MI 48840; (517) 339-2478.

Real-time Writer

This is the original ENFI environment. It runs on a local-area network and is near real time; "conversation" scrolls on screen as new messages are received. It has database searching capability.

Available from Real Time Learning Systems, 2700 Connecticut Avenue, N.W., Washington, DC 20008-5330; (800) 832-2472.

TeamFocus

This is the most complex but the richest environment. This set of tools was developed for group decision support, but it is also used as a sequence of environments to support groups going through a writing process. It is available on local-area networks.

Available from the IBM TeamFocus Support Center, Endicott, NY. Also, contact Trent Batson, Gallaudet University, Washington, DC.

APPENDIX B: GENERAL READINGS

Amdahl, M. (1992). Aspects 1.0. [Review]. *Computers and Composition 10*(1), 89-92.

This contains a review of Aspects, one program that allows an ENFI environment to be created through shared text files on networked machines.

[The entire November 1992 issue of *Computers and Composition* is recommended to writing teachers seeking information about software for composition.]

Barker, T.T., & Kemp, F.O. (1990). Network theory: A postmodern pedagogy for the writing classroom. In C. Handa (Ed.), *Computers and community* (pp. 1-27). Portsmouth, NH: Boynton/Cook.

Barker and Kemp compare the traditional "proscenium" (teacher centered) classroom with a new, postmodern approach to writing instruction based on what they call "network theory." They provide a model for classroom pedagogy that encourages shared knowledge, collaboration, and student enfranchisement.

Batson, T. (1988). The ENFI Project: A Networked classroom approach to writing instruction. *Academic Computing*, 2(5), 32-33, 55-56.

Batson details the rationale and findings of the ENFI Project, a 3-year study of classes at five universities in which students using ENFI software were compared with those in traditional classrooms.

Batson, T., & Peyton, J.K. (1986, November). *ENFI project report 1985-1986*. Unpublished manuscript available from the ENFI Project, Gallaudet University, 800 Florida Ave. NE, Washington, DC 20002.

This is a more detailed version of the above study. A comprehensive bibliography is also available upon request.

Brown, L.F. (1992). The Daedalus Integrated Writing Environment. [Review]. *Computers and Composition, 10*(1), 77-88.

This is a review of the latest incarnation of Daedalus's five program-writing software bundle, formerly known as DIScourse. One of the programs, Interchange, has been widely used to create ENFI environments in writing classrooms.

Bruce, B., Peyton J.K., & Batson T. (1993). *Network-based classrooms: Promises and realities*. New York: Cambridge University Press.

Bump, J. (1990). Radical changes in class discussion using networked computers. *Computers and the Humanities, 49*, 49-65.

Bump describes the ways in which ENFI-based written discussions changed the dynamics of classroom participation and his students' attitudes toward writing.

Bump, J. (1990, May) Presentation at the Computers and Writing Conference, Austin, TX.

Burns, H. (1992). "Teaching composition in tomorrow's multimedia, multinetworked classrooms." In G.E. Hawisher & P. LeBlanc (Eds.), *Re-imagining computers and composition: Teaching and research in the virtual age* (pp. 115-130). Portsmouth, NH: Boynton/Cook.

Burns discusses the strengths and weaknesses of using multimedia and multinetworking, a kind of long-distance ENFI, to link writing classes at remote sites.

Cooper, M., & Selfe, C.L. (1990). Computer conferences and learning: Authority, resistance, and internally persuasive discourse. *College English, 52*, 847-869.

Eldred, J., & Fortune, R. (1992). Exploring the implications of metaphors for computer networks and hypermedia. In G.E. Hawisher & P. LeBlanc (Eds.), *Re-imagining computers and composition: Teaching and research in the virtual age* (pp. 58-73). Portsmouth, NH: Boynton/Cook.

Eldred and Fortune situate electronic conferencing within the metaphorical structures we use to describe communicative forms. They problematize the notion that ENFI is purely written communication by showing how teachers discussing "written conversation" are "continually thrown back into the language or metaphor of speech" (p. 63).

Faigley, L. (1990). Subverting the electronic network: Teaching writing using networked computers. In D. A. Daiker & M. Morenberg (Eds.), *The writing teacher as researcher: Essays in the theory and practice of class-based research* (pp. 290-311). Portsmouth, NH: Boynton/Cook.

In a study somewhat similar to Bump's, Faigley discusses his experiences using ENFI with writing classes. Faigley's findings indicate that "reading and writing are inherently social," that in ENFI-based discussion, "the many voices act out Bakhtin's principle of dialogism," and that "computers joined in a network can be a means of liberation, particularly for those students who are often marginalized in American classrooms."

Hawisher, G.E. (1992) Electronic meetings of the minds: Research, electronic conferences, and composition studies. In G.E. Hawisher & P. LeBlanc (Eds.), *Re-imagining computers and composition: Teaching and research in the virtual age* (pp. 81-101). Portsmouth, NH: Boynton/Cook.

Hawisher situates electronic conferencing, both synchronous and asynchronous, within the larger frameworks of composition pedagogy and social constructionism. Her section on the advantages and disadvantages of using electronic conferences will be especially valuable to writing teachers.

Hawisher, G.E. & Selfe, C.L. (1991). The rhetoric of technology and the electronic writing class. *College Composition and Communication, 42,* 55-65.

Hawisher, G.E. & P. LeBlanc (Eds.). (1991). *Re-imagining computers and composition: Teaching and research in the virtual age.* Portsmouth, NH: Boynton/Cook.

A must-read for computer-using writing teachers. These essays reassess the present state of computer-assisted writing instruction, with a look toward the future. Most notably, they challenge our assumptions about what writing is, and what composition pedagogy should be.

Kaplan, N. (1991) Ideology, technology, and the future of writing instruction. In G.E. Hawisher & C.L. Selfe (Eds.), *Evolving perspectives on computers and composition studies: Questions for the 1990s* (pp. 11-42). Urbana, IL, and Houghton, MI: NCTE and Computers and Composition Press.

Kaplan argues that software and pedagogies for computer based writing instruction, like other tools and pedagogies, are based on often-unstated social conventions and assumptions about authority and power. Because there is no such thing as a value-free or neutral program or approach, we must be aware of the possibilities for exclusion or disenfranchisement inherent in any approach.

Kemp, F. (1992). Who programmed this? Examining the instructional attitudes of writing-support software. *Computers and Composition, 10*(1), 9-24.

This article contains a section that examines computer-mediated communication's role in changing assumptions about writing and composition pedagogy. Kemp argues that students' use of CMC in the writing classroom is "less a passive reception of knowledge and more an active generation of skills (p. 19), and that "such networked pedagogy challenges the notion that writing is either strictly formal or strictly personal (p. 19).

Klem, E., & Moran, C. (1991). Computers and instructional strategies in the teaching of writing. In G.E. Hawisher & C.L. Selfe (Eds.), *Evolving perspectives on computers and composition studies: Questions for the 1990s* (pp. 132-149). Urbana, IL, and Houghton, MI: NCTE and Computers and Composition Press.

This article also contains a section on CMC in the networked writing classroom that discusses the possibilities for interactive and collaborative work and CMC's potential to shift the locus of power from teachers to students.

Langston, M.D., & Batson, T. (1990). The social shifts invited by working collaboratively on computer networks: The ENFI project. In C. Handa (Ed.), *Computers and community* (pp. 140-159). Portsmouth, NH: Boynton/Cook.

A detailed examination of some of the social shifts that often occur in ENFI classrooms, this article contains a short sample of an ENFI session transcript and shows how the adoption of ENFI can move classrooms from "presentational to environmental, "can shift the teacher from evaluator to participator, can move classroom activity from "recitation to collaboration," and can change composition from an "individual to [a] social" act.

Mason, R. & Kaye, A. (Eds.). (1989). *Mindweave: Communication, computers and distance education.* New York: Pergamon Press.

Although it deals primarily with electronic conferencing in distance education, this text makes an important contribution to network theory in its suggestion that electronic conferences have the potential to weave together multiple perspectives and sources of information from participants, a phenomenon Mason and Kaye call "mindweave."

Moran, C. (1992). Computers and the writing classroom: A look to the future. In G.E. Hawisher & P.LeBlanc (Eds.), *Re-imagining computers and composition: Teaching and research in the virtual age* (pp. 7-23). Portsmouth, NH: Boynton/Cook.

The section of Moran's article dealing with the online classroom provides a detailed description of the CMC-using electronic university of the future. Although he outlines some of the benefits of the online classroom, Moran is careful to mention the major drawback of CMC: that it lacks the visual cues of face-to-face communication. He is optimistic, however, "that we will develop new conventions—such as the 'emoticons' of e-mail correspondence—once we have learned to live and work in our virtual classrooms" (p.19).

Neuwirth, C. et al. (1993). Why write—together—concurrently on a computer network? In B. Bruce, J.K. Peyton and T. Batson (Eds.), *Network-based classrooms: Promises and realities*. New York: Cambridge University Press.

Schriner, D.K., & Rice, W.C. (1989). Computer conferencing and collaborative learning: A discourse community at work. *College Composition and Communication, 40*, 472-478.

Selfe, C.L., & Meyer, P.R. (1991). Testing claims for online conferences.

Written Communication, 8, 163-198.

Spitzer, M. (1989). Computer conferencing: An emerging technology. In G.E. Hawisher & C.L. Selfe, (Eds.), *Critical perspectives on computers and composition instruction* (pp. 187-200). New York: Teachers College Press.

Spitzer, M. (1990). Local and global networking: Implications for the future. In D.H. Holdstein & C.L. Selfe (Eds.), *Computers and writing: Theory, research, practice* (pp. 58-79). New York: Modern Language Association of America.

This article deals with both local and long-distance CMC and discusses a wide range of possible effects of ENFI on writing classrooms.

Taylor, P. (1992). Social epistemic rhetoric and chaotic discourse. In G.E. Hawisher & P. LeBlanc (Eds.), *Re-imagining computers and composition: Teaching and research in the virtual age* (pp. 131-148). Portsmouth, NH: Boynton/Cook.

Taylor relates synchronous conferencing (ENFI) to chaos theory in order to show how the communal text and synergistic interactions generated by such conferencing challenge our notions of originality, authorship, and coherence.

Thomson, D. (1988). Interactive networking: Creating bridges between speech, writing, and composition. *Computers and Composition, 5*(3), 17-22.

Tuman, M. (1992). *Word perfect: Literacy in the computer age.* Pittsburgh: University of Pittsburgh Press.

In his chapter titled "The New Writing," Tuman contextualizes classroom CMC efforts, such as ENFI, in terms of their cultural implications. He discusses and problematizes the potential for critical thought, collaboration, and consensus in a CMC environment.

Chapter Three

Patterns of Social Interaction and Learning to Write: Some Effects of Network Technologies*

Karen Hartman, Christine M. Neuwirth
Sara Kiesler, Lee Sproull
Cynthia Cochran, Michael Palmquist
and David Zubrow

In 1981, Emig challenged the dominant educational model in the schools, a model that viewed writing as "exclusively a silent and solitary activity," and called upon teachers to view writing as an activity that "can be enhanced by working in, and with a group of other writers, perhaps especially a teacher, who give vital response, including advice" (p. 27). A decade later, teachers who have adopted collaborative approaches to writing no longer lecture exclusively. In addition, they talk with stu-

*This research was funded in part by Committee on Social Science Research in Computing (CSSRC), Carnegie Mellon University, and by the Annenberg/CPB Project as part of the Electronic Networks for Interaction (ENFI) Consortium. This chapter originally appeared in *Written Communication*, *8*(1), 79-113, and is reprinted here with permission of Sage Publications.

dents to monitor what they are learning and to understand how best to structure collaborative activities. In practice, however, learning to write in collaboration with others is difficult. In the traditional writing classroom, time constraints and routines are counterproductive of collaboration. For example, a group of teachers who were named as outstanding teachers of writing reported that student conferencing is extremely valuable but difficult to arrange with any frequency (Freedman, 1987). The teacher in a traditional classroom is constrained because logistically it is easier to have everyone on the same time clock. Everyone turns in papers at the same time and receives comments at the same time. It is also hard to arrange for students to give and receive comments from their classmates. It is expensive to reproduce papers for circulation and it is time-consuming to coordinate the sharing of papers.

In the past, these problems have plagued collaborative writing programs. But a new technology, word processing plus computer-mediated communication, may help to alleviate some of them. Computer-mediated communication is a text-based tool (e.g., electronic mail, bulletin boards) that can be synchronous or, more frequently, is asynchronous. Unlike computer-based tools for writing that allow an author to check or improve his or her work by interacting only with computer programs or databases (such as text analyzers or dictionaries), this technology is entirely devoted to letting people communicate with one another. Several characteristics make it uniquely suited to increasing interaction and to expediting collaboration among teachers and students. First, both synchronous and asynchronous computer-mediated communication overcome physical barriers. Teacher and students do not have to be in the same place (e.g., the teacher's office, the classroom, a dormitory room) to communicate. Of course, the telephone permits interaction over space—but not over time. Moreover, people cannot read over the telephone, and providing detailed comments over the telephone is difficult, particularly when only one person has a physical copy of the paper as is often the case. Second, asynchronous computer-mediated communication is convenient. Senders and receivers do not have to coordinate their communications jointly. Students do not have to wait for a class meeting or an arranged appointment to offer a paper for feedback or to ask questions. Responses from classmates and teachers can be requested when they are most needed. Third, computer-mediated communication, particularly electronic mail, greatly reduces social context cues, even when participants do not use pseudonyms (Dubrovsky, Kiesler, & Sethna, in press; Sproull & Kiesler, 1986). It reduces static social cues such as clothing and furniture that remind people of social definitions and social distinctions. It reduces dynamic social cues such as smiling, frowning and hesitating that remind people they are being evaluated. Students who might be anxious or shy about going to the teacher's office or contacting a classmate might feel more confident communicating electronically (Finholt, Kiesler, & Sproull, 1986). Finally, group computer communication tools such as electronic bulletin boards and distributive mail lists make it easy to communicate with many people simultaneously over distance, providing students with opportunities to communicate in real contexts to a wider audience than just the teacher, both locally, within a classroom or school (Rubin & Bruce, 1986), and globally, throughout the country or world (Cohen & Riel, 1989; Levin, Riel, Boruta, & Rowe, 1984).

Increased interest in using collaborative activities to teach writing (Bruffee, 1973, 1985; Gere, 1987), increased use of computers to prepare text, and increased access to computer-mediated communication tools has led to the use of asynchronous electronic bulletin boards and electronic mail to extend the writing classroom (Hiltz, 1986; Payne, 1987) and to the use of synchronous electronic communication to give real-time writing feedback (Batson, 1988). However, our understanding of how computer-mediated communication affects patterns of interaction in writing classes is limited (Sheingold, Hawkins, & Char, 1984). The primary goal of the field experiment reported here was to begin exploring this process by comparing interaction in writing classes that had access to networked communication tools with interaction in classes that used traditional modes of communication.

HYPOTHESES

We examined the following hypotheses:

H1. When the technology is easily accessible and sanctioned, teachers will communicate more with students and students will communicate more with each other because computer-mediated communication may increase opportunities for interaction and decrease its costs. In other words, we expected total communication to increase with the availability and teacher sanctioning of networked communication tools; we did not expect communication via traditional modes to decrease as electronic communication increased.

In addition to examining the overall effects of the availability of computer-mediated communication on interaction, we examined the role of several potential mediating variables—in particular, variables relating to performance, ability, anxiety, and behavioral consistency.

While the present study is not designed as a test of any theory of social interaction in learning to write, we used ideas from models of motivational and structuring processes and their effects on social interaction (Turner, 1988) to hypothesize the following consequences of computer-mediated communication for individual students:

H2a. Less able or poorer performing students will be the primary beneficiaries of increased opportunities for communication. On the one hand, the classroom ecology literature suggests that brighter, better performing students dominate traditional modes of communication such as face-to-face by choosing the front and center classroom seats where interaction is greatest (e.g., Adams & Biddle, 1970; Becker, Sommer, Bee, & Oxley, 1973; Breed & Colaiuta,1974; Sommer, 1967; see Montello, 1988, for a review). Perhaps these students would also dominate these new ways to communicate as well. However, we expected network communication tools to provide less able or poorer performing students with communication opportunities that they might not have in the regular classroom because of efforts to maintain self-esteem, shyness, or slower reaction times.

H2b. Students with higher writing anxiety will interact less about their writing with their teachers and other students via traditional modes of communication than students with lower anxiety. Although a definite cause of writing anxiety has not been established, it seems likely that anxiety over evaluation plays a role (Hillocks, 1986) and, if this is the case, we would expect high anxiety students to avoid situations in which their writing may be evaluated. In addition, this negative relationship between anxiety and interaction will be less for communication via computer-mediated modes because it takes place without an exchange of nonverbal cues and social context information that (1) reminds students they are being evaluated and (2) makes it easier for students to manage self-presentation.

H2c. Students with higher computer anxiety will interact less about their writing via computer-mediated communication modes than students with lower computer anxiety. In an experimental setting, high levels of computer anxiety were shown to be related to poorer task performance, greater state anxiety, self-reported physiological arousal, and debilitative thoughts (Heinssen, Glass, & Knight, 1987). Hence, we expect high levels of computer anxiety to lead to avoidance of using computers.

H2d. Students who communicate more with their teacher and other students at the beginning of the semester will communicate more with their teacher and other students at the end of the semester. The fact that social interactions are repeated across time gives rise to structuring in social interactions. This is an hypothesis of simple behavioral consistency or "routinization" as a predictor of amount of interaction (cf. Turner, 1988).

Finally, and somewhat speculatively, we hypothesized the following about individual teachers:

H2e. More experienced teachers and their students will use electronic communication modes more than less experienced teachers. New computer technologies do not, in and of themselves, create educational improvements; instead, they create opportunities for improvements. Realizing such opportunities typically requires teachers and students to reconceptualize ways of teaching and learning in order to exploit the technology's potential for enhancing classroom goals. As Rubin and Bruce (1990) observe, ". . . in general, teachers and students create *new practices* that reflect complex and situation-specific combinations of old and new approaches" (p. 2). If realizing a technological innovation is a complex problem-solving process in which teachers and their students must reason about the potential of the new technology in order to create practices that meet classroom goals, then we might expect that experienced teachers will be more effective in realizing the potentials of new technologies. Research suggests that experienced teachers have more developed knowledge structures about learning, teaching, and students that allow them to reason more effectively about classroom events than inexperienced teachers; inexperienced teachers seem to lack the conceptual structures or seem to have simple, undifferentiated structures (cf. Clark & Peterson, 1986).

We explored these hypotheses in a field experiment that compared two types of collaborative writing classes, one in which students and teachers used traditional modes of communication and computer word processing, the other in which teachers and students used, in addition, a distributed computer network having special applications for collaborative work, a document "comments program," a program for simultaneous discussion via computer, electronic bulletin boards, and electronic mail.

METHOD

The data for this study were collected from four sections of a freshman writing course at Carnegie Mellon University (CMU) in the spring of 1988. The course is a university-wide core requirement for all students who do not qualify for an exemption based on SAT and AP scores. (In the academic year '87-'88, approximately 12% of the freshmen were exempt.) All sections emphasized collaborative approaches to writing. Two sections used network communication tools in their writing tasks. Each networked section met in a computer laboratory once a week and in the regular classroom twice a week. When the networked classes met in the computer laboratory, students and teachers used traditional modes of communication (e.g., face-to-face) as well as electronic modes. The two regular sections met three times a week in a regular classroom. Although the networked section met in the computer laboratory only once a week, students and teachers in the networked sections (and in the regular classrooms as well) had access to the electronic modes of communication outside the classroom at any time. Thus, the primary difference between the networked sections and the regular sections was that in the networked sections, teachers sanctioned the use of electronic modes of communication by meeting in the computer laboratory once a week and encouraging—and on some occasions requiring—students to use the electronic modes outside the classroom.

Participants

Students were randomly assigned to the sections, subject only to constraints of scheduling and achieving a mix of majors in each section. Both the networked and regular sections contained a balance of fine arts students (architecture and art) and science and engineering students. (Freshmen liberal arts students take this course in the fall.) There were no significant differences in average SAT verbal scores across sections as indicated by a one-way ANOVA, $F(3,70) = .29$, n.s. Thirty-seven students were placed in the networked sections, and forty-four students were assigned to the regular sections. All entering CMU students take a Computer Skills Workshop (CSW) that teaches three computer systems, including the system on which the networked writing tools are implemented. In CSW, students learn to use electronic mail and bulletin boards. All thirty-seven students in the networked sections had completed the Computer Skills Workshop prior to the writing class. All but three students in the regular sections had taken the workshop prior to beginning the writing class. All sections were told that the English Department was studying collaboration in writing.

The two teachers in the networked sections were interested in teaching networked sections of the course.[1] One was a beginning teacher with only several semesters part-time experience; the other had several years full-time experience in teaching, administration, and tutoring. The teachers in the regular sections were targeted for recruitment into the study on the basis of teaching experience comparable with that of teachers interested in teaching the networked sections. This targeted recruitment resulted in one teacher being a beginner with one semester prior experience; the other had several years full-time prior experience in teaching, administration, and tutoring. All teachers were recruited on the basis of their interest in collaborative approaches to writing and were randomly assigned to their sections. All teachers used word processing regularly and were at least acquainted with using the campus wide network. The teachers using the computer network to support collaborative writing in their sections were also given computer technical support.

Course Structure and Writing Assignments

The writing course emphasized the process of writing, strategies for producing particular types of writing, discussions, feedback, and revision. Each student in this course wrote and revised three papers during the semester. The three writing assignments were (1) the statement of a problem and an analysis of its aspects, (2) defining a thesis and supporting it, and (3) a proposal with a problem-solution structure. Students also examined how each of these three kinds of writing functions in its academic, public, and professional contexts. Because of course constraints, the assignments were not counterbalanced and are thus treated separately in subsequent analyses.

The instructors followed a common course outline with identical writing assignments, but specific activities in their individual classes were left to their discretion. Each pair of instructors (networked vs. regular) had weekly meetings with a supervisor to discuss collaborative approaches to writing. Collaborative activities discussed included all aspects of the composing process: monitoring and orchestrating writing processes, representing the writing task, purpose and audience, acquiring knowledge, generating ideas, setting goals, and so forth. The instructors reported a similar mix of activities and requirements across the four sections. All four teachers required students to attend one face-to-face conference about their first paper, and all were available for optional conferences for the remainder of the semester. As students planned each paper, they

[1]The English department typically runs networked sections on the basis of teacher interest.

engaged in interactions and group exercises both inside and outside the classroom. In addition, students typically wrote at least one draft on which the teacher and classmates commented before writing a final draft. Although students collaborated on many writing processes, students drafted their papers individually and were assigned individual grades.

Network Tools

While all four sections engaged in traditional (e.g., face-to-face) collaborative activities, the networked sections also used the following network communication tools for collaborative communication: *Comments* (Neuwirth, Kaufer, Keim & Gillespie, 1988) and Talk (Neuwirth, Palmquist & Gillespie, 1988a, b), electronic bulletin boards, and electronic mail. *Comments* is a menu-driven computer program that permits authors to send electronic versions of papers for comment to an unlimited number of respondents (see Figure 3.1). The author of a paper notifies a recipient by an electronic mail message that he or she would like the recipient to comment on the paper. The recipient can read the paper online or print a hard copy, but, except to add comments, normally cannot change the electronic copy sent by the author. *Comments* provides a special window in which the reader writes comments, much as the reviewer of a paper document might write comments in the margin of that document. To make a comment, the reader uses a mouse to point to a location in the text or selects a region of text and chooses *Make Comment* from a menu. An icon appears in the text marking the region the reader is commenting on. The reader can make as many comments as desired. He or she may also have access to comments written by others (perhaps by the author or other readers) and can comment on those by pointing to the location within the comment and again choosing *Make Comment*. When the reader is done, he or she notifies the author that the paper is available by an electronic mail message. At that point, if the author does not understand a comment or disagrees with it, the author can ask for elaboration by sending the paper back to the commenter, continuing a dialog. The *Comments* program is similar to some other text annotation programs that support collaborative writing (Edwards, Levine, & Kurland, 1986; Fish, Kraut, Leland, & Cohen, 1988), but it is integrated with the CMU campus-wide, distributed personal computing network that allows students and teachers to access their files from any workstation on campus.[2] Students in the networked section were introduced to this program during the first weeks of the semester and could

[2]CMU's campus-wide network is based on a distributed personal computing environment of advanced function workstations called *Andrew* (Morris, et al.,1986).

access it in the computer laboratory and at other locations on campus at any time. That is, students' use of the *Comments* program was not limited to the one day they met in the laboratory; students could access all electronic communication modes 24 hours a day, 7 days a week. They were sometimes assigned tasks that required them to use the program to comment on each other's writing and to "hand in" intermediate and final drafts to their teachers. They were encouraged to use the program to contact their teachers if they had a "quick question" about their intermediate drafts while composing. Students often used *Comments* outside the classroom.

The networked writing students also used *Talk*, a communication program designed for synchronous conversation and brainstorming. *Talk* puts a window on a workstation screen for each participant in the conver-

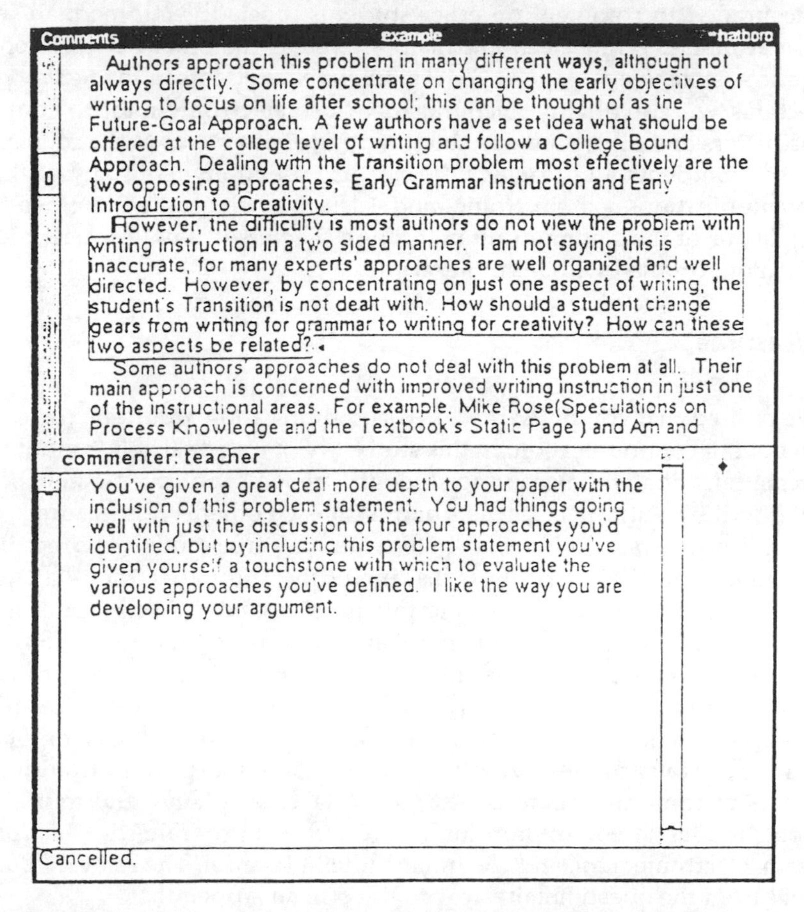

Figure 3.1. Comments program screen with a student's text in the upper panel and a teacher's comment in the lower panel

sation. It splits each window into panels, one for each participant. Each participant can compose and read messages in his or her own panel and can read the messages of other participants in all the other panels. Participants do not need to wait to read other messages before composing and sending their own. All messages are sent character-by-character, the instant participants type them. *Talk* also stores on the disk a record of the conversation that students could access or print. *Talk* was used primarily during the class sessions held in the computer laboratory for required activities structured by the instructor (e.g., brainstorming or role-playing types of readers), though like *Comments*, students could access it from any workstation on campus and occasionally used it outside the classroom.

Students in the networked sections were also assigned tasks to be posted on the section's electronic bulletin board (B-board) and were encouraged to comment on other students' posts. Electronic mail was also available. While electronic mail (as well as the other network tools) are accessible to everyone at CMU at all times, students in the networked sections were explicitly encouraged to use electronic mail to contact instructors and other students about writing assignments in the course.

Students and teachers did not use pseudonyms in any of their communications via electronic modes. Each of the tools identifies the originator of the communication through the person's unique user identification, coupled with his or her name.

Measures

We posited that computer-mediated communication would increase the amount of communication. In this study, we operationalized "amount of communication" by measuring students' frequency of interaction about their writing with their teachers and with each other. We measured frequency of interaction by asking students how frequently they received comments on their writing tasks, including the paper they had just turned in. Students were asked to rate on seven point Likert scales how often their instructors and other students had communicated with them via various modes of communication. We also asked students to rate how helpful the comments were "for becoming a better writer," in order to obtain one indicator of the quality of the interactions that took place via the various modes. Questions were asked about three traditional modes of communication (paper, face-to-face, telephone) and four electronic modes of communication (the *Comments* program, the *Talk* program, electronic mail, and electronic bulletin boards). The relevant questions from the questionnaire are provided in an Appendix.

We hypothesized that less able or poorer performing students would be the primary beneficiaries of increased opportunities for communication. We used verbal SAT as a general indicator of ability. We collected two measures of students' writing performance. The first was the grade assigned by the instructors to the papers. Since grades are known to teachers and the students who receive them, this measure can be expected to be relevant to students' efforts to maintain self-esteem. Grades ranged from D- to A+ and were translated into a simple 12-point variable (i.e., D- =1, D=2, D+ =3, C- =4, etc.). In theory, this measure should reflect only the quality of writing, but because teachers interact with students in many ways other than by reading their writing assignments, it is possible that factors in addition to the quality of the written assignment partially determined the grades. Moreover, students in the different sections were graded by different instructors, making it difficult to compare grades of students across sections.

Therefore, the second measure of students' writing performance was holistic scores assessed by four independent sets of judges who did not know the students. The judges were asked to perform holistic evaluations based on assignment-specific course criteria. Judges were trained on a set of practice papers following the procedures outlined by Jacobs et al. (1981). Two sets of judges consisted of three doctoral students in English, two acting as primary judges and one as a "tiebreaker." The other two sets of judges consisted of five doctoral students each. The judges' assessments were made in two stages. First, one set of two judges made rough evaluations of the first papers by placing them into four quartiles with the third judge acting as a "tiebreaker" to insure that papers were distributed equally into the four quartiles. The reliability of the first two judges (Spearman's correlation) was .61. The other set of three judges did the same for the last papers (Spearman's correlation for the two primary judges = .48). Second, one set of five judges read all of the first papers within each quartile and ranked them from best to worst. The average of the rankings of the five judges was used to generate one rank per paper. The reliability of this summary measure (Cronbach's alpha) was .63. Thus, when the rankings were combined, the entire set of first papers was ranked from the best to the worst. The same procedure was followed by the other set of five judges for the last papers (Cronbach's alpha = .56).[3] Although the interrater reliability scores are on the low side, the reliability of the resulting summary measures and hence their empirical validity (i.e., the correlation between them and

[3]Only 4 of the 5 judges' rankings were used in forming the summary measure for the last set of papers. Preliminary analyses indicated that the rankings of the 5th judge correlated negatively with those of each of the other 4 judges. This discrepancy may be due to the judge having made an error in data recording (accidentally reversing the scales) or to the judge using different criteria than the other 4 judges (and to the criteria the judge had used in the training session). Because a large amount of time had elapsed between the collection of the ranking data and

another observed variable) may be higher than what is indicated by the interrater reliability scores (Bohrnstedt, 1983).[4]

We hypothesized that writing anxiety and computer anxiety would mediate students' interactions. We operationalized writing anxiety with the Daly-Miller writing apprehension scale (Daly & Miller, 1975) and computer anxiety with the Computer Anxiety Rating Scale (Heinssen, et al., 1987).

Finally, we hypothesized that teacher experience would affect interaction in electronic modes. We assessed teachers' experience through an examination of their departmental records and interviews.

Procedures and Analyses

We collected data using two questionnaires. The first asked about high school writing experience and prior computing experience, and it included the Daly-Miller writing apprehension scale and the Computer Anxiety Rating Scale. It was administered during the initial week of classes.

The second questionnaire assessed students' perceptions of frequency of interaction via three distinct traditional modes of communication and four distinct electronic modes of communication as well as the helpfulness of the various modes. Because we were primarily concerned with change in use of the different modes of communication across the semester, the second questionnaire was administered two times: after students had turned in their first paper and had received a grade for it, about six weeks into the semester, and again when the students turned in their last paper but before they had received a grade, at the very the end of the semester.[5]

---

the preliminary analyses, it was infeasible to obtain additional evidence concerning the issue by asking the judge. Had we retained this discrepant judge's rankings in the summary measure, the reliability coefficient would have been near 0.

[4]This is because the measures are a summative composite of the judges' individual rankings and, while each of the judges' individual rankings may deviate from the "true" ranking, some deviations from the true ranking are likely to be positive, others are likely to be negative, and the total will tend to cancel. Thus, in such a summative composite, the reliability is partially a function of the number of individual judges used, and Cronbach's alpha is a lower bound to its reliability. Moreover, in a study that examines relationships among variables, high reliability is important in reducing false negative errors (i.e., of failing to find a relationship when one is there), but has less relevance to reducing false positive errors. If a significant relationship *is* found between a measure and another variable, the fact that the reliability of the measure is only moderate does not automatically invalidate the finding, provided that the correlation can be interpreted as indicating that the measure has criterion-related validity.

[5]The fact that students' responded to the questionnaire *after* receiving a grade on the first essay but *prior* to receiving a grade on the third essay is likely to have introduced a response bias (Bradburn, 1983). For example, students who were

To evaluate the first hypothesis—(When the technology is easily accessible and sanctioned, teachers will communicate more with students and students will communicate more with each other)—we used a repeated-measures ANOVA to examine the frequency of interaction data across the different types of classrooms via the two modes at two times. When we turned to individual differences in the use of the different modes of communication and examined the mediating relationships postulated in the second hypothesis, we began with simple correlations to examine teachers' use of communication modes at T2 and the two performance measures, grade and holistic scores. To further explore the relationship in hypothesis two in the light of other mediating variables (writing anxiety, computer anxiety, behavioral consistency, and teacher experience), we used multiple regression analysis to assess the independent effects of students' general ability and writing performance on interaction at Time 2 while controlling for the mediating variables.

RESULTS

Students' Interaction with their Teachers

Our first analysis examined differences in students' ratings of their frequency of interaction with their teachers in the two types of sections—networked and regular—and for two communication modes, traditional and electronic. To insure greater reliability, we defined the two communication modes by adding together students' ratings of their interaction frequencies for the following individual modes: paper, face-to-face and telephone (traditional); electronic mail, bulletin boards, and *Comments* and *Talk* programs (electronic). There are two times: Time 1, immediate-

---

expecting to receive a higher grade on the third essay than they actually received may have rated the modes of interaction more helpful than if they had rated the modes after receiving a grade. However, since students rated the modes in relationship to each other, it is likely that any such response bias would affect students' ratings of all the modes—that is, it would affect the students' rating of traditional as well as electronic modes. In the same way, students in regular and networked sections would be affected equally by any such bias. Thus, it is unlikely that any response bias introduced by the procedure affected the results. Although undesirable—other things being equal, the difference in procedure was necessary because we wanted to administer the first questionnaire to all sections at the same time, in order to avoid having students who had filled it out talking to students who had not. Since the sections were not on exactly the same schedules and teachers did not wish to delay giving students their grades, we waited until all students had received grades before administering the questionnaire the first time. It was impossible to duplicate the procedure on the second administration because students did not receive grades on the third paper until after the semester had ended and many of them would have already dispersed.

ly after students turned in their first paper (the early part of the semester, approximately six weeks), and Time 2, immediately after students turned in the third and last paper (at the end of the semester). We analyzed the data with a 2 (networked vs. regular sections) x 2 (traditional vs. electronic modes of communication) x 2 (Time 1 vs. Time 2) repeated measures ANOVA, with the first factor between subjects and the last two factors within subjects. All three main effects were significant. Over all subjects, there was more total interaction in the networked than the regular classes, $F(1,73) = 22.49$, $p < .001$ (see Table 3.1 and the top panel of Figure 3.2),[6] more use of the traditional modes of communication than the electronic modes, $F(1,73) = 118.05$, $p < .001$ (compare the bottom left panel of Figure 3.2 to the bottom right panel), and slightly more interaction at Time 2 than at Time 1, $F(1,73) = 4.27$, $p < .05$.

All three of these main effects are qualified by a highly significant 3-way interaction, $F(1,73) = 19.71$, $p < .001$. The nature of this interaction is seen clearly in the bottom two panels of Figure 3.2. During the early part of the semester, at T1, there was no significant difference in the frequency with which the teachers in the networked and regular sections used traditional communication modes to provide writing feedback (means of 7.5 and 8.3, respectively). Over time, however, there was a slight (though nonsignificant) decrease in the networked teachers' use of the traditional modes (from 7.5 to 7.1) while teachers in the regular sections marginally increased their use of traditional communication modes over time (from 8.3 to 9.3). Thus by Time 2, the end of the semester, teachers in the regular sections were using the traditional communication modes more than teachers in the networked sections (9.3 vs 7.1).

The picture is very different for electronic communication (bottom right, Figure 3.2). Teachers in the networked sections substantially increased their use of electronic communication over time (from 4.8 to 6.8). This increase in electronic communication did not come at the expense of traditional communication, however, because the networked teachers did not significantly change their use of traditional communication modes over the course of the semester. Thus the data suggest that teachers in the networked sections maintained most communication via traditional modes and added to their repertoire of tools for communication by using electronic communication modes to give feedback on writing. On the other hand, teachers in the regular section rarely used the electronic modes to communicate with students at any time during the semester.[7]

---

[6]The numbers in Figures 3.2 and 3.3 reflect a recoding of the Likert-type scale variables (from 1 = never. . . 7 = very frequently to 0 = never. . . 6 = very frequently) so that the graphs in these figures would have origins at zero.

[7]Only a few students reported any use of the electronic communication modes in the regular sections.

Table 3.1. Analysis of Variance: Student-Teacher Interaction

Effect	*df*	*F*	*p*
Type of Classroom (C)	1,73	22.49	.001
Mode of Communication (M)	1,73	118.05	.001
Time (T)	1,73	4.27	.042
CxM	1,73	90.13	.001
CxT	1,73	1.97	.164
MxT	1,73	2.89	.094
CxMxT	1,73	19.71	.001

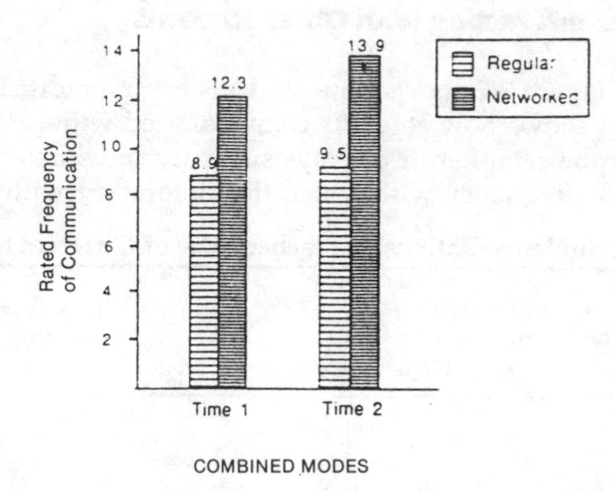

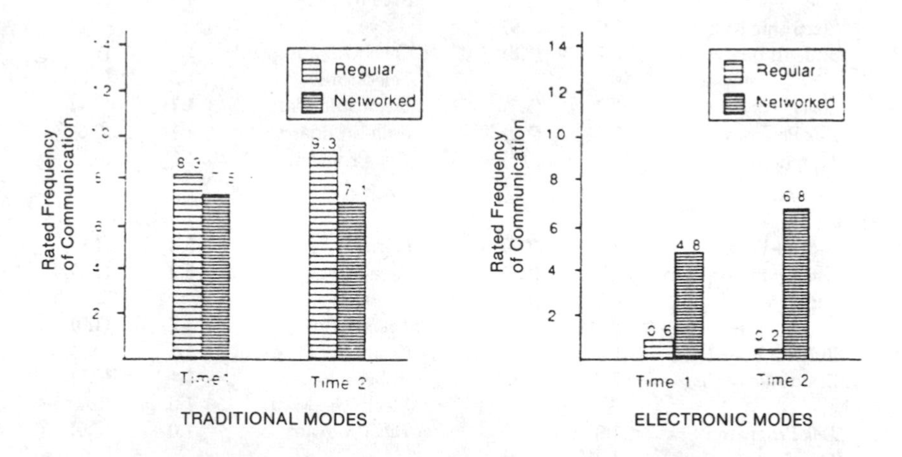

Figure 3.2. Student's ratings of frequency of communication with their teachers at Time 1 (sixth week) and Time 2 (end of semester) in regular and networked classrooms for combined, traditional, and electronic modes

Table 3.2 presents a more detailed view of the data discussed above. The means and standard deviations for the seven individual modes that compose the traditional and electronic summary scales are displayed. Early in the semester, paper and face-to-face interaction were the most frequently used communication modes, even for the teachers in the networked sections. This pattern was sustained over time by the teachers in the regular sections. This pattern was broken, however, by the teachers in the networked sections who later in the semester used the *Comments* program as frequently as face-to-face interaction and paper to provide feedback on students' writing.

Students' Interaction with Other Students

Whereas Figure 3.2 shows how students communicated with teachers, Figure 3.3 shows how students communicated with *each other* over the course of the semester. It displays summary measures of students' ratings of the frequency with which they interacted with other students

Table 3.2. Students' Ratings of Teachers' Use of Different Modes in Detail

	Networked (n = 36)			Regular (n = 39)	
Mode	Use	(SD)	Mode	Use	(SD)
Time 1					
Paper	5.0	(1.6)	Paper	5.5	(1.6)
Face-to-Face	4.5	(1.3)			
			Face-to-Face	4.7	(1.7)
Electronic Mail	3.0	(1.9)			
Bulletin Board	2.7	(1.8)	*Comments* Program	1.5	(1.3)
			Telephone	1.3	(0.7)
Comments Program	1.7	(1.2)	Electronic Mail	1.1	(0.4)
Talk Program	1.4	(1.2)	Bulletin Board	1.1	(0.6)
Telephone	1.1	(0.5)	*Talk* Program	1.0	(0.2)
Time 2					
Face-to-Face	4.8	(1.3)	Paper	5.4	(1.9)
Comments Program	4.5	(1.8)	Face-to-Face	5.2	(1.1)
Paper	4.0	(1.5)			
			Telephone	1.7	(1.0)
Bulletin Board	2.4	(1.7)	*Comments* Program	1.1	(0.7)
Electronic Mail	2.3	(1.6)	Bulletin Board	1.1	(0.5)
			Electronic Mail	1.0	(0.2
Talk Program	1.8	(1.3)	*Talk* Program	1.0	(0.0)
Telephone	1.3	(0.8)			

Note: Blank spaces between modes indicate that students' ratings of teachers' use of modes were significantly different ($p < .05$), using selected paired comparisons.

about their writing, using traditional and electronic communication. Again, these interaction rates were analyzed with a 2 (networked vs. regular sections) x 2 (traditional vs. electronic modes of communication) x 2 (Time 1 vs. Time 2) repeated measures ANOVA (see Table 3.3). There were two significant main effects. As with teacher-student interaction, total student-student interaction was greater in the networked sections both at Time 1 (12.9 vs 8.1) and Time 2 (13.8 vs 8.7), $F(1,73) = 30.75$, $p < .001$. Likewise, there was more student-student interaction via the traditional modes than the electronic modes, $F(1,73) = 44.80$, $p < .001$ (compare the bottom left panel of Figure 3.3 to the bottom right panel).

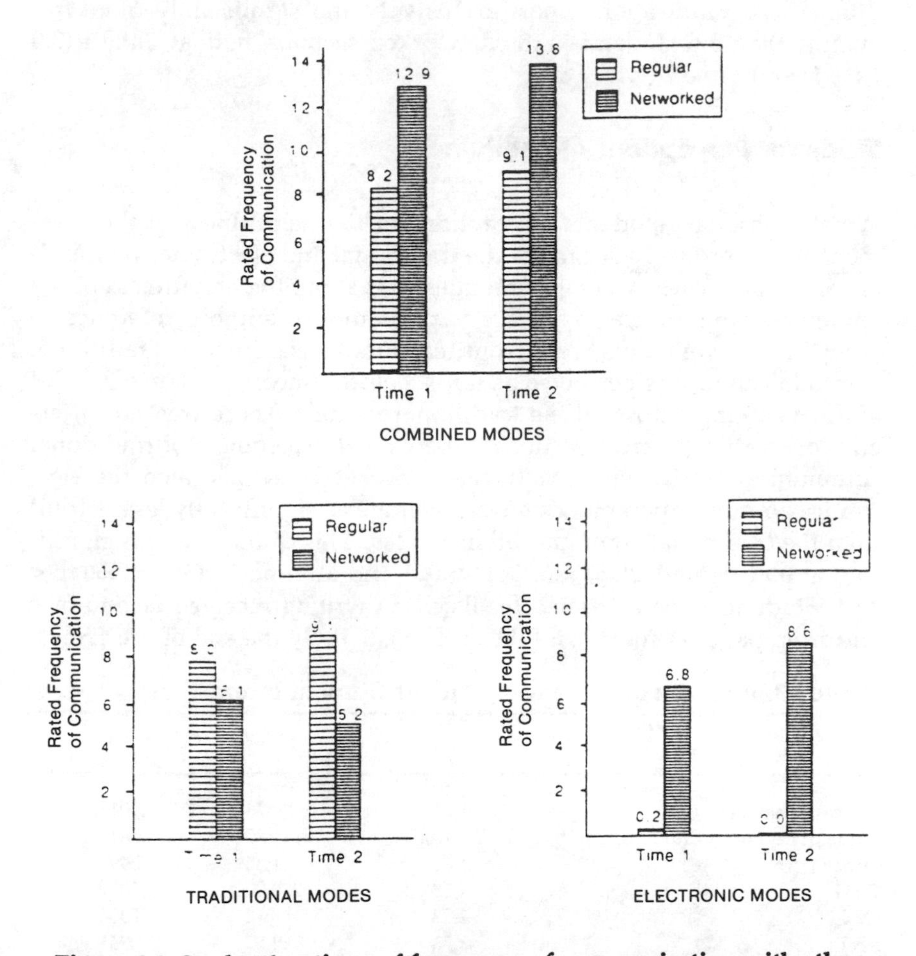

Figure 3.3. Student's ratings of frequency of communication with other students at Time 1 (sixth week) and Time 2 (end of semester) in regular and networked classrooms for combined, traditional, and electronic modes

Once again these main effects must be qualified by a highly significant 3-way interaction, $F(1,73) = 11.84$, $p < .001$. Students in the networked sections, like their teachers, increased their electronic communication with each other over the course of the semester (from 6.8 to 8.6). In contrast to their teachers, however, students seem to have *substituted* electronic communication for the traditional modes, as use of the traditional modes decreased about as much as use of the electronic communication modes increased (from 6.1 to 5.2). In particular, the networked students used paper less frequently to provide feedback to other students and increased their use of the *Comments* and *Talk* programs (see Table 3.4). In the regular sections, on the other hand, students used traditional communication almost exclusively and significantly more frequently than did students in the networked sections, both at Time 1 (8.0 vs. 6.1) and Time 2 (9.1 vs. 5.2).

Students' Perceptions of Helpfulness

We also assessed students' perceptions of the helpfulness of the comments they received via each of the traditional and electronic communication modes. These were general questions about the helpfulness of the comments communicated via the various modes without reference to whether the comments were from teachers or classmates. Traditional communication was perceived as fairly helpful (mean = 5.0 on a 7-point scale averaging across all the traditional modes). There was no difference over time or across sections in perceived helpfulness of traditional communication. But students in the networked sections rated the electronic communication modes on the average as significantly less helpful than the traditional communication modes. This difference was significant at both Time 1, $t(35) = 6.10$, $p < .001$ and at Time 2, $t(36) = 3.56$, $p < .001$. Students generally rated feedback on writing received face-to-face and from paper as most helpful (see Table 3.5). By the end of the semes-

Table 3.3. Analysis of Variance: Student-Student Interaction

Effect	*df*	*F*	*p*
Type of Classroom (C)	1,73	30.75	.001
Mode of Communication (M)	1,73	44.80	.001
Time (T)	1,73	1.35	.249
CxM	1,73	270.99	.001
CxT	1,73	.12	.733
MxT	1,73	2.87	.094
CxMxT	1,73	11.84	.001

Table 3.4. Students' Ratings of Classmates' Use of Different Modes in Detail

	Networked (*n* = 36)			Regular (*n* = 39)	
Mode	*Use*	*(SD)*	*Mode*	*Use*	*(SD)*
Time 1					
Face-to-Face	4.2	(1.6)	Face-to-Face	5.5	(1.5)
Comments Program	3.7	(1.7)	Paper	4.1	(2.3)
Paper	3.6	(1.8)			
			Telephone	1.5	(1.2
Electronic Mail	2.5	(1.7)	*Comments* Program	1.1	(0.5)
Bulletin Board	2.5	(1.7)	Electronic Mail	1.0	(0.2)
Talk Program	2.2	(1.6)	Bulletin Board	1.0	(0.2)
			Talk Program	1.0	(0.2)
Telephone	1.3	(0.8)			
Time 2					
Face-to-Face	4.3	(1.5)	Face-to-Face	5.7	(1.4)
Comments	4.2	(1.6)			
Talk Program	4.1	(1.8)	Paper	4.1	(2.2)
Paper	2.4	(1.4)	Telephone	2.1	(1.7)
Bulletin Board	2.3	(1.7)			
Electronic Mail	2.0	(1.4)	*Comments* Program	1.0	(0.0)
			Electronic Mail	1.0	(0.0)
Telephone	1.6	(0.9)	Bulletin Board	1.0	(0.0)
			Talk Program	1.0	(0.0)

Note: Blank spaces between modes indicate that students' ratings of classmates' use of modes were significantly different ($p < .05$), using selected paired comparisons.

ter, however, after students in the networked sections had sufficient experience with the *Comments* program, they rated it as helpful as face-to-face interaction and paper.

In sum, the availability of electronic modes of communication increased total student-teacher interaction, but not total student-student interaction. Students in the networked sections seemed to prefer face-to-face and paper modes initially, but shifted over time to include the *Comments* program among their preferred modes. However, these results do not address whether electronic communication aided certain types of students or teachers and not others.

Individual Differences

We hypothesized that teachers would use different modes to communicate with students who had performed less well and that these students would use different modes to communicate with each other. We first examined the simple correlations between the teachers' use of different individual communication modes at Time 2, the end of the semester, and student performance as measured by teacher grades and by the holistic rankings assigned to the first and last papers (see Table 3.6).[8] The pattern of correlations for the teachers in the regular sections is overwhelmingly positive, suggesting either that these teachers communicated more with students who had performed well, or that students who performed well sought out their teachers more often. The pattern of correlations displayed in the left column of Table 3.6 (11 out of 12 positive) is significantly different from chance according to a binomial test, $p < .003$.[9]

Table 3.5. Students' Ratings of Helpfulness of Different Modes in Detail

	Networked				Regular		
Mode	*Use*	*(SD)*	*n*	*Mode*	*Use*	*(SD)*	*n*
Time 1							
Face-to-Face	5.5	(1.4)	35	Face-to-Face	5.9	(1.3)	39
Paper	5.0	(1.4)	36	Paper	5.2	(1.7)	38
Electronic Mail	3.8	(1.7)	21	Telephone	3.0	(2.0)	14
Comments Program	3.6	(1.6)	33				
Bulletin Board	3.3	(1.5)	22	*Comments* Program	2.2	(2.0)	10
Talk Program	3.0	(1.6)	21				
Electronic Mail	1.0	(0.0)	7				
Telephone	2.7	(1.9)	9	Bulletin Board	1.0	(0.0)	7
				Talk Program	1.0	(0.0)	6
Time 2							
Face-to-Face	5.8	(1.4)	35	Face-to-Face	5.7	(1.6)	39
Comments Program	5.0	(1.5)	36	Paper	5.6	(1.6)	37
Paper	4.6	(1.1)	34	Telephone	3.3	(2.3)	25
Talk Program	3.8	(1.5)	33	Electronic Mail	1.1	(0.7)	17
Electronic Mail	2.7	(1.7)	22	*Comments* Program	1.0	(0.0)	16
Telephone	2.6	(1.6)	20	Bulletin Board	1.0	(0.0)	16
Bulletin Board	2.2	(1.4)	23	*Talk* Program	1.0	(0.0)	16

Note: Blank spaces between modes indicate that students' ratings of helpfulness of modes were significantly different ($p < .05$), using selected paired comparisons.

[8]We also examined an analogous set of correlations for interactions between classmates, but no interesting pattern of correlations resulted.)

[9]Because the grade assigned by the teacher and the panel of experts' ranking score were based on the same paper, these two measures are not completely independent and therefore a binomial test based on both sets of correlations may

The pattern of correlations for the networked sections includes many more negative correlations (9 of 16), significantly more than the regular sections, $\chi^2(1) = 6.86$, $p < .01$. That is, teachers in the networked sections communicated more with lower performing students as defined by the teachers' grades and by scores of the independent judges. This pattern is strongest when communication was by paper and through the *Comments* program. We cannot know from these data if teachers in the networked sections sought out lower performing students or if lower performing students sought out the teacher. It is clear that teacher-student interaction patterns in the networked sections differed from teacher-student interaction patterns in the regular sections.

Notice the association in the regular sections is strongest between teacher face-to-face communication and students who were given high grades by the teacher. The association is much weaker between teacher face-to-face communication and the holistic rankings. The different magnitudes of correlations observed between the teacher's grade and holistic ranking in the regular section for face-to-face communication and the absence of such differences for face-to-face communication in the networked sections suggest that processes of self-esteem maintenance and social influence may be operating in teacher's assignment of grades: Students who know that they have performed well at Time 1 experience a reduction in evaluation anxiety and interact more than students who received a low grade, possibly appearing more interested in class. Teachers reward this increased interaction with higher grades, especially if the student is perceived as sincere (Bean & Kuh, 1984).

The negative associations displayed in Table 3.6 between student writing performance and interaction with the teacher in the networked sections ran counter to the pattern of teacher-student interaction reported in the literature. Such zero order correlations, however, preclude drawing strong inferences because many possible "third variables" confound the relationships reported in Table 3.6. Therefore, to assess the independent effects of student performance and teacher experience on interaction (controlling for several plausible mediating variables), we regressed summary scales of the students' ratings of their frequency of interaction with teachers via the electronic and traditional modes at Time 2—the end of the semester—on grade on the first paper, SAT verbal score, the writing anxiety scale, the computer anxiety scale, frequency of interaction at Time 1—the sixth week—and teacher quality. We included grade on the first paper as the measure of performance

---

not be appropriate. Looking only at the grades given by the teacher, 6 out of 6 correlations are positive. This pattern is significantly different from chance, $p < .02$. Considering only the holistic ranking, 5 of the 6 correlations are positive. This pattern is significantly different from chance, $p < .10$.

Table 3.6. Associations Between Students' Frequency of Communication with their Teachers at Time 2 and Measures of Students' Writing Performance

	Regular Sections Modes at Time 2			Networked Sections Modes at Time 2			
Writing Performance	Face-to-Face	Paper	Telephone	Face-to-Face	Paper	Telephone	Comments
First Paper (Time 1)							
Teacher's Grade	.49**	.15	.17	.19	-.28*	-.03	-.06
Holistic Ranking	-.02	.36**	.11	.20	-.22	.18	-.43***
Third Paper (Time 2)							
Teacher's Grade	.47**	.18	.31*	.09	-.43***	.27	-.08
Holistic Ranking	.19	.19	.27*	.002	-.40**	.51***	-.21

Note: Table entries are Pearson correlations.
* $p < .10$; ** $p < .05$; *** $p < .01$.

(which was known to the teachers and students at T1) and SAT verbal score as a measure of general ability. With both of these variables included in the regression equation we could look at the independent effects of performance and ability on interaction, at least as these concepts were operationalized here. We expected students with higher levels of writing anxiety compared to those with lower levels to interact less with their teachers via traditional communication modes. We expected this negative relationship to be weaker for communication via the electronic modes because cues that remind us we are being evaluated, for example smiling and frowning, are missing in computer-mediated communication. Additionally, we predicted that higher levels of computer anxiety would have a detrimental effect on electronic communication. Because we were interested in changes in interaction over time, we also needed to include interaction behavior at Time 1 as a predictor. Finally, we included teacher experience in the regression equation because we thought teachers defined as more or less experienced might differ in how they communicated with their students. We also wondered whether the teachers differed in the extent to which they encouraged their students to interact with each other via the various communication modes. Hence we conducted these same analyses on the summary scales of students ratings of their frequency of interaction between classmates. Results of the analyses are displayed in Table 3.7.

Several aspects of the data are notable. First, holding other variables constant, SAT verbal score was a significant predictor of electronic communication. The lower the students' SAT verbal scores were, the more they interacted electronically with teachers and classmates. Second, the teacher defined as more experienced in the networked sections differed in how he communicated writing feedback. The more experienced teacher communicated more electronically. Indeed, this more experienced teacher communicated more frequently in all modes, but the effect was strongest for the electronic media. Also, this teacher's students communicated more with each other electronically.

We expected writing anxiety to be more strongly related to use of traditional communication modes than to use of electronic communication. This pattern was observed for students in the networked sections although the difference in the regression weights was not significant. The higher their writing anxiety, the less students in the networked sections communicated with their teacher and classmates via the traditional modes. Writing anxiety was also negatively related to teacher-student interaction via the electronic modes. As expected, this relationship was weaker than the relationship of writing anxiety to traditional communi-

Table 3.7. Factors Predicting Students' Frequency of Interaction with Their Teachers and with Other Students at Time 2

Factor	Regular Sections	Networked Sections	
	Traditional Modes	Traditional Modes	Electronic Modes
Student-Teacher Interaction			
SAT Verbal	-.12	-.29	-.48***
Teacher Experience	.02	.22	.37**
Writing Anxiety	-.04	-.35**	-.27*
Computer Anxiety	-.28*	-.13	-.27*
Time 1 Interaction	.27	.30	.27
Grade on Paper 1	.30*	-.01	.03
n	37	36	36
Adjusted R^2	.22	.18	.42
Student-Student Interaction			
SAT Verbal	-.17	-.03	-.41**
Teacher Experience	-.10	.10	.63***
Writing Anxiety	-.27	-.36**	-.06
Computer Anxiety	.04	.02	-.18
Time 1 Interaction	.30*	.43***	-.06
Grade on Paper 1	-.14	.12	.22
n	37	36	36
Adjusted R^2	.05	.25	.32

Note: Table entries are standardized regression weights.
*$p < .10$; **$p < .05$; ***$p < .01$.

cation. Computer anxiety was also a significant predictor of electronic teacher-student interaction. The higher their computer anxiety, the less frequently the networked students communicated electronically. Unexpectedly, computer anxiety was also negatively associated with traditional communication in the regular and networked sections.

In general, interaction at the sixth week (Time 1) was positively associated with interaction at the end of the semester (Time 2) although this effect reached conventional levels of significance only for traditional student-student communication. The effect of simple behavioral consistency, which usually is the most important predictor in any longitudinal study, was weaker than expected. Certainly, styles of collaboration and of interaction with classmates and teachers about writing are much less habitual than many other behaviors performed in school. Thus the relative novelty of the activity, particularly in the networked sections, helps explain the low coefficients for prior behavior.

Finally, the pattern of correlations between student performance and teacher-student interaction reported in Table 3.6 is also evident in the regressions. A student's grade on the first paper was significantly associated with communication via the traditional modes in the regular sections, even after the effects of all the other variables in the equation were controlled ($p < .09$). Its effect was positive, and it is the most important predictor in the equation. Grade on the first paper was unrelated to teacher-student interaction in the networked sections, but the negative relationships noted in Table 3.6 were picked up by SAT verbal scores in the regressions. As already discussed, this relationship was highly significant for use of the electronic modes and approached significance ($p < .17$) for the traditional modes.

DISCUSSION

The social effects of computing are contingent not only upon the particular computer system, for example a network and its associated tools, but also upon its social context: characteristics of individuals, user groups, the larger organizational and social structure in which the technology is embedded all play a role (Kling, 1980; Markus, 1983). We took care to describe characteristics of the social context that previous theory and research suggest are relevant: The teachers and students were relatively computer literate, the teachers worked actively to find ways in which network technology could enhance their course objectives and communicated their goals and the reasons for using particular methods to achieve them to students, and teachers and students had easy access to network tools because of the campus wide network. We believe these results will transfer to similar social contexts. Although many schools do not yet have such sophisticated campus wide networks, such networks and their associated tools are clearly valuable and becoming increasingly widespread.

This study examined the use and effects of computer-mediated communication in a context in which it may prove to be most helpful, a classroom in which collaborative learning is encouraged. In such a classroom, working together is valued, not penalized. Network technology and collaborative writing tools support student efforts to become better writers by providing opportunities for practice and for receiving feedback from an audience that includes both teachers and classmates. Because computer-mediated communication crosses space and time, the teacher is no longer a scarce resource for students when the technology is available. Critics of the use of electronic communication tools in education worry that highly valued aspects of the teacher-student relationship will be eliminated. They fear in particular that face-to-face interaction will decrease as more "impersonal" modes of interaction, such as networked communication, increase. This was not the case in our study. We found that using network communication tools to support collaborative learning and writing did not replace traditional forms of communication with teachers, but in fact, total teacher-student communication about writing increased. In particular, face-to-face communication between student and teacher increased over the course of the semester whether students and teacher were networked or not.

The most important practical implications of our findings have to do with the effect computer-mediated communication had on the distribution of teachers' attention in the classroom. We know from the educational literature that better students are more likely to volunteer answers and comments than poorer students (Brophy, 1983) and that they tend to sit in the area of the classroom that captures teacher attention and interaction opportunities. We suggested that network technology might modify this pattern, providing poorer students and their teachers with psychologically and physically low-cost alternative communication modes not found in the regular classroom. We found that less able students communicated more with teachers and classmates electronically than more able students. The availability of electronic communication, in a sense, allowed a more equitable distribution of attention, especially from the more experienced teacher. Interestingly, research in organizational communication suggests similar effects. Computer-mediated communication permits peripheral members of organizations more access to work and social activities. As a result, such people feel more central to the organization and more committed to it (Eveland & Bikson, 1988; Huff, Sproull, & Kiesler, 1989; Sproull & Kiesler, 1990).

Because the data reported here are correlational, we do not know if the changes in focus of attention that we observed were due to the networked teachers and students seeking out less able students or if less able students initiated more contacts. Most likely, this relationship is bidirectional. Less able students probably feel anxious about interactions concerning their writing skills and, therefore, they can benefit from electronic communication, which reduces the social cues that remind them they are being evaluated. Thus less able students might feel more comfortable interacting electronically with others about their writing than they feel in person. Likewise, teachers are probably more anxious about interactions that convey criticism, albeit constructive, and they might feel more comfortable delivering their feedback electronically to students.

One striking result of this study was the strong relationship between teacher experience and the use of electronic communication. The more experienced teacher in the networked condition communicated electronically with students and somehow encouraged students to communicate with each other electronically. This finding highlights a limitation of this study that can be redressed in future research. Teacher experience was not manipulated. Obviously, for ethical reasons, we cannot deliberately assign students to less experienced teachers (or manipulate levels of writing anxiety and computer anxiety). But we would have more confidence in our finding if we had studied more teachers. With only two teachers in the networked sections, we do not know if the results say something representative of more and less experienced teachers (and electronic communication), or if the results are idiosyncratic to the individuals involved. A replication of this finding with as many teachers as possible is clearly warranted to assess the generalizability of the teacher experience effect we found in this study.

In the study reported here, we operationalized "amount of communication" as students' ratings of their frequency of interaction. Given that we found effects with this measure, it seems reasonable to carry out further research using more expensive, direct observation measures.[10] Although much of our knowledge about people's behavior is based on such verbal self-reports (Schwarz, 1990), direct observation measures could provide us not only with an additional measure of the frequency of interaction, but also with information that can shed light on important questions about duration (e.g., Did teachers in the networked sections spend more time on classes than teachers in the regular sections?) and form of the interactions (e.g., What did the electronic modes of interaction with low ability students look like?). Such information is, of course, crucial in creating independent judgments about the interaction process

---

[10]While it is less expensive to gather direct observation information for the electronic communication modes, gathering *comparable* information is expensive for traditional modes.

itself and the quality of interaction.. Both kinds of judgments are needed in order to form a more complete model of the effects of network technologies upon social interactions and learning to write. In the absence of such information, we focused on the processes of social interaction rather than on performance outcomes. Although clearly such outcomes are of ultimate interest, we believe that in the absence of a more detailed model, such a focus is likely to generate more heat than light.

CONCLUSION

Educational theory and research suggest that students learn through active participation in tasks that closely represent the real-world situation in which they are embedded (Cohen, 1972; Brown, Collins, & Duguid, 1989). Computer-mediated communication can facilitate these processes. It provides students who are learning to be better writers increased opportunities for interaction with the heterogeneous audience they are likely to encounter in the real world. It may change interaction patterns and patterns of attention in the classroom. Because less able students are often the most disenfranchised members of the classroom, a technology that redistributes teacher and classmate attention so that these less able students can become more active participants may ultimately have a profound impact on learning outcomes. We have no evidence that more able students will suffer any less attention as a result. In our study, there was more teacher-student communication in the networked sections throughout the semester. Computer-mediated communication did not just redistribute shares of a constant pie, it actually increased the size of the pie.

APPENDIX: SELECTED QUESTIONS FROM THE SECOND QUESTIONNAIRE

This questionnaire asks you about your experience in the class so far this semester. Many of the questions ask you about "your writing" for the class. By "your writing," we mean all of your writing assignments and activities in the class, including but not limited to problem statements, purpose of audience analyses, writing process descriptions, paper plans, sketches, as well as intermediate and final drafts. We are interested in UNIT I,[11] from the beginning of the semester to your problem analysis paper. Please read and answer all of the questions carefully. Your instructor will not see your answers which will be kept completely confidential. Thank you for your participation.

---

[11]When the questionnaire was administered the second time, it referred to UNIT III.

Writing Experience

Instructor Activities. The following questions ask about the role your instructor played in the production of your writing. For each question, fill in the blank(s) with a number from the following scale:

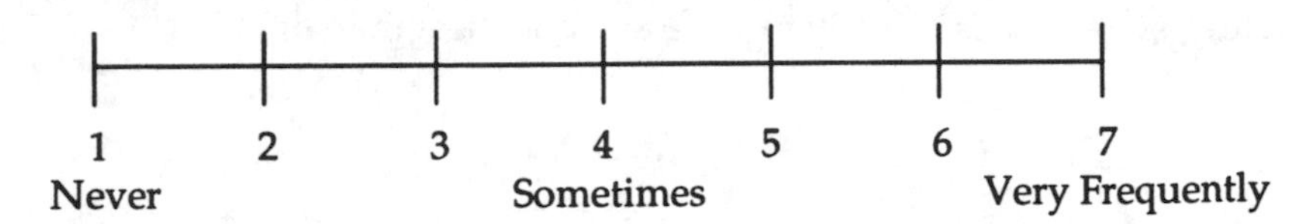

Q. For the comments you received from your instructor, how frequently did your instructor use each of the following means of communication to give you comments?

Written via paper	______	Face-to-face	______
Written via e-mail	______	Over the phone	______
Written via b-boards	______	Interactively via computer	______
Written via *Comments* program	______	(talk or co-op programs)	______

Classmates' and Friends' Activities. The following questions ask about the role your classmates and friends played in the production of your writing. For each question, fill in the blank)s) with a number from the following scale:

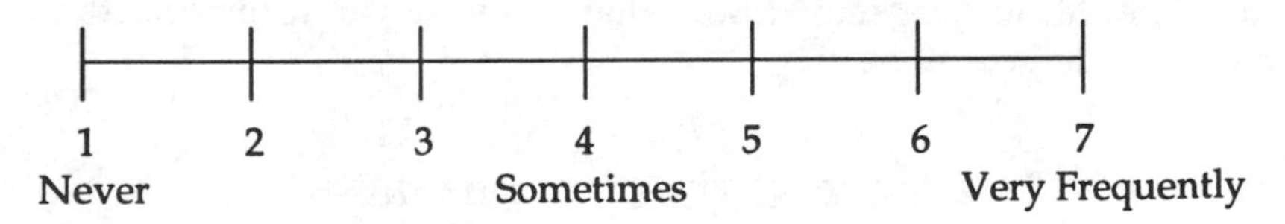

Q. For the comments you did receive from your classmates, how frequently did your classmates use each of the following means of communication to give you comments?

Written via paper	______	Face-to-face	______
Written via e-mail	______	Over the phone	______
Written via b-boards	______	Interactively via computer	______
Written via *Comments* program	______	(talk or co-op programs)	______

Helpfulness of Activities and Feedback

The next section asks about how helpful various activities were for becoming a better writer. For each question, fill in the blank with a number from the following scale:

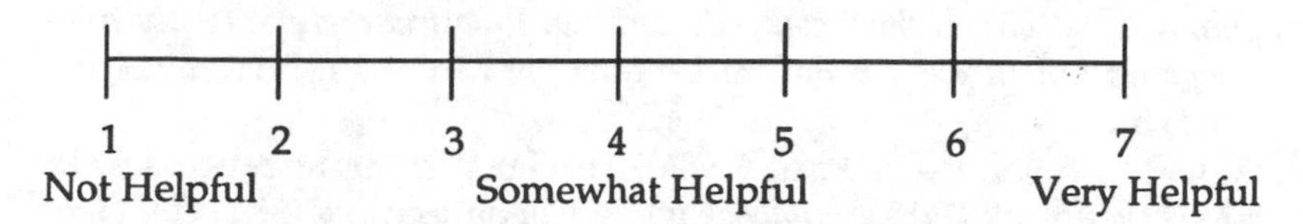

Not Helpful Somewhat Helpful Very Helpful

Q. How helpful were the following means of communication?

Written via paper	_____	Face-to-face	_____
Written via e-mail	_____	Over the phone	_____
Written via b-boards	_____	Interactively via computer	_____
Written via *Comments* program	_____	(talk or co-op programs)	_____

NOTE: Put a "0" in the blank if the question is not applicable to you, for example, if you never engaged in that activity.

REFERENCES

Adams, R.S., & Biddle, B.J. (1970). *Realities of teaching: Explorations with video tape*. New York: Holt, Rinehart, & Winston.

Batson, T. (1988). The ENFI project: A networked classroom approach to writing instruction. *Academic Computing, 2*, 55-56.

Bean, J., & Kuh, G. (1984). The reciprocity between student-faculty informal contact and academic performance of university undergraduate students. *Research in Higher Education, 21*, 461-477.

Becker, F., Sommer, R., Bee, J., & Oxley, B. (1973). College classroom ecology. *Sociometry, 36*, 514-525.

Bohrnstedt, G.W. (1983). Measurement. In P.H. Rossi, J.D. Wright, & A.B. Anderson (Eds.), *Handbook of survey research* (pp. 69-121) . San Diego, CA: Academic Press.

Bradburn, N.M. (1983). Response effects. In P.H. Rossi, J.D. Wright, & A.B. Anderson (Eds.), *Handbook of survey research* (pp. 289-328). San Diego, CA: Academic Press.

Breed, G., & Colaiuta, V. (1974). Looking, blinking, and sitting: Nonverbal dynamics in the classroom. *Journal of Communication, 24*, 75-81.

Brophy, J. (1983). Research on the self-fulfilling prophecy and teacher expectations. *Journal of Educational Psychology, 75,* 631-661.

Brown, J., Collins, A., & Duguid, P. (1989). Situated cognition and the culture of learning. *Educational Researcher, 18,* 4-13.

Bruffee, K.A. (1973). Collaborative learning: Some practical models. *College English, 34*(5), 579-586.

Bruffee, K.A. (1985). *A short course in writing: Practical rhetoric for teaching composition through collaborative learning* (3rd ed.). Boston: Little, Brown.

Clark, C. M., & Peterson, P. L. (1986). Teachers' thought processes. In M.C. Wittrock (Ed.), *Handbook of research on teaching* (3rd ed.). New York: Macmillan.

Cohen, E. (1972). Sociology and the classroom: Setting the conditions for teacher-student interaction. *Review of Educational Research, 42,* 441-452.

Cohen, E., & Benton, J. (1988). Making groupwork work. American Educator: *The Professional Journal of the American Federation of Teachers, 12,* 10-17.

Cohen, E., Lockheed, M., & Lohman, M. (1976). The center for interracial cooperation: A field experiment. *Sociology of Education, 49,* 49-58.

Cohen, M., & Riel, M. (1989). The effect of distant audiences on students' writing. *American Educational Research Journal, 26,* 143-159.

Daly, J.A., & Miller, M.D. (1975). The empirical development of an instrument to measure writing apprehension. *Research in the Teaching of English, 9,* 242-249.

Dubrovsky, V.J., Kiesler, S.B., & Sethna, B.N. (in press). The equalization phenomenon: Status effects in computer-mediated and face-to-face decision making groups. *Human Computer Interaction.*

Edwards, M.R., Levine, J.A., & Kurland, D.M. (1986). *ForComment* (Computer program). San Rafael, CA: Broderbund.

Emig, J. (1981). Non-magical thinking: Presenting writing developmentally in schools. In C.H. Frederiksen & J.F. Dominic (Eds.), *Writing: The nature, development, and teaching of written communication* (Vol. 2, pp. 21-30). Hillsdale, NJ: Lawrence Erlbaum.

Eveland, J.D., & Bikson, T.K. (1988). Work group structures and computer support: A field experiment. *Transactions on Office Information Systems, 5,* 354-379.

Finholt, T., Kiesler, S., & Sproull, L. (1986). *An electronic classroom.* Working paper, Carnegie Mellon University, Pittsburgh, PA.

Fish, R.S., Kraut, R.E., Leland, M.D.P., & Cohen, M. (1988). Quilt: A collaborative tool for cooperative writing. *Proceedings of the COIS '88 Conference on Office Information Systems* (pp. 30-37). Baltimore, MD: Association for Computing Machinery.

Freedman, S.W. (1987). *Response to student writing.* Urbana, IL: National

Council of Teacher of English.

Gere, A.R. (1987). *Writing groups: History, theory and implications.* Carbondale, IL: Southern Illinois University Press.

Heinssen, R.K., Glass, C.R., & Knight, L.A. (1987). Assessing computer anxiety: Development and validation of the computer anxiety rating scale. *Computers in Human Behavior, 3,* 49-59.

Hillocks, G., Jr. (1986). *Research on written composition: New directions for teaching.* Urbana, IL: ERIC Clearinghouse on Reading and Communication Skills.

Hiltz, S.R. (1986). The 'Virtual Classroom:' Using computer-mediated communication for university teaching. *Journal of Communication, 36,* 295-304.

Huff, C., Sproull, L., & Kiesler, S. (1989). Computer communication and organizational commitment: Tracing the relationship in a city government. *Journal of Applied Social Psychology, 19,* 1371-1391.

Jacobs, H.L, Zinkgraf, S.A., Wormugh, D.R., Harfiel, V.F., & Hughey, J B. (1981). *Testing ESL composition: A practical approach.* Rowley, MA: Newbury House.

Kling, R. (1980). Social analyses of computing: Theoretical perspectives in recent empirical research. *Computing Surveys, 12,* 61-110.

Levin, J.A., Riel, M., Boruta, M., & Rowe, R. (1984). Muktuk meets jaccuzi: Computer networks and elementary schools. In S. Freedman (Ed.), *The acquisition of written language* (pp. 160-171). Norwood, NJ: Ablex.

Marcus, M.L. (1983). Power, politics, and MIS implementation. *Communications of the ACM, 26,* 430-444.

Montello, D. (1988). Classroom seating, location, and its effect on course achievement, participation, and attitudes. *Journal of Environmental Psychology, 8,* 149-157.

Morris, J.H., Satyanarayanan, J., Conner, M.H., Howard, J.H., Rosenthal, D.S., & Smith, F.D. Andrew: A distributed personal computing environment. *Communications of the ACM, 29,* 184-201.

Neuwirth, C.M., Kaufer, D.S., Keim, G., & Gillespie, T. (1988, January). *The Comments program: Computer support for response to writing.* (Tech. Rep. No. CMU-CECE-TR-2). Pittsburgh, PA: Carnegie Mellon University, Department of English, Center for Educational Computing in English.

Neuwirth, C.M., Palmquist, M., & Gillespie, T. (1988a, June). *An instructor's guide to collaborative writing with CECE Talk: A computer network tool.* (Tech. Rep. No. CMU-CECE-TR-8). Pittsburgh, PA: Carnegie Mellon University, Department of English, Center for Educational Computing in English.

Neuwirth, C.M., Palmquist, M., & Gillespie, T. (1988b, June). *A student's guide to collaborative writing with CECE Talk: A computer network tool.*

(Tech. Rep. No. CMU-CECE-TR-7). Pittsburgh, PA: Carnegie Mellon University, Department of English, Center for Educational Computing in English.

Payne, D. (1987). Computer-extended audiences for student writers. In L. Gerrard (Ed.), *Writing at century's end: Essays on computer-assisted composition*. New York: Random House.

Rubin, A., & Bruce, B. (1986). Learning with Quill: Lessons for students, teachers, and software designers. In T.E. Raphael & R.E. Reynolds (Eds.), *Contexts of situation based literacy*. New York: Random House.

Rubin, A., & Bruce, B. (1990). *Alternative realizations of purpose in computer-supported writing*. (Technical Report No. 492). Champaign, IL: University of Illinois at Urbana-Champaign, Center for the Study of Reading.

Schwarz, N. (1990). Assessing frequency reports of mundane behaviors: Contributions of cognitive psychology to questionnaire construction. In C. Hendrick & M.S. Clark (Eds.), *Research methods in personality and social psychology* (pp. 98-119). Newbury Park, CA: Sage.

Sheingold, K., Hawkins, J., & Char, C. (1984). I'm the thinkist, you're the typist: The interaction of technology and the social life of classrooms. *Journal of Social Issues, 40*, 49-61.

Sommer, R. (1967). Classroom ecology. *Journal of Applied Behavioral Science, 3*, 489-503.

Sproull, L., & Kiesler, S. (1986). Reducing social context cues: Electronic mail in organizational communication. *Management Science, 32*, 1492-1512.

Sproull, L., & Kiesler, S. (1990). *Connections: New ways of working in the networked organization*. Manuscript under review.

Turner, J.H. (1988). *A theory of social interaction*. Stanford, CA: Stanford University Press.

Chapter
Four

Computers and Urban Commuters in an Introductory Literature Class*

Helen Schwartz
Indiana University
Purdue University at Indianapolis

Several important questions need to be asked when using computers in education: How and why should technology be used in a particular discipline? and how does it serve urban commuters in particular? This chapter explores the evolutionary process of answering these questions for an introductory literature class in the course of five semesters. At first students used computers in and out of class to discuss course work as a supplement to face-to-face classes. These experiences helped shape procedures in a distance-education course, with subsequent replanning. My current conclusions are presented here, but any teachers who learn from them must also evolve and discover their own answers.

*We are grateful to IBM for a grant that made the community loaner progam possible.

WHO ARE THE STUDENTS?

The growth in the number of New Majority students has forced us to see that pedagogical theory cannot be considered out of context. New Majority students can be defined as those who are over 25 years old or part-time students with jobs or family responsibilities. Their numbers have grown—both absolutely and as a percentage of total college enrollment. The traditional timing, location, and architecture of teaching at a residential college does not fit the needs of a student whose children have a different schedule of holidays or whose job requires trips out of town (airline personnel or business people). The five versions of the introductory literature class described in this chapter were developed at my own commuter institution—Indiana University-Purdue University at Indianapolis (IUPUI)—and illustrate both the needs of New Majority students and the ways computer-mediated communication supports their learning.

Our campus in the heart of Indianapolis serves over 20,000 undergraduate students, of whom 98% are commuters, 72% are over 20 years old, 11% are minority, 31% are married, 59% are female, and 60% are employed full time or part time. The literature class, English L115 (Literature for Today), can run 14 weeks in Fall and Spring or six weeks in one of the summer time periods. Because the course can count toward fulfilling the humanities requirement for graduation (part of the general education requirements for all undergraduates), the classes can contain students of very diverse ages, academic majors, and socioeconomic status. Although my sections varied according to the time and teaching module (as discussed later), the classes were overwhelmingly female (about 90%), with only 10% minority students.

WHAT IS TAUGHT IN AN INTRODUCTORY LITERATURE CLASS

The goals for this introductory class were two-fold:

> Goal 1: to introduce students to the ways an author conveys meaning (for example, through plot, characterization, and symbolism) in a variety of different genres (specifically, in fiction, drama, and poetry).
> Goal 2: to show why readers may legitimately differ in their interpretations and the importance of this difference in the reader's enjoyment of literature.

All instructors were to include the writing of formal essays as one means of evaluating student learning, and they were encouraged to develop a way to use a portfolio of work in evaluation. These guidelines are rather typical of introductory classes to help students better understand and enjoy literature.

To reach Goal 1, students need guidance in identifying how literature makes meaning and regular practice in applying analytic techniques. Reading literature is not linear but involves making hypotheses or noting questions or discrepancies, linking evidence to previous information or patterns, and recognizing implications that are often too complex, too rich (that is, apparently contradictory) to be stated simply in a straightforward manner. Apparently "wrong" or idiosyncratic reactions can make sense if a student can explain the links they made; or by explaining the "logic" of their emotional response, students may understand the need to change their views. The traditional classroom can provide models of good interpretation but cannot easily give detailed, timely, individual feedback. Computer-assisted instruction with simple answer checking is bound to be inadequate; multiple-choice questions contradict Goal 2 of showing that there can be more than one correct choice.

To reach Goal 2, students need to hear a variety of different but arguable interpretations. Here the traditional classroom often sends mixed messages. Teachers say interpretations can be different, but students often do not see the work of others—they hear the teacher's view, their own, and the teacher's response to theirs.

For these reasons, introductory literature classes now often assign informal writing in journals (so that students respond to literature holistically) and spend class time in peer review (to expose students to the views of others and to stress the process of developing ideas in writing and discussion).

My teaching methods assume that active student involvement and group work in learning are essential—through informal writing and through peer (and instructor) review of an essay draft before the final draft is due. Therefore, I evaluate students on the basis of prediscussion writing (graded only on timeliness, not quality, during the semester), formal essays (with peer review of a draft required before the final submission of each), and a portfolio of writing (graded on its quality) based on informal writings that were revised by students before resubmission. The syllabus starts out thematically with units on Coming of Age, Family Relations, and Love and Sexuality. In the first three versions of the class, a unit on literary conventions asks students to read and write modern fairy tales or beast fables to see what is traditional in the form and how conventions might be changed. Those classes also contain a special section on poetry as well as include clusters of poems in the topical units. Although the preponderance of the literature is modern, we also study Shakespeare's *Midsummer Night's Dream* and some poetry from the Renaissance and the 19th century.

Traditionally these goals have been met adequately, often brilliantly, in only a blackboard-equipped classroom where a teacher lectures and engages students in discussion.

WHY SHOULD COMPUTER-MEDIATED COMMUNICATION (CMC) BE USED IN TEACHING COLLEGE LITERATURE COURSES?

Increasingly, analysts of media have claimed that hypertext and electronic communication uniquely fit literary theory and the study of literature (Bolter, 1991; Landow, 1992). Selfe (1989) argues in "Redefining Literacy: The Multilayered Grammars of Computers," that the conventions of a medium (such as arrangement, structure, form, and appearance of text) form its "grammar." She cites theorists Gumpert and Cathcart (1985), McLuhan (1967), and Ong (1982) "who claim that the conventions associated with specific media determine not only how we see text but how we view the world as a whole and how we construct our reality" (p. 5). As an example, she cites the development of indexes as a spatial strategy of retrieving information only after print presents a collection of pages that can be searched linearly. Furthermore, because people observe media conventions and internalize them, they later begin to use media conventions as "tools of thought" in unrelated areas. Consider, for example, the way people now use "instant replay" outside the context of televised football. What, then, does the "grammar" of computer-mediated communication contribute to literary study?

Computers help provide all the conditions of learning described here as desirable for literary study with the flexibility that urban commuters need. A computer-assisted instruction (CAI) program helps model expert practice for reaching Goal 1, but it also allows collaboration that shares information and supports peer review. A discussion on a local area network during class time or discussion out of class on a wide-area network electronic conference can help "decenter" the classroom, moving the teacher from the podium of authority to a roving guide or equal-access participant. Students, therefore, can see each other's work without massive photocopying and distribution. Pacing can be individualized, depending on the ability and personal situation of the student. The storage capacity of computers can help students record and manage the process of growth.

HOW CAN COMPUTERS BE USED IN A LITERATURE CLASS (LOGISTICS)

Let me first describe the logistics of five different learning situations and then give qualitative results in order to support the claims that computers support literary study with the flexibility that urban commuter students need.

The Community Group

A pilot project, called the Interactive Learning Community (ILC), aimed to engage students in learning by supplementing face-to-face interaction in the classroom with computer access to each other using loaner computers. In Fall 1991, 20 students met twice a week as a class, once in a computer classroom with a local-area network and once in a traditional classroom. The loaner computers allowed out-of-class access to each other, not only through individual e-mail messages, but also by establishing a group conference through what Santoro calls an e-mail "exploder" (using the Listserve program on the wide-area network BITNET). Students were trained in the computer classroom by a student monitor who attended every class. (Student monitors help in all computer-based classes to free teachers from computer consulting and to support part-time instructors who have very limited access to computers outside of class.) At this time, the local-area network was not connected to the wide-area network (BITnet).

The Weekly Group

Could the advantages of the Community Group be made available without the expense of using loaner computers with a class of predominantly "mature" students (that is, over 25 years old) meeting once a week? In Spring 1992, 20 students met on Wednesday nights for the full 2 1/2 hours in the computer classroom. In addition, each student was trained in using the wide-area network (although the computer classroom remained unconnected to the wide-area network until the last two weeks of class). Students had weekly assignments to post at least two days before the class meeting. (Very few students had modem-equipped computers available at home or work, and so they came to the computer facilities open on campus to all students.) Instead of using the "exploder" type group conference (which requires each person to receive and process each piece of e-mail sent to the group), we used what Santoro calls a "conference management system"—named

VAXNotes. Unlike the "in-basket" approach of a Listserv, this type of conference functions like an electronic bulletin board, allowing each person to choose what he or she will read, and at the same time keeping other items available for later reading without stacking up in the student's e-mail box.

The Broadcast Group

Could people off campus join the modeling of expert behavior through broadcast of the lecture discussion in the on-campus class, at the same time joining the community through shared network-managed writing? As part of IUPUI's Community Learning Network (funded partially by Annenberg/CPB as part of the New Pathways Initiative), I taught a 6-week course that met 3 nights a week in Summer 1992. Each night, a 1-hour broadcast over educational cable television linked two students at the Hispanic Wholistic Center (HWC) with four students and me on campus for an hour. The HWC students could ask questions through an open telephone line. Then students at both sites wrote their responses which were shared on the electronic bulletin board (VAXNotes) with our on-campus local-area network finally linked to the wide-area network. On campus, a student monitor answered computer questions; off campus, an undergraduate student mentor helped students both with coursework and computer questions. Tapes of the class were available at the HWC in case students had missed a class. In addition, each HWC student got a "voicemail" address on campus so that I could send them messages, and their papers were sent to me by fax. Another electronic bulletin board linked me with student mentors and other technical support staff.

The Triads Group

The Broadcast Group offered no real advantage to off-campus students unless their time commitment could be made more flexible. Furthermore, as long as all students had to meet at the same time, we had an obvious problem with access to computer facilities. But what would my role be if the students worked independent of me? In Fall 1992, I piloted a strategy for independent student work in groups of three, following the example of my colleague Professor Edwin Casebeer. My role as teacher was to create the worksheets: some questions were to be completed at home before class (usually factual or guiding what the student noticed as he or she read) and others were to be discussed in the triads in class and written on the handouts (and later revised selectively for the portfolio). Twenty students met twice a week. I would make announcements or clarifications at the beginning or end of class, but otherwise, I simply circulated among the groups. No computers were used in this class; my focus was on the quality of interaction in the triads. If students could conduct high-quality discussion with only minimal mentoring, then the students could meet at different times in triads with student mentors, as long as conclusions were shared with a larger group through CMC. If the triads worked without computers, I planned to use triads in a distance education course as a way for as few as three students to work at a site, with community established through writing posted on the wide-area network.

Broadcast Triads

One problem of the generally successful Triads Group was a need for greater expert modeling. Another lurking problem was the cost of small classes. Meanwhile, Professor Casebeer has been adapting a video-based correspondence course (Literary Visions developed through an Annenberg/CPB grant) by using it in class with triad groups. His goal is to teach in conjunction with undergraduate student mentors a large-enrollment class that feels like a small class. In Fall 1993, we intend to collaborate. He will teach the regularly scheduled noncomputer class, and I will teach a distance-education course in which students watch (or tape for later viewing) two half-hour segments of the Literary Visions videotapes broadcast on educational cable television, do the reading and self-tests at home, come for a triad meeting (and test) for 1-hour per week, and communicate with the larger group through 1 hour of computer use per week. In addition, Professor Casebeer and I, along with the student mentors in his class and my triads, will tape and broadcast a half-hour segment that will discuss common problems or outstanding student contributions made during the preceding week.

The facilities, timing, location, assignments, and support staff necessary for these five configurations of the course are summarized in Figure 1.

HOW CAN COMPUTERS SUPPORT LEARNING IN LITERATURE CLASSES? (ADVANTAGES, ASSIGNMENTS, AND EXPERIENCES)

Modeling Expert Behavior with CAI

SEEN is a computer program I have developed that prompts response to open-ended questions and then allows students to save their work on

Figure 1: Pedagogy and Delivery of an Introductory Literature Class

	Learning Structure	Time Module	Evaluation	Support Needed
Comm	--2 Classes face-to-face/week, one in a local-area networked (LAN) classroom --Lecture/discussion/small groups --Loaner computers so all have home access	--Twice weekly 1-1/4 hrs./day (14 week semester)	--3 papers, informal writing & group work --Portfolio of selected and revised informal writing --Exchange on an computer conference	--In-class student monitor --Support available for problems with computer conference on wide-area network (WAN) --Student accounts on WAN --Loaner computers
Weekly	--1 Class/wk., face-to face in LAN classroom --Lecture/discussion/small groups --Post homework on electronic bulletin bd. 2 days before class.	--Once weekly 2-1/2 hours (14 week semester)	--3 papers, informal writing & group work --Portfolio of selected and revised informal writing	--In-class student monitor --Support for problems with wide-area network --Student accounts on WAN --Computer facilities for drop-in access to elec. b.bd. (WAN)
B.cast	3 classes/wk., simultaneously meeting on campus and at off-campus sites --1 hr. broadcast live (& taped) --1 hr. on electronic bull. bd. at LAN connected to WAN	--2 hrs. thrice weekly (6 weeks)	--3 papers, informal writing & group work --Portfolio of selected and revised informal writing	--In-class student monitor (campus) --Student mentor off-site --Student accounts on WAN --Fax & voice mail for off-campus students --Broadcast studio
Triad	--2 classes face-to-face/wk. --Worksheets and triad discussion groups with 15-30 min. of lecture.	--Twice weekly 1-1/4 hrs/class (14 wk. semester)	--2 papers --1 exam --Portfolio of selected & revised informal writings	
Br Triads	--1 hr. triad discussion & testing/week --Three 1/2 hour video broadcasts (mixture of prepared tapes and local response tapes) --Worksheets for reading, viewing & discussion --Essay (expanding on triad notes) posted weekly on elec. bulltn. bd.	--1 hr. triad meeting/wk. --1/2 hr. computer access/wk --Home viewing of video	--Informal writing --Weekly quizzes --Weekly response on computer --Portfolio of selected & revised responses	--Mentor/6 triads (=18 students) --Broadcast facilities --Student accounts on WAN --Fax and voice mail

Figure 4.1: Pedagogy and Delivery of an Introductory Literature Class

their own disk for further work on a word processor, to print their file, and to post their ideas on a bulletin board that is part of the program. The program SEEN, winner of a Distinguished Software Award from EDUCOM/NCRIPTAL, comes with tutorials, including ones on characterization in literature, plotting, and general exploratory response. Students in the Community, Weekly, and Broadcast groups used the program on the local-area network or at the off-campus site. (Although a distance-learning version is being prepared by the publisher CONDUIT, communication among sites in the interim is arranged by uploading all students' responses to the electronic bulletin board.) SEEN tutorials model the kinds of evidence and arguments used in the analysis of literature. The student's choice of subject is inserted into generic questions to help individualize student inquiries. For example, in the characterization tutorial, after the student has chosen a character (for example, Bottom) in a work (*Midsummer Night's Dream*) and a thesis ("too egotistical to be harmed by the magic"), the tutorial asks for evidence of this thesis in what the character says and does, how others respond to the character, how he compares to others in a similar situation, and so on. The student is then asked to consider exceptions to the thesis and then to choose the most interesting idea from the session as a possible paper topic. With repeated use, students internalize the questions in their reading technique (Schwartz, 1984).

SEEN also allows students to see each other's work and to comment on it, with the program keeping a record of who has done what activities (for teacher management). Students can share work without necessarily requiring the teacher to read and comment on every student's writing.

The use of several different tutorials illustrated the idea of "heuristics"—a procedure likely to generate ideas, but not guaranteed (as in the case of a formula or algorithm) to arrive at a correct or workable answer. In the Weekly Group, we worked in the poetry unit to generate heuristics, and one group for their final project wrote a script for a SEEN tutorial on poetry, which is available for use by subsequent classes. Taylor (1980) talks about the potential of computer software as tutor, tool, and tutee. SEEN functioned as all three: a tutor of expert questioning, a tool for peer review and collaboration, and a tutee for students' metacognitive exploration of poetry analysis.

"Divergent Thinking" Modeled in a Decentered Class

In the classroom, students got used to sharing their ideas on SEEN's bulletin board or with "real-time chat" on Interchange (a feature of the Daedalus system used in our IBM-based local-area network). With

Interchange, the students respond to a central question composed on the top part of a split screen and then "post" it to a scrolling text file available to all participants through the local-area network and shown on the bottom part of the screen. This technology supports "divergent thinking" that stresses a multiplicity of possible answers, rather than enforcing uniform, "convergent thinking" with one correct answer. After one use of Interchange in the Weekly Group, students made three comments: First, they felt they worked more than in a traditional classroom (although I felt we had "covered" less). Second, all could participate comfortably because the give-and-take proceeded at each student's speed of reading and response. Third, once students realized that postings were identified with the writer's name, they felt a need to get to know each other.

Perhaps more important, decentered discussion changed students into more active learners without undermining the teacher's authority as an expert. The teacher became more of a guide than an oracle, and this relationship was an announced goal of the class. Active learning was especially prevalent in the Community group. Home access to asynchronous communication on the electronic conference helped form an active learning community. Although the majority of IUPUI students do not now have home access (without provision of loaner computers), in the not too distant future, this option will be more viable, and our experience pioneered the kind of pedagogy that works well to supplement face-to-face classes.

Unlike an electronic bulletin board, a Listserv requires all participants to process all messages, even if they only throw them out like hastily opened junk mail. It was hard to separate responses to homework from more general notes. I used this feature as an asset by modeling a holistic community in which comments about class could be intermixed with news about current events or personal information. Students formed a community because their shared referents included more than common reading assignments. Sharon talked about her son Ian standing up for the first time in his playpen. Wendy shared her questions, wondering why an at-risk infant taken off life support should live, whereas her middle-aged aunt died of cancer. AIDS entered our reflections with reaction to Magic Johnson's announcement. These shared experiences became real-life touchstones in our discussion of poetry—what it can and should deal with.

Students helped each other with computer problems and then with homework problems. For example, one student in the Community Group excelled as an "asker"—for example, she requested help in understanding Shakespeare and the reading assignment. Her question was answered by three different students before I ever saw it, and I have shared the students' advice in subsequent classes. Research has shown that the locus of control is more distributed on an Interactive Learning

Community Listserv than in an in-class discussion in a traditional seminar room (Robertson, 1990). The research taped two classes, a week apart, in a 200-level literature class, and then compared interaction in person to that on the computer conference. Students initiated discussions twice as often on the Listserv (60% as compared to 30% face to face). Because a posted question might be answered by a student before the instructor or technical consultant chimed in, students got used to taking control.

Students were required to send certain postings to the electronic conference so that all had to participate. But students varied in their nonrequired behavior, with some students "lurking" (reading but not responding) and others contributing continually, in spurts or minimally.

Assignments evolved as I came to understand what the electronic conference supported. For example, one time students had to describe an unusual cultural practice of the Ibo, described in Chinua Achebe's *Things Fall Apart*, and then explain how that practice was functionally similar to another practice in 20th-century American culture. Another time, as we studied fairy tales and beast fables, each student had to write and post a "modern" fairy tale or beast fable; the following week, each person had to comment on the work of two fellow students, showing what was conventional and what was "modern" in each story. These informal assignments were ungraded (except for timeliness), yet they could be stored and subsequently revised for inclusion in their portfolios. Another assignment was to summarize class discussion; this not only helped reinforce learning or show what needed clarification, it also helped students who had missed class. One Community student broke her leg but was able to stay current with assignments through these postings.

The more structured form of the electronic bulletin board was less helpful in creating community but less time-consuming for students with limited access to the computer, as in the Weekly and Broadcast Groups. (For some Weekly students, posting meant an extra trip to campus. Most chose to post rather than send their assignment by U.S. mail and then bring copies to class.) Here, assigning comment on other students' work (as with the fairy tales assignment) insured that students would read widely, even though the conference structure did not have a required "in-basket" of notes. With a bulletin board, all posted notes remain available online, each with a unique number as an address. Therefore, I started a thread on "Models" in which I continually added comments on a few posted notes that fulfilled the assignment well. Students could read my detailed praise, then look at the note to which I referred, and subsequently review their own work. Whenever possible, I used different people as positive models. This "honor roll" provided criticism through praise, thus helping to keep the wide-area electronic conference as a place for experimentation and community.

Timing as a Learning Aid

Wide-area computer conferencing helps extend the class beyond the classroom, bringing wonderful flexibility and enrichment. Especially with an electronic conference, but also with a bulletin board, people can post information that was omitted in class or reflections or questions. One student in the Community Group posted a response to Denise Levertov's poem about Vietnam, "What Were They Like?" stating that although the analysis in class had clarified the meaning, she still felt it was important to express sadness as an emotional response to the poem. Her comment brought us back to a holistic view of the poem and increased our enjoyment of it.

Posting assignments two days before the Weekly class forced the students to complete the bulk of their assignment over the weekend and not during their coffee breaks on the day of the class.

Most important for me was the ability to design classroom discussion on the questions and ideas that emerged before class from postings. For example, on the electronic bulletin board, Weekly students explained why they felt Okonkwo, the main character in *Things Fall Apart*, was a success or a failure. The rich variety of their answers showed the need for various definitions of success, an approach I would not have taken without seeing their responses.

Managing the Process of Learning

Without an emphasis on differing interpretations and the process of learning, students may only get tenable interpretations of the assigned works (interpretations that I will probably change the next time I teach the literary work) and fail to develop interpretive skills for independent work. The syllabus can combine with the storage capacity of computers to help students track their developing ideas. Word processing takes the drudgery out of extensively revising a draft. The storage of discussions on local-area or wide-area networks allows students to remember discussions more accurately than notes of oral debate.

Moreover, the portfolio requirement allows students to track the development of their most interesting thoughts at the end of the semester, or someone else's ideas. Is it wrong for one student to start from, or include, the idea of another? I think not, if the debt is acknowledged. Collaborative learning provides a micromodel of scholarship using secondary sources. Furthermore, with flexible time limits for posting assignments, weak or marginal students can see the work of stronger students who have already posted their work. Because everyone can see all the postings, there is no question of "cheating." Instead, cheating needs to be redefined in the collaborative class as a withholding of opinion or engagement.

FUTURE DIRECTIONS

How can computer-mediated learning become easier and more accessible? Software and hardware designers still have a long way to go to make computers easy to use. And facilities are inequitably available, even with an increase in on-campus facilities. ILC classes allowed us to develop pedagogy with the full socioeconomic range of IUPUI students, but without loaners, students may find computer-based assignments difficult to complete. In the Community Group, over one-third of the message sending occurred between 9 p.m. and 8 a.m.—that is, during hours when presence was impractical at a commuter school (275 messages out of 767). And over 20% of the time, computer use took place when most campus computer facilities were closed—that is, between 10 p.m.-8 a.m. (163 out of 767 messages).

Can distance education provide the collaboration necessary for seeing different interpretations? Can costs per student and in faculty time equal on-campus education or help realize savings while extending access? I have no answer to these questions. However, I do know that my attitude as a teacher has changed. Initially I feared broadcast as a part of distance education for two reasons. First, broadcast that includes a changing public audience on cable television raised fears of self-imposed censorship. Did I really want to explicate Donne's "On His Mistress Going to Bed" on public access television in the unit on love and sexuality? What I discovered was a way to depersonalize the topic, both for a public audience and the students being asked to respond on camera or microphone. I assigned about 13 poems discussing various attitudes toward love and sex: innocent sexuality in Marlowe's "The Passionate Shepherd to the Nymph," a celebration of married sexuality and parenthood in Galway Kinnell's "After Making Love We Hear Footsteps," promiscuity considered in Sharon Olds's "Sex without Love," and so on. Each student was responsible for expressing the views of a poem's speaker (not their own views) in response to questions such as: Can love last? What is the relation of sexuality and love? This approach freed students of self-consciousness and focused attention on the ideas and techniques of the poets, rather than on personal views.

Second, I feared the loss of freedom that a staff of technical and teaching helpers seemed to entail. In anticipation, I felt like a carefree flapper used to a free-swinging chemise who was suddenly asked to wear the constricting hoops and wigs of Marie Antoinette. With conventional media of communication, this fear might have been realized, but collaboration with others on an electronic bulletin board, especially with student mentors and fellow faculty, added a rich and reflective dimension to teaching that makes small-class teaching seem lonely by comparison.

At this time, computer-mediated communication offers tremendous opportunities and challenges. The "grammar" of various media used in CMC provides a way to provide expert modeling along with collaboration that teaches and helps manage the learning process. Larger questions of access will test our society's political commitments as much as the technological ingenuity of emerging technologies.

REFERENCES

Bolter, J. (1991). *Writing space: The computer, hypertext and the history of writing*. Hillsdale, NJ: Erlbaum.

Gumpert, G., & Cathcart, R. (1985). Media grammars, generations, and media gaps. *Critical Studies in Mass Communication, 2*, 23-35.

Landow, G.P. (1992). *Hypertext: The convergence of contemporary critical theory and technology*. Baltimore: Johns Hopkins University Press.

McLuhan, M. (1967). *The medium is the message: An inventory of effects*. New York: Random House.

Ong, W. (1982). *Orality and literacy: The technologizing of the word*. London: Methuen.

Robertson, L. (1990, March). *Writing for action: Texts for an activist learning community*. Paper presented at Conference on College Composition and Communication, Boston.

Schwartz, H. (1984). SEEN: A tutorial and user network for hypothesis testing. In W. Wresch (Ed.), *The computer in composition instruction: A writer's tool* (pp. 47-62). Urbana, IL: National Council of Teachers of English.

Selfe, C. (1989). Redefining literacy: The multilayered grammars of computers. In G. Hawisher & C. Selfe (Eds.), *Critical perspectives on computers and composition instruction* (pp. 3-15). New York: Teachers College Press.

Taylor, R. (1980). *The computer in the school: Tutor, tool, tutee*. New York: Teachers College Press.

Chapter
Five

Collaborative Investigation Online: Eighteenth-Century Literature Moves to the Computer Lab

Russell A. Hunt
St. Thomas University

BACKGROUND: THE PROBLEM

In spite of powerful and dramatic developments in theories of how people learn language and literacy, the "default mode" of university teaching remains today essentially unchanged from what it has been for the past century: students read a textbook, listen to lectures, engage in occasional class discussions, infrequently write a paper, and regularly take an examination (more often quantitative and machine scoreable than essay type). And this method works about as well as it always has: that is, it favors those who need help least, separating out those who come prepared to learn in spite of the method from those who, for whatever reasons, could profit from educational methods that took more account of the nature of learning.

COLLABORATIVE INVESTIGATION AT ST. THOMAS

There are some signs, however, that things are changing. The spread of new ideas, public calls for curriculum reform, university initiatives to support and reward teaching, and the advent of new technology are beginning to make inroads in traditional practice. One instance that I can describe in some detail is what is called unofficially the "collaborative investigation" program at St. Thomas University. After more than eight years of development, this work is beginning to receive increasingly widespread attention (see the appended list of references for publications and conference presentations arising out of it).

Although details vary from teacher to teacher and from discipline to discipline, certain principles are widely accepted, whether the course is introductory psychology, Native American Religions, an 18th-century literature seminar, or a senior-level class in the theory and applications of rhetoric. In each case student research and writing are the central activities of the course, largely displacing textbook reading, attendance at lectures, taking and studying class notes, and group discussion. But it is student writing of a rather different kind than is normally found in classrooms. Students write neither traditional term papers nor essay exams. They do not, that is, write in order to demonstrate the acquisition of knowledge or for the teacher in the role of examiner. Writing in these classes, insofar as possible, has authentically social purposes. Students write to amuse or interest or inform or persuade a known audience—an audience capable of being, in actuality, amused, interested, informed, or persuaded. Another way to say this is that insofar as possible the written language is what is described by Bakhtin (1973, 1986) as *dialogic*—that is, it originates in, and constitutes a response to, someone else's query, assertion, or argument, and it is written in anticipation of someone else responding to it.

The following is an illustrative example of this contrast: A few years ago in my own class, I might have asked on an examination, or as an essay topic, why Jonathan Swift is an important author. Now, the class as a whole asks each other, who are the important authors in the 18th century, and whom should we read, and why? Based on wide (individually selected) readings in a range of textbooks, literary histories, guides to literary study, and so forth, groups of class members come up with lists of important writers and write arguments for reading some as opposed to others. (Most of the groups usually include Swift; it's difficult to read background material on the 18th century without seeing that there is a consensus that he is an important writer.) The class reads all the arguments and makes the decisions about whom to read based on whether they were persuaded by them. The arguments are not read by the teacher and evaluated. They are not overtly evaluated, even by the students' classmates. They either achieve their end—persuasion—or don't. That is, people are either persuaded to read and study the author, or they are not. We select a "short list" of writers, and one group investigates Jonathan Swift's reputation and work. They then persuade the rest of the class to read specific works of Swift. Again, people choose what to read (and what everyone should read) on the basis of the arguments and information presented.

To use written language in these ways in a classroom context involves some fundamental changes in the structure of the teaching process and in the means by which it is organized and conducted. For example, much time that conventionally would be spent in class discussion or lecture is spent in reading or in writing. Often students read the teacher's photocopied written assignments and explanations rather than listen to oral explanations of assignments or organizational strategies; or they might write impromptu texts on a given issue or subject, which are then circulated around small groups or to the whole class for reading and response—a form of written discussion referred to as "inkshedding." Similarly, time that could have been spent reading a course textbook might in this case be spent in the library, reading in a selection of textbooks, or, more important, in the public literature of the discipline. Class time is regularly given up for library work or for groups to assemble reports or arguments, or for such reports to be read and responded to. The instructor's time is distributed differently, as well. For example, written "prompts" are composed, printed, and photocopied rather than lectures prepared. Regularly, a great deal of student writing must be distributed quickly to multiple readers. Sometimes this can be accomplished by circulating individual copies around a group; more often it entails massive amounts of photocopying. Organizing this sort of thing takes time that might otherwise be used in marking papers or planning classes.

It became clear a number of years ago that there are important practical, procedural, and logistic problems associated with utilizing writing in these ways. Circulating written text by means of photocopies is not only expensive, but time-consuming and awkward. Individual access to the writing of others—especially at the time you need it most—is logistically complicated and often inconvenient. Consistent production of originals, which are susceptible of photocopying (dark enough, clearly enough handwritten), is not a trivial difficulty. Responding to the writing of others entails creating at least somewhat legible marginal comments, or extra sheets of paper, paper-clipped, stapled, or stuck to the original. And keeping track of all the paper—making sure that there is a central record of who has written what, and who has responded to whose writing—poses serious mechanical difficulties.

Computerizing Collaborative Investigation

For such a course and such a concept the next logical step was clear. Computer word processing technology and computer networking clearly have a great deal to offer in such a situation. Since 1987 we have been moving toward a situation in which we could take advantage of the technology in pursuit of these aims. During the 1989-1990 year, St. Thomas University installed a local-area network on the PCs in the university computer lab. It was a Novell network, running a classroom software program distributed by IBM, called ICLAS. After some initial startup problems, it became clear that such a course could be based on such a network. Particularly important considerations included the ease of signing on, the availability of a uniform and easily learned word processing program, and the general accessibility of the technology. Accordingly, after Christmas I began encouraging my year-long 18th-century literature class to use the account I had set up for the course (students all signed on to the same account, "18C"). Although the computer-based aspect of the course had not been announced in advance, and could hardly be required, by the end of the academic year at least 17 of the 26 students had submitted or edited files on the LAN (in some cases by composing on other computers and arranging to have them loaded onto the server). Although we had not found ways to computerize most of the kinds of writing characteristic of a collaborative investigation, we had managed to put the entire corpus of reports for the "course book"—in excess of 50 files, ranging from 2 pages to 10 or more in length—on the network. Many of these files had been radically revised, or constituted separate reports combined into single files, by individuals or groups. At the end of the course, each was copyedited, usually by two other members of the class, and the whole was printed using the network printer in the lab. As finally combined, the course book took up half a megabyte of disk space (557739 kilobytes, to be exact) and printed out at over 200 8-1/2 by 11 pages.

The logistic problems, however, remained great. Even though students generally found it possible to learn to handle the lab and the software, it was often difficult for them to get access to the lab, which was not only small, but was used for teaching computer literacy courses and for other purposes as well. This contributed to a decision to delay completion of the book until after classes were over. The physical difficulties of getting files from my own computer, in my third-floor office, to the lab in the basement and back, and maintaining the account, were considerable. There were extremely time-consuming problems with duplicate files (often, copies existed on individual student disks, on my computer, and on the classroom server; occasionally it was very difficult to tell which had been edited and which should be discarded as obsolete; often we had need for backup files because errors were made on the files on the classroom server, etc.).

It was clear, however, that the results of this trial were encouraging. In large part the computer technology actually did facilitate the work of the course—the dialogic exchange and use of written text—rather than being only a difficulty to be overcome. It was also clear that by using only slightly more elaborate technology, a great deal more could be achieved. Many of the other genres and purposes of writing typically used in such classrooms could, it was apparent, be facilitated by the computer. Over the years since, in fact, our experience suggests that virtually all of these ways can be implemented without overwhelming expenditures in hardware or software. Here is how we worked out methods of rendering such strategies more easily through the network.

Technological Issues

Some major hard- and software issues that have been addressed since that first trial are the following:

1. The network has been physically extended beyond the lab to include the machines in teachers' offices. This has had profound effects, including the possibility of using e-mail for virtually synchronous assistance with problems, and the elimination of the problem of duplicate files on various machines: All are now on the server, and teachers have access to the same common directories as students. In the near future the lab will be extended to student residences and will be provided with dial-in access, which will make it accessible from home computers, on telephone lines. Obviously, this will make communication even more easy.
2. An elegant shareware mail system (Pegasus Mail) has been installed on the network. This has not only made collaboration easier, but it has facilitated communication between teachers and students. The fact that it is an extremely simple program to use has eased the initiation of many students into computer use.
3. During one year, we had a usable bulletin board program (that freeware program, BrainStorm, has since been replaced by an unusable commercial version, and we are currently searching for a replacement).
4. Abandoning ICLAS allowed us to facilitate student-to-student communication and collaboration; a simpler menu program allowed us easily to set up a directory structure that promoted

these activities and allowed students easily to share files and exchange messages.

5. A specific room has been designated as the collaborative investigation classroom, and cabled appropriately. In this particular case, it operates on the same server as the larger, university lab, and students can use either. The Collaborative Investigation (CI) lab has six or seven (depending on how many are functioning; some are aging 8088-based machines) computers in it, and the larger lab a dozen or 15. We expect to expand both, but at the moment this serves with some difficulty the needs of the hundred or so students currently using the network for CI courses. The network now has a server with 1.4 gigabytes of storage, of which a third is dedicated to student and other user files. The server runs Novell version 3.11 and currently uses a shareware program called DougMenu as a user interface.

Because of the creation of this smaller lab, it turned out there were serendipitous benefits. Groups meet in the lab not only for electronic editing, but for more informal and wide-ranging oral discussions. The lab, over the course of the term, becomes a regular meeting place. Not only is the electronic medium used for collaboration, so is the cork bulletin board (print documents with handwritten annotations are regularly posted there), the top of the filing cabinet (boxes of printed bulletin board strands are left there for annotation) and the chalkboards (graffiti of various kinds accumulate steadily).

Generic Issues

Similarly, there are a number of ways in which we have found that genres of writing that these courses promote can be facilitated on the network.

1. Teacher's messages, instructions, and assignments to the class ("Prompts"). Much of the organization and conduct of such courses, particularly at the beginning of the year, is accomplished through written "prompts" which are photocopied and handed out at the beginning of a class meeting or posted in an envelope on a bulletin board or on the instructor's office door if class isn't meeting. Over the course of the year in the prenetwork 18th century course, for example, there were over 80 such documents composed, printed, duplicated, and distributed, in 30-35 copies each (some ran to two or three pages). Currently, however, such documents can be written and held

in a read-only file on the computer network. This not only saves a great deal of photocopying (students make their own printed copies as and if they need them), but the prompts are permanently accessible for reference. Further, questions regarding them can be posted through e-mail as they arise and dealt with immediately. And, in fact, although the difficulties of structuring the network to make that sort of access possible turned out to be greater than we had anticipated, once achieved, the process turned out to be extremely productive. Although finding a reliable and user-friendly bulletin board program to run on a Novell network has not been easy, students have proved eager to engage in such discussions.

2. Transactionally embedded impromptu writing ("inksheds"). Regularly, as I have described, in-class impromptu writing is generated and circulated as a way of strengthening and structuring discussion, testing ideas, sharing responses to presentations or papers, and so on. Although it seemed obvious it would be difficult to computerize the writing that is done physically in the classroom (unless there were 20 or more keyboards in the room), such writing is often scheduled to be done between one class meeting and another. Students with access to the lab could compose such writing on the computer and print it for circulation. Even more important, it seemed likely that the principle could be extended by establishing running conversations in accumulative files on an electronic bulletin board; this could be done entirely outside of class time and printed and distributed to the class at intervals (or read online). Again, this proved to be much easier than we had anticipated: Although many of the details of reading and commenting on each others' writing were modified, almost all of this is readily achieved on a bulletin board, or, even more simply, by setting up a common read-write file to which students add their own comments.
3. Group reports. Besides the research reports, which are the central material of the course, there are proposals for study, annotated lists of questions to be explored, proposals for scheduling, and so forth. Without the network, these were done in traditional ways—individuals drafted sections, and editorial groups or individuals combined sections, revises, and edited hard copy. Finally, "designated secretaries" from the group arranged for final copy—either typescript or computer file. The final copies were photocopied and distributed, sometimes prior to class by being posted on the board outside my office, some-

times at a class meeting. Access to the LAN greatly facilitated this process. Just as computer word processing programs afford revision, they make collaboration easier. Files are written individually and combined electronically; spell checkers and editing software are used; hard copies are printed as needed.

4. Responding to reports. Regularly, when a report is circulated, everyone in the class reads it and responds in writing—in my own courses, usually with a set of questions for clarification or further information. Before the network, texts were usually turned in to me by the responders, whereupon I assembled them into packages according to the report being responded to and distributed them to the authors. The authors then revised their report, using the questions in whatever way they found appropriate. This was a very difficult process to administer, especially when the reports and responses were not tightly synchronized (it was particularly difficult to keep records of who had responded to which reports). But it is perhaps the most powerful aspect of the writing process in a collaborative investigation course: The questions are a very effective way in which students can tell whether their report has been understood and an extremely productive stimulus for revision. If the reports were on read-only files on the computer, we thought, students could enter their questions in associated files, enabling them to avoid duplication and to elaborate or reinforce questions already asked (because they would automatically have access to all the questions already asked of a given report); it would also provide an automatic record of who had read and asked questions about which reports. Although this too turned out to be more difficult than we had anticipated because of the peculiarities of the network software, eventually we found a method for creating easily accessible read-only and read-write directories for students.
5. Revisions of group reports. Each such report is (at least potentially) revised in light of the questions posed by others in the class. What happened previously was that the group who wrote the original report might take all the questions and a copy of the report and work with all of that at a meeting—editing, recasting, perhaps doing more research. At the end of the process a secretary would be designated to retype or rekey the report. Putting all the files involved on the computer network obviously makes such a process easier and involves more students more actively. The processes of passing the questions and the various annotated copies of the report

among the members of the group are, if not eliminated, rendered much less confusing.

6. Question and Topic Generation. Regularly, everyone in such a class proposes lists of questions, topics, or subjects to be studied. The process of discussing and deciding among such proposals is often a complex and confusing (although in important ways productive) one. If, for example, 25 students each come to class with different lists of five or six Restoration writers they wish to argue the class should read, and short arguments for each, circulating the information around the class and helping everyone to make an informed decision can entail a great deal of paper shuffling and reorganizing of groups. It seemed clear that if each recommendation were loaded into a database and sorted according to the author recommended (or question asked, or topic proposed), it would be easy to arrange for everyone to read all the recommendations before making a decision. This, so far, has not proved possible. No database of which we are aware is easy enough to use to allow such manipulations for the computer novices in our classes.
7. Individual correspondence. Because a great deal of the work of a class like this is carried out in writing, I regularly encourage students to write me with questions or comments about the course or the subject matter before we meet (if necessary) to discuss things. Sometimes I ask specific questions or raise specific concerns and invite comment. I encouraged them to pin notes to the literal cork bulletin board outside my office (in envelopes if they were private). I wrote responses and pinned those to the bulletin board in turn. It was obvious, and it has turned out to be the case, that this literal cork bulletin board could be made more flexible and convenient by being converted into an electronic one. Messages could either be private or public, depending on the concerns; a network mailing system (Pegasus Mail, as it turned out) could be set up for correspondence between student and teacher (and between student and student), as well as a bulletin board for concerns that might be of interest to everyone.
8. Book publication. As I have described, what is in some ways the focal activity of the course is the preparation of a "course book." Usually this book constitutes a permanent record of what the course's subject matter and is the result of varying amounts of revision and copyediting of reports prepared by individuals and groups during the course. Such reports were photocopied (from typed, printed, or handwritten originals) and permanently bound. Many of the ways in which this

activity could be enhanced and made more convenient by putting the course on computer were obvious, and indeed had already been demonstrated through the computerization of the course book, *The Eighteenth Century Frame: Studies in the Literature and its Contexts*, during the spring term of 1990. More students can be instrumentally involved in more aspects of the book's production; moreover, the final copy can take advantage of the techniques of desktop publication and can be laid out attractively and typeset uniformly, rather than being created out of assembled photocopies of whatever individuals or groups submit.

9. Evaluation. One of the most significant aspects of collaborative investigation teaching as it has developed at St. Thomas has been a novel approach to evaluation. Traditional courses evaluate students primarily on the basis of an instructor's judgment about performance on specific tasks—essays, examinations, or class discussion. Because an important aspect of collaborative investigation involves decreasing the extent to which the instructor is at the center of all discourse transactions in the class, methods of evaluation have evolved that also move the instructor away from the center. Also important is the extent to which the course depends on students learning from, and teaching, each other. Thus, typically, two factors become central to a new sort of evaluation: (a) exhaustive records of the extent to which students are actively involved in the sequences of assignments and tasks which make up the course, and (b) the students' evaluations of each other's contributions—in writing, in class discussion, or in editorial committees and group work—to their learning. These evaluations typically involve relatively complex forms, photocopied by the students, filled out by individual students, and turned in inside sealed envelopes.

   Both of these matters posed some problems which could, it seemed clear, be at least in part solved by computerization. For example, it is much easier to keep accurate records of student participation in tasks such as writing questions on reports, proposing subjects for study or questions for investigation, or writing, revising, and editing reports. In spite of all its limitations, IBM's ICLAS made such recordkeeping virtually effortless. The basic Novell network software and menu system we are currently using is not quite so forthcoming, but currently we are exploring possibilities of using its accounting capabilities for such purposes. Perhaps equally important, peer evaluations could be greatly simplified if they were put on computer files from the beginning: Such files could easily be converted to databases that would allow the instructor to see readily all the ratings for a given student in any area. This has worked well, in spite of my own misgivings about the public nature of composing onscreen in a public lab.

AN EXAMPLE OF A COURSE

What happens, then, in a given, specific course? In my case, as in most, it all begins with handing everyone a long, written introduction to the course and giving everyone time to read it silently. I also hand out, as I do at the beginning of most sessions, a document headed "In Class Today." In September 1991, that document said, in part:

> As you'll discover, one of my central beliefs as a teacher is that reading and writing are powerful tools, and ones we don't use as often as we might. One of the ways in which that belief is acted out in my teaching is that I write a lot, ask you to read it, and expect you to write a lot and expect others (including me, sometimes) to read it. But I don't expect that the writing is going to be used in the way most educational writing is used—that is, as a basis for evaluating the writer (can she write? does she know what she's supposed to know?). I expect it's going to be used the way you'll use most of these handouts—to see what I have to say, and respond to it in some meaningful way (by doing what it asks, or arguing that what it asks doesn't make sense, for example).

That handout also asked everyone to write about the 18th century for 10 or 15 minutes.

> The second part of the class will involve everyone writing about the literature of the eighteenth century, reading each other's writing, and generating responses and questions. This is a way of ascertaining the sorts of things we all know, and need to know, about the period, about its literature, and about literary study, and generating some issues and concerns that we're going to be addressing over the first few weeks.

After everyone had written, the texts were read in groups, preliminary questions were written and shared, and we began moving toward a discussion of the questions that seemed primary. Between then and the second session, the class generated a set of questions about the 18th century. At the end of that class, we divided the questions into three categories: (a) those that no one expected could be answered, (b) those that could only be answered after a good deal of study and learning, and (c) those that might be answered by a group of two or three students who spent some time in the library over the next week. I divided the class into groups, the groups picked a question of the third type (they included questions on comedy in the period, on changes between this period and the 17th century, on what an ode was, and on who were important playwrights at the time), and we were off. Next week, each group had completed a draft of a report and keyed it into the network server.

In the meantime, we began a running conversation on the electronic bulletin board. Everyone was required to log on and read the board—and contribute something—each week. Over the year, contributions varied from Merry Christmas messages and complaints about the heat in the computer lab to an extended, multivoiced discussion of whether Moll Flanders should be regarded as primarily the author of her own fate or a victim of society. Everyone was also required to touch base with me once a week through the more private electronic mail system. Letters there varied from "nothing to report this week" to long exchanges about the reasons why some people find it harder to participate in oral discussions than in written ones (that one, in fact, expanded into a bulletin board discussion).

Between then and April, according to my estimate, the 13 students in that course generated well over 40,000 words on the bulletin board and over 30,000 words in electronic notes to me. How much they may have generated in notes to each other I have no way of knowing, but it probably was considerable. Even without that, the total works out to a bit over 5,000 words per student.

Beyond that, of course, there is a great deal of noncomputer writing—inkshedding, question generating, commenting on other people's reports, questioning them, and so forth—which I have no way of counting or tracking.

But also, of course, and most important, there is all the electronic writing done in the more formal context of written reports to the rest of the class, and comments on and reactions to those reports by their readers. Although the mechanics of this varied as the course (and our familiarity with the computer network) developed, the last cycle of reports, all of which had to do with some facet of the class's reading of various texts of Pope and Johnson, were handled this way. Questions and issues were discussed (in part through in- and out-of-class inksheddings) and then proposed individually, in files in a common directory on the network. Each person in the class was invited to read the questions posed by all the others and add comments and suggestions to the individual files. As the comments accumulated, the authors read them; in some cases these led to modifications of the questions, and in some the authors were offered strategies for finding answers; in most there was a good deal of comment suggesting that others were interested in the questions. Over the next week or so, as the authors began finding answers to their questions, they began putting drafts into the same file, immediately following the sets of questions and comments. As the drafts lengthened, others read them and added comments on, and questions and suggestions about, the drafts in the same files, following the drafts. As authors checked back on the responses to their work, they regularly edited and changed the drafts in response to their audience's questions. Comments on the bulletin board suggested that this was, from most of the students' point of view, the most successful way of managing this collaborative form of writing we had yet tried.

It is difficult in a few pages to give any flavor of the discussion in these files. I did not work fast enough to arrange to archive the original drafts, so as I go through the files it is not clear how the comments on first drafts affected subsequent modifications, but let me pull a few examples out of one such file. It's the one that began with this question, from Darice (all names have been changed):

> My question has to do with Pope's repulsiveness both physically and personality wise as I feel his ability to write satiric literature may be connected (simply because I'm sure since he is described as looking like a toad that he knew that people found him repulsive and therefore promoted this repulsiveness in his personality, which ultimately led to an ingenious ability to compose satiric literature as a way to overcome the public's view of him). I may be way off, but I feel that this may be the case as Russ explained in class that Pope used to get very irate if someone had said his parents had been poor and also that not many people who knew Pope liked him. If I'm unable to get any information upon this connection between his physical and personality repulsive character which may have influenced his poetic ability, then I thought I might just pursue the reasons behind his physical deformity.
>
> Any suggestions? What do you think: a dead path or possibility? I realize this is not a question orientated specifically to historical background, but more a background on Pope (Russ is this o.k.)?

Some of the comments on this question included the following:

> Darice: This sounds interesting. It's nice to get another side of things—a background, or at least some kind of sense of this sort of thing. —Pat
>
> There are arguments about some of these issues (different biographers have different views). One way to focus it would be to present

some views of it, specifically ascribed to the authors; it's certainly a question worth asking. —Russ

Darice, I didn't pick up on the fact that Pope wasn't a 'very handsome' fella, or as you say "repulsive"! I think you might have to look at Biographies etc to see what his background was like and family life which might have influenced his personality, but, (not to discourage) I think it would be difficult to determine that someone's physical appearance affected their personality. —Greta

Darice, I just read something that described when Pope developed his disease and the pain it caused him. The book relates that as a young man Pope was first stricken with the disease and was convinced he was dying. He even went so far as to write letters of goodbye to his friends. Perhaps the constant expectance of death influenced his nasty attitudes and helped sharpen his satirical tongue. —Tamara

I just read something else about him too: a description of him at fourteen: "He is small and pale, fragile, and already not quite straight in the back . . . , but he has a frighteningly sensitive face, large wondering eyes, and an enchanting voice which will earn him the name of 'the little nightingale'". I don't know if this is relevant to what you are doing, but I thought it might be nice to hear a pleasant description of the poor guy. —Tamara

Pope was often described in quite attractive terms by his friends, often quite similar to what you found, Tamara. (Who is that, by the way?) —Russ

I took the quote from Bonamy Dobree's book Alexander Pope, published in 1952. —Tamara

In response to those questions, Darice produced an 850-word report on Pope's early life, drawn primarily from George Sherburn's and John Russo's books. Her report included passages like this (just to give you a sense of the tone):

> Since they were Catholics at a time when England's religion was Protestant, the Pope's were forced by antipapist legislation to move often, which prompted Mr. Pope to retire from his successful linen business. There is little known of Pope as a child, except that he experienced several traumatic experiences. Although Pope was not physically deformed as a child, his half sister, Mr. Rackett informed Pope's biographer, Mr. Spence that when he was between the age of three and five "a wild cow that was driven by the place where he was filling a little cart with stones struck at him with her horns, tore off his hat which was tied under the chin, wounded him in the throat, beat him down, and trampled over him" (Russo, p. 27). Further Pope studied under four priests, one of which was said to have whipped and ill-used him for writing a satire (isn't that ironic!).

Most of the comments on the report were appreciative; a few raised further questions. For instance:

> Darice,
>
> I enjoyed this report very much; it was an interesting way to look at Pope and his work. However, I think you may have overlooked something of relative importance: what can explain his friends' kind attitudes towards him? Surely, he must have had some attractive qualities. For instance, his voice was quite enchanting—could that have affected his ability to create such rhythmic, lyrical verses? Perhaps not, but I do think his positive attributes should also be explored.—Tamara
>
> Darice, I have been fascinated with the physical descriptions of Pope since reading about him. This report is very helpful in giving me a more vivid picture. Have you read Johnson's "From the Lives of Poets", the section on Pope? I read it for this week and I must say, it is a very informative piece. Not only does it talk about his works, but about his personal life too. It said that he "never took tea without a stratagem"—his mind was always on the go. It also said he thought quite highly of himself. My question is, "did his brilliantly sharp mind and maybe, his somewhat conceited air have something to do with his physical deformities—was his mind compensating for something else? Something to think about and you should read it if you have not already—its really interesting. —Barb

That there is change occurring, and that it involves learning about writing as well as about the 18th century, seems to me clear. Toward the end of the course, in preparing for a conference presentation, I asked the students to look back over the writing they did for the course in the first few weeks and at what they had done more recently, and reflect on what differences they saw (with examples, if possible). Here is one example, chosen by Barb as typical of her writing in September:

> Ultimately, the relationship between comedy and its audience cannot be measured because society is not homogeneous in nature; there can be no absolute because there is no universal standard.

About that sentence, Barb said:

> I found my initial report to be very formal. I think we were trying to impress you, the professor, rather than our classmates because that is what we are used to doing. I think when we write essays we tend to try to aspire to academic heights and we try to sound as academic as possible. When we write for the benefit of our classmates, we

> know that they are at the same academic level, so we don't have to sound so professional. The writing in class is more friendly; more personal and less formal.
>
> I think, too, I am more relaxed in my writing because there isn't the pressure of a paper that is worth 40% of the mark. With this type of class, I am able to relax and this changes my writing style, I believe.

Here is the sentence she chose from her more recent writing.

> From what I've read about the often diseased food at the time, I don't think I would have wanted to have eaten back then.

As an instructor, I do not want to contend that that second sentence represents "better" writing than the first. I am not arguing that it has a more authentic voice, that it's more concrete and personal and therefore more effective, or that the student has found a superior register in which she should now attempt to produce her papers for her other literature courses. I believe the first kind of writing is as necessary and as useful as the second, and, further, that the only criteria that could possibly be used to judge which is "better" writing are functions of the situation in which the composing occurs. What I would argue, and what I think the student is arguing, is that the second kind of writing is "better" in a situation in which what she is doing is writing to engage and inform the other students in the class. Now, the first piece was written, as well, in just such a situation—but it is clear, I think, that she had not yet begun to make the sorts of adjustment that are apparent when you contrast the two.

I think, as well, there is evidence of similar learning going on in other situations in this class. One place I find it most obvious is in the postings to the electronic bulletin board. Besides the growing concreteness and specificity of the messages, what I am struck with is the new consciousness of this medium as a device for forging and maintaining social relationships, as well as carrying on an intellectual discussion. There is strikingly more casual and efficient references to the positions of others ("The question was originally brought up by Barb") to other documents in the class ("When you consider Tanya's report on employment for women"); there are in-jokes ("for any Soc. people out there"), and so on. All these suggest a context and relation between writer and readers very different from what is implied in those early, formal messages, written in obvious consciousness of the teacher reading over the author's shoulder.

There is an increasing consensus (at least among the educational writers and practitioners for whom I have the most respect) that the best sort of teaching is the kind that engages people in what Smith (1983; see also Dixon & Stratta, 1984) calls "an enterprise" and then observes closely to see what they can do, what they actually do, what—as Vygotsky (1962, 1986) insisted—they can almost do, and can do with a little help from their friends, and then finds ways to promote learning that is specific to where each learner is and to where he or she needs to be. I think, in general, that is what's going on in classes conducted like the one I have described. The computer network facilitates this in ways that seem to be fulfilling some of the long-promised and long-delayed benefits of computers in education.

REFERENCES

Bakhtin, M.M. (1973). *Marxism and the philosophy of language.* ["By V. N. Volosinov"] (Trans. L. Matejka & I. R. Titunik). New York: Seminar Press [Harvard University Press].

Bakhtin, M.M. (1986). *Speech genres and other late essays* (Trans. V. W. McGee, eds. C. Emerson & M. Holquist). Austin: University of Texas Press.

Dixon, J., & Stratta, L. (1984). Student enterprises with personal and social value. *Series B: Writing 14 to 18, Discussion Booklet 3.* ERIC Document No. ED268522.

Smith, F. (1983). *Essays into literacy.* London: Heinemann.

Vygotsky, L.S. (1962). *Thought and language.* (Eds. and trans. E. Hanfmann & G. Vakar). Cambridge, MA: MIT Press.

Vygotsky, L.S. (1986). *Thought and language.* (Trans. A. Kozulin). Cambridge, MA: MIT Press.

SUGGESTED READINGS ON COLLABORATIVE INVESTIGATION

Hunt, R. A. (1987). 'Could you put in lots of holes?' Modes of response to writing. *Language Arts, 64*(2), 229-232.

Hunt, R. A. (1989a). A horse named Hans, a boy named Shawn: The Herr von Osten theory of response to writing. In C.M. Anson (Ed.), *Writing and response: Theory, practice, and research* (pp. 80-100). Champaign-Urbana, IL: National Council of Teachers of English.

Hunt, R. A. (1989b). Learning to converse with texts: Some real readers, some real texts, and the pragmatic situation. *SPIEL: Siegener periodicum zur internationalen empirischen literaturwissenschaft, 8*(1), 107-130.

Hunt, R.A. (1990). *Society, the individual and the teacher: Mediating the demands through collaborative investigation*. Paper presented at the Conference on College Composition and Communication, Chicago.

Hunt, R.A. (1991a). Foreword. In J. Newman (Ed.), *Interwoven conversations: Learning and teaching through critical reflection* (pp. vii-xii). Toronto: OISE Press.

Hunt, R.A. (1991b). Modes of reading, and modes of reading Swift. In J. Clifford (Ed.), *The experience of reading: Louise Rosenblatt and reader-response theory* (pp. 105- 126). Portsmouth, NH: Heinemann-Boynton/Cook.

Hunt, R.A. (1991c). R Texts Us? *Inkshed, 10*(1), 5-6.

Hunt, R.A. (1991d). Subverting the literary system: Nonhegemonic literary socialization. In E. Ibsch, D. Schram, & G. Steen (Eds.), *Proceedings of the Second IGEL Conference: Amsterdam 1991* (pp. 175-180). Amsterdam: Rodopi.

Hunt, R.A. (1992). Utterance in the classroom: Dialogic motives for invention. *Resources in Education:* ERIC Microfiche Card ED 345 271.

Hunt, R.A. (1993). Texts, textoids and utterances: Writing and reading for meaning, in and out of classrooms. In D. Bogdan & S. B. Straw (Eds.), *Constructive reading: Teaching beyond communication* (pp. 113-129). Portsmouth, NH: Heinemann-Boynton/Cook.

Hunt, R.A. (in press). Speech genres, writing genres, school genres and computer genres. In A. Freedman & P. Medway (Eds.), *Genres in education*. Portsmouth, NH: Boynton/Cook Heinemann.

Hunt, R.A., & Brown, K. (1992). *Collaborative investigation across the disciplines*. Paper presented at the Society for Teaching and Learning in Higher Education Annual Meeting, Toronto.

Hunt, R.A., & Reither, J.A. (1992, September 4). *Beyond portfolios: Scenes for dialogic reading and writing*. Miami University conference on the teaching of writing: New Directions in Portfolio Assessment. Oxford, OH.

Reither, J.A. (1985). Writing and knowing: Toward redefining the writing process. *College English, 47*(6), 620-628.

Reither, J.A. (1990). The writing *student* as researcher: Learning from our students. In D. Daiker & M. Morenberg (Eds.), *The writing teacher as researcher: Essays in the theory and practice of class-based research* (pp. 247-255). Portsmouth, NH: Boynton/Cook Heinemann.

Reither, J.A., Hunt, R.A., Parkhill, T., & Vipond, D. (1990). *Knowledge in the making: Celebrating diversity in writing, English, and other content courses*. Paper presented at the Conference on College Composition and Communication, Chicago.

Reither, J.A., and Vipond, D. (1989). Writing as collaboration. *College English, 51*(8), 855-867.

Chapter Six

NEOS and the Development of the Electronic Classroom at MIT*

Edward Barrett
Massachusetts Institute of Technology

INTRODUCTION: WHAT IS THE ELECTRONIC CLASSROOM?

Six years ago, MIT's Program in Writing and Humanistic Studies, in collaboration with Project Athena (with grants from IBM and Digital Equipment Corporation) and Information Systems at MIT, developed the first university electronic classroom for teaching writing and other subjects in a fully distributed computing environment. Since then most colleges and universities in the United States have begun development of electronic classrooms because of their usefulness as teaching tools. Every major university now has some form of networked classroom, usually localized within one or several buildings. Some have much more extensive online environments or are planning to implement them. And networked, computer-mediated instruction easily ranges across the curricu-

*Initial development of NEOS was a collaborative effort between members of the Program in Writing and Humanistic Studies (WHS) and staff of Project Athena, with supporting grants from IBM and Digital Equipment Corporation. The current windowed version of NEOS was developed in collaboration between members of WHS and staff of Information Systems at MIT.

lum: The success of the electronic classroom and its associated software at MIT has led to its use in 20 different classes in the schools of humanities, science, and engineering.

What is an electronic classroom? Is it just a room with some computers in it where students go after class to crunch numbers, do word processing, or review foreign language exercises? What is the role of "the computer" in educational environments? A surprisingly large number of faculty and administrators fear some monolithic "teaching machine" (the phrase is Skinner's who wrote about computers in education in the1960s), programming students to learn in a rigid, algorithmic fashion, perhaps like Skinner's pigeons. Or they imagine computerized expert systems, artificial intelligences that think for students rather than with them.

But for faculty in writing at MIT, the concept of the electronic classroom was more. In the design and implementation of our software and in the physical layout of the classroom space, we wanted to support a web of social interactions that we felt defined an educational community. We wanted to use networked computers not in place of teaching but as a means by which students could interact with each other, with faculty, and with online information. We wanted "the computer" to become a transparent tool for helping students synthesize their own ideas out of the welter of information and course material with which they are presented. We thought a writing class would be the ideal place to experiment with such a system because writing is by nature a synthesizing activity. Writing is thinking: It allows students to see what—and how—they know something.

An electronic classroom, therefore, is more than a conventional classroom outfitted with computers: It is a "virtual" space that resides within four walls during scheduled class time *and* also exists asynchronously outside those four walls, to be invoked anytime, anywhere, by any class member to suit her or his educational needs. In essence, any subject supported by an electronic classroom is always in session, just not always in one place with all class members present. An electronic classroom is a human, social construct—a verbal communications matrix supported by computational technology, not constrained by it.

Six years ago, and especially in the field of writing instruction, such an insight was not generally shared. My colleagues and I, however, felt that most educational software available at the time lent too much authority to "the computer." Available software marched students through a set of preprogrammed educational steps that supposedly were equivalent to the cognitive states "expert" writers possessed at different stages of writing (or indeed of personal development). To make matters worse, "computer labs" were usually classroom add-ons, a place students were sent to outside of class hours for self-paced tutorial work, a workspace defined by one student interacting with one computer but not with anyone else in the class. There students could trace and retrace certain preprogrammed learning loops until they, presumably, internalized the promptings of the machine. Sometimes these loops might contain a finite set of subloops to give the appearance of intellectual searching within an otherwise closed system.

But was that writing? Was that education? We felt strongly that education was not programming an individual to follow a set pattern of intellectual insights, no matter how well that pattern might match any "educated" person's ways of thinking or creating. We did not want to use the computer to simulate a fictive expert; we wanted to use technology to support the varying, complex, private, and social activities that make up the educational process.

Our chief design contribution to the future of educational computing is in that conclusion: take the notion of a society of mind and turn it inside out so that we shift focus from how the mind might be arranged in certain cognitive states to how the private and social processes of investigating, positing, arguing, and reviewing take place in a diverse community. Pay attention to the social content of the classroom and the surrounding environment, rather than fixate on how to model the mind in a machine. The computer can store any number of combinations of information, accessible in unbounded ways. And a fully distributed computing network supports an unlimited communication of ideas and recombinations of information into new ways of looking at anything. It seemed best to us not to use the computer to model some hypothetical notion of the mind, but rather to model the complex interactions of people sharing ideas.

NEOS

This design choice allowed us to create educational software, NEOS (Networked Educational Online System), that never attempted to intrude on an individual's private world of sense making by dictating a process of investigation, or an end to that investigation. NEOS supported the processes that, we felt, defined education in any subject area. These processes include the creation of texts (in which "texts" can mean an essay or math problem, a poem or program code), the exchange of these texts among students and instructors, the review and annotation of these texts by everyone in a class, and the public and private display of texts in and out of class. NEOS also supports online textbooks and the storing and dissemination of other curricular materials over the network.

NEOS changed "the computer" from a monolithic "teaching

machine" into a virtual meeting place for the sharing of ideas, if by "sharing" one means the difficult process of studying databases for information, imagining new constructs, and communicating those new ideas to others for their review and whatever new cycle of imaginings that review invokes. The NEOS interface, therefore, never prompts a student to do anything; instead, it simply enables the student to call up his or her own work in conjunction with the work of others. It gives us a supple means to annotate that work, and it supports these activities in real class time and outside of class at anytime.

When students or instructors log on to NEOS, they are presented with a simple editing window from which they may access other material stored online or from which they may communicate with others. Above that editor window students may click on various icons or buttons to perform certain operations. They may click on "turnin" or "pickup" to share work for comment or to see what comments have been made on their work. They may click on a "handout" button for access to online curricular materials. An "exchange" button allows students to distribute, pick up, and comment on each others' work in and out of class. Another icon calls up an online textbook facility, whereas another "help" button accesses technical documentation for all aspects of the software for a neophyte user.

An important part of NEOS is the annotation facility because writing—indeed, any subject—is a process of thinking, sharing, and rethinking over time and through a topic. Texts are exchanged in and out of class for comments by the instructor and by student colleagues. Commentators may place an online equivalent to a post-it note anywhere in a student's text—a scrollable window that allows them to write comments of any length. Each comment window is identified by the commentator's name so that students may inquire of that person further if they are puzzled or disagree with any comment. From these pop-up annotation windows anyone may refer any other writer to all other curricular material (handouts and texts) stored online.

This user ID at the top of the annotation window is the only means for differentiating an instructor's comment from comments by students. Because writing classes in the electronic classroom at MIT are generally small (usually 16 students), everyone knows everyone else's user name, so students can easily identify the instructor's ID at the top of a comment window. In practice, a student will usually turn in two electronic copies of a draft: one to the instructor's turn-in bin, the other to the student exchange bin for peer review. The instructor's copy would be returned directly to the student "pickup" bin. Peer reviews would be returned to the exchange bin for student authors to retrieve. Students rarely report being confused as to who is making a comment.

NEOS, therefore, creates a kind of hypercontext in which the ongoing conversation of questioning minds takes place unfettered by the limitations of four walls or the clock. Students can turn in, and others may review, at any time the products of their thinking and investigations into any subject. Instead of assignments and due dates, NEOS gives us intellectual questioning, attempts at resolution, revision, or reimagination of subject matter in any course across the curriculum. There is no "expert system," no programmed path leading to a right way, just the give and take of students and instructors using texts to create meanings.

A typical class using NEOS and the electronic classroom, therefore, will be defined by the needs of the students. In my practice a classroom scenario can take any shape, so no one class is typical. We may begin by looking at several pieces of writing that students have turned in out of class since the last meeting: We look at these texts at our individual workstations and on a large-screen projection. These texts may have been commented on by just the instructor, or by the instructor and a student's peer group, or reviewed by the whole class. Changes may be suggested during class discussion, and we can see the effects these suggestions have by manipulating the text on the large-screen display. Our experience using the electronic classroom suggests that the best physical layout will have a central seminar table at which students may engage in face-to-face conversation about a text. Students should also be able to turn from this central seminar table to their computers, which ring the periphery of the room. The instructor's workstation should be integrated seamlessly into this concentric ring, in contrast to the usual podium stage in the conventional classroom, so that no visual clues suggest that the instructor is predominant in these in-class discussions. The electronic classroom empowers students to think for themselves; the instructor intervenes either as a peer or because her or his experience adds to the discussion. No visual clues suggest that the instructor a priori should lead these exchanges.

From this group discussion, my class might then turn to their computers to experiment with one or more of the strategies we have discussed. Perhaps a sample text will be picked up from online handouts, or we may focus on one or more student essays, or they may be asked to create something new on the spot. Students favor this movement from discussion to writing because it allows them to integrate theory and practice in real class time. Besides, it breaks the typical student tedium of being the passive recipient of ideas and lectures. They, and I, see what effects certain strategies of thought may or may not have. The class develops a feel for the reality of intellectual discussion, and they see how their input affects another's performance—surely an important lesson for nascent engineers and scientists whose professional development is so closely tied to peer review and communal ideas of discourse.

Outside of class the same freedom to turn in, review, discuss, and recreate one's ideas is supported by NEOS. Students may turn in texts for comment by the instructor, by peer groups, or by the whole class. The heavy grid of class schedules is submerged within this continuing dialogue. It has not been unusual for students to turn in an essay for my commentary, have it returned, then resubmit another draft before the due date for the original draft has been reached. In other words, students focus more on the developmental process of writing and thinking rather than on the usual pattern of assignment-performance-grade that predominates in much university teaching and learning. Of course, final drafts are due, and final grades are assigned. But the intellectual effort of arriving at that point is now defined by discussion, consensus, and understanding, instead of expectation and either disappointment or celebration. The obsession with a grade is replaced by engagement with the process of discovery.

But do students "learn better" in the electronic classroom? Are they "better writers" at the end of the semester? Are electronic classrooms worth the time and money?

Anecdotal evidence in the form of anonymous student responses to questionnaires about the classroom suggests that a majority of students prefer working in this online environment—and that preference usually translates into working harder at their writing. Good writers don't all have great talent, they just practice more. Students say the quick feedback loops that NEOS supports in and out of class helps them "get" the point of a particular criticism of their writing and drives them to do more revisions. As one student wrote, the online environment "helped me think about my thinking." This drafting-revising cycle also involves greater peer review, in and out of class, and students express their preference for this increased communication among peers.

They also express favorable reactions to the mix of theory and practice in the electronic classroom: the switching back and forth from discussion to writing to review in real class time. In surveys of my class, students unanimously stated that this was one of the chief benefits of the electronic classroom because, they felt, this cycle of in-class review had lasting effects on their writing outside class. The word students repeatedly use to describe this online review cycle is *natural*. By natural they seem to be expressing their developing sense that good writing is simply an extension of thinking through a problem, rather than a dead product, an "assignment" to finish and hand in. Student responses indicate that they feel they write more, and more effectively, at the end of a semester using the online environment, that they feel more comfortable approaching a writing task, and that their style of writing is "more natural," closer to their own voice than ever before. Surely these subjective impressions indicate that students are more comfortable with the process of writing and more willing to practice this art as a natural extension of their professional lives.

In terms of our original design goals—to support the social processes of learning—the electronic classroom is a success. NEOS and the online environment support greater communication through writing and speech, thus increasing the practice of using language to make a point. And the electronic classroom integrates theory with practice in real time so that writing seems less academic, less removed from one's own real concerns. Students are less passive in and out of class in this new environment; they are less rote learners and more collaborators with the instructor and each other.

But numbers alone cannot really measure success in writing in which one's effectiveness is a result of so many changing factors. Two years ago, MIT participated in a nationwide survey of college expository writing students in traditional and electronic classrooms conducted by researchers at the City University of New York. Results of pre- and posttesting in knowledge of grammar and syntax and holistic scoring of essays seemed to demonstrate a slightly better performance by students in the electronic classroom. But this study was fundamentally flawed because not all electronic and traditional classrooms were identical in structure and approach. Yet each semester in every university instructors do assign grades and certify levels of performance based on their extensive knowledge of different kinds of writing and effectiveness within those forms. On that basis, I can make certain large-scale comments on improvements in my students' writing.

Each year I teach an advanced essay class composed mainly of first- and second-year students and an advanced seminar in scientific and engineering writing. Both classes are held in the electronic classroom using NEOS. Students are rarely in need of remedial work on grammar and syntax, but neither have they developed distinctive styles of expression or argumentation in their writing. Because of the increased number of drafts they can write, and by having students comment on each other's writing more frequently, their willingness to argue in prose—to state a position and defend it—seems to mature. They begin to use language that is simpler yet more supple, more expressive of finer points of distinction than at the start of the semester. The length of essays also increases, not because of wordiness, but because of a greater depth of understanding of their own experience, now more accessible to them through the constant questioning of their topics and ways of arguing in essays. It becomes easier for them to discover a topic because they have more people reading and asking them questions about what they want to write about and how they will support their ideas. As students write more they inevitably experiment with the form of the essay, moving from the stock 5-paragraph essay to forms dictated more by the subject about which they are writing. As they write in this engaged way, it becomes more enjoyable reading their work—now it is less an assignment and more an actual journey of discovery.

Rapid in-class writing and extensive peer review out of class helps students in my technical writing class to develop a style that is concise, less bloated with personal narrative or extraneous discussions, and more focused on the needs of the audience trying to receive complicated technical information in a coherent form. Because NEOS supports the *process* of writing, my technical writing students are more involved with the typical document stream of proposals, progress reports, or final reports that defines any scientific or engineering project. These document types are reviewed in class and outside of class in peer groups, so my technical writing students develop a more developed critical language for interpreting complex documents and for suggesting revisions in a professional, collegial manner.

LIMITATIONS

Then what are the limitations to NEOS and our version of the electronic classroom? Or, perhaps a better way of asking this question is, once we had secured financial support for development and implementation, what limitations have we noted? NEOS was supported by grants from Project Athena at MIT, and Project Athena was supported by generous grants from IBM and DEC. Given our economy, we may never see corporate sponsorship on that level again. Too bad, because as Zuboff writes, the computer textualizes the workplace (Zuboff, 1988)—and what better way to develop such a "textualizing" tool than in the academy where "texts" are our bread and butter? What better place, I would go on to say, than in the traditional fields of the humanities because humanists—far more than computer scientists—receive the best training in the study of texts? I'll go one step further: Humanists must textualize the computer (see Barrett, 1989).

But I was talking about limitations: The first year anyone moves from a hardcopy format for instruction to an electronic format should be a year of massive release time. Reconfiguring for the computer means objectifying every intuitional move, every ingrained conviction, every unthought action, and every prejudice you have developed throughout a teaching career. It is like learning a new language: One wants to use the new language to discuss large ideas, but he or she is still stumbling over the word for "spoon." At MIT—perhaps because it is MIT and "technology" is such a shibboleth—many a faculty member in humanities simply will not endure this time sink. They cannot: Tenure and promotion policies still do not favor heavy investment in computational initiatives within the humanities.

Another limitation—at least within humanities—may be the programmer. If one is developing his or her own software and must hire programming staff, one is threatened with a loss of control over development and implementation. Programmers—some at least—simply do not understand that it is not the computer that is important, but the educational practice that the computer supports. Development of NEOS has always been a struggle between world views: the faculty who want the computer to be transparent, to disappear at the point at which it brings subject matter into view, and the programmer whose delight is in the computer itself. One especially vexing form of this struggle in an open, fully distributed computing environment is that teaching must take place within a constantly evolving context of development. "Evolving" may be the wrong word—discontinuity, sudden disappearance of species may be more like it as "improvements" muscle their way in, not over years, but over the course of a semester.

For a writing class another limitation of the electronic classroom is that at some point one has to download to hardcopy format to see what one has. We still live in a hardcopy world—"the book" is still our chief form of intellectual property. Online writing produces a blizzard of drafts, encourages change and adaptability, and threatens the neophyte writer with the blankness of hyperspace. With so many opportunities to change a text, why settle on this one rather than that one? Why printout at all—aren't online databases more complete? And, of course, they are not; writing is thinking, and thinking is not a totally rootless, unhierarchical intellectual mall that one browses through. Virtual realms can be like that: mental arcades in opposition to the light outside. And while I am within this metaphor it is important to note the analogy between the interior world of the computer screen and Plato's cave. Who is throwing those shadows on the cave wall? No database or virtual realm in the computer is unowned. Someone created it, placed dimension within it. The escape from authorial imperative in virtual worlds is a potent myth.

Yet in the real world other constraints apply, such as number. My writing classes in the electronic classroom are limited to 16 students—a design choice that would force an administrative decision to keep writing classes small. What about the other real world where writing classes may be as large as 20 or 30 students and where instructors must teach several such sections a semester? What happens in the electronic classroom then?

The electronic classroom can be a more effective tool for managing large sections. First of all, the computer does nothing better than count and archive, so papers do not get lost as easily as hardcopy. Software, certainly NEOS, helps the instructor sort and classify sections. So electronic bookkeeping is already a plus. More importantly, NEOS can be used to filter the drift of coursework. Peer groups can be set up more efficiently online so that early drafts of papers are reviewed there more intensely. The instructor can designate a changing cadre of student peer group leaders to report on traffic within the group. In essence, the online environment is an effective on-the-job training course for this revolving band of students.

In my capacity as director of the undergraduate technical writing cooperative at MIT (a joint program in which writing program staff participate in science and engineering classes, focusing on student documentation) I have used NEOS to review as many as 200 papers from a variety of classes across the curriculum. Obviously, I do not want online access to clog the rest of my academic life, and reviewing a constantly blossoming field of drafts and revisions would be impossible, so several gates are placed between me and direct access in this context. First, students are asked to review online curricular material and style guides, including sample papers to help them articulate what they view as a problem in their writing. Students are then encouraged to ask their lab partners and technical instructors for feedback. Finally, they may send that portion of their report (usually reports are 10 to 12 pages long) giving them trouble, along with a brief statement of their difficulty.

In other words, I use NEOS in this case as a heuristic device: It encourages students to assess their own work first (and presents them with several comparative models and style analyses) before they submit it to the writing instructor, who is now viewed as a last, not first, resort. Is this a distancing tool? Not at all: Sometimes students are too quick to surrender to the innate difficulties of writing and want quick fixes, instant diagnoses of problems (and, of course, instant solutions). In this case, NEOS supports greater thinking through of writing problems and also encourages greater connection with peers and technical instructors (always a sore spot with students at MIT). Of course, without the campus-wide computing environment this sort of electronic community would not be possible.

WHERE TO GO FROM HERE

Without focusing on the need for greater refinement in this or that software interface (including NEOS), or the constant search for financial support for development and experimentation, there are several large-scale directions for development I would identify.

The first is more transparent communication between hardware and software platforms. The academy loses room for negotiation with vendors because it is in general locked into a particular operating system. The academy has to articulate its needs apart from a contract with providers. Until they can think beyond the four walls of the classroom—and into the library, the dormitory, the university library in the next state, and the copyright laws which hinder massive online regeneration of textual research—we will remain merely consumers of technology, rather than providers of expertise, our more typical role.

The electronic classroom which so effectively melts the four wall dimension of teaching and extends the class community in space and time is nevertheless defeated at every turn by the lack of supple curricular databases within and across individual disciplines. No one—not the student in history or literature, not the mechanical engineering student, nor the mathematics student—is educated in isolation from other bodies of knowledge. Students should be able to browse extensively in online fields of texts, with and without direction. Just as a student in my writing class can walk away with a complete online portfolio on diskette of her or his essays at semester's end, so too should students be able to graduate with their own individually tailored sets of textbooks, notes, or lecture materials that will continue to serve them in their careers. Who owns ideas?

No piece of technology will ever replace imagination, depth of experience, and engagement as the best teaching "tools." But the electronic classroom helps to create an environment in which students and teachers can exercise their intelligence and creativity more freely and with greater interaction than ever before. Properly designed, the electronic classroom can fulfill expectations of what a university can and should be, a place for the exchange of information and ideas in pursuit of personal and shared knowledge.

REFERENCES

Barrett, E. (1989). Thought and language in a virtual environment. In E. Barrett (Ed.), *The society of text*. Cambridge, MA: MIT Press.

Zuboff, S. (1988). *In the age of the smart machine: The future of work and power*. New York: Basic Books.

Chapter
Seven

Computer-Mediated Communications Applications in Selected Psychology and Political Science Courses

Cecilia G. Manrique
Harry W. Gardiner
University of Wisconsin-La Crosse

When BITnet was introduced at the University of Wisconsin-La Crosse, campus faculty and administrators were reluctant to invest the time and effort required to learn the system. Little attention had been given to training, dissemination, and support for previous efforts for computing, let alone communicating via computers.

Today, with the linking of the Wisconsin university system via WISCNET and the Internet, faculty, staff, administrators, and students are becoming well acquainted with the value of internal and external communication using electronic mail. In fact, support for the use of these systems has been organized in such a way that it is easy for any user to obtain documentation, training, and support (Raleigh, 1991).

Current concerns focus on efforts to increase the effective use of computer-mediated communications (CMC) within the classroom. During the past year, increasing numbers of faculty have discovered that electronic mail can be an effective means for communicating with students by encouraging them to increase and improve their writing skills without their conscious awareness of it, as well as for getting students to communicate with peers from other countries. In this way, electronic mail has been an effective venue for fulfilling an institution's trilateral goals (see Figure 7.1) of trying to bring together computing, writing, and internationalizing the curriculum (Manrique, 1990a).

This chapter describes some of the ways in which faculty members at the University of Wisconsin-La Crosse have employed electronic mail and computer-mediated communications in fulfilling the following curricular goals: (a) to widen student experience through communications with peers from other countries (internationalization), (b) to encourage students to practice their ability to communicate through writing (writing across the curriculum), and (c) to introduce the usefulness of computing as a tool for enhancing students' knowledge base (computing across the curriculum). The experiences recounted herein are those of faculty who have had their students communicate with others in foreign countries for an Asian Government and Politics course, a general education Global Issues course, and Cross-Cultural Psychology courses.

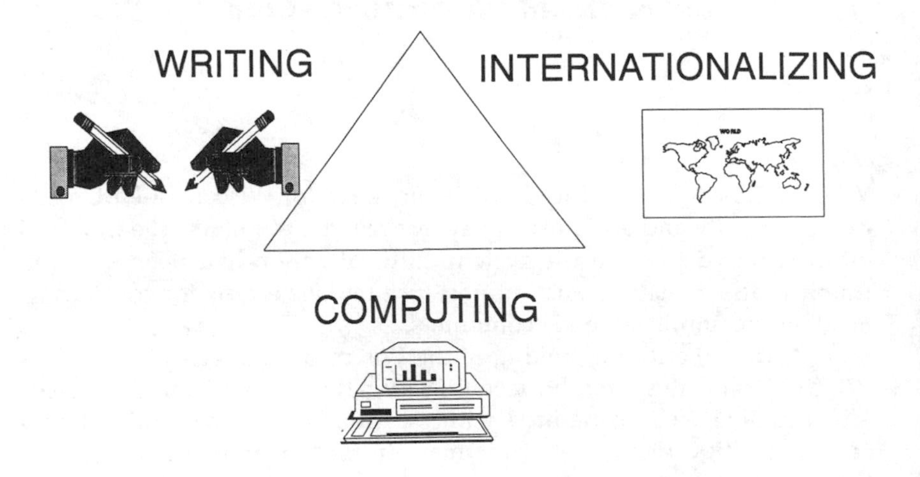

Figure 7.1. Envisioning the trilateral goals

Attention is given to some of the advantages and disadvantages of using electronic mail in specific courses, showing where it has been successful, as well as noting some of the pitfalls that accompany such a nontraditional method of delivering education. Suggestions are made for incorporating electronic mail into a variety of courses through resources available to students and faculty in "netland" that can make the computing learning experience more exciting. This means discussing listservs on BITnet, Telnetting into different campus libraries via the Internet, and exploring such resources as the Dow Jones News Retrieval Service and the Cleveland Freenet for *USA Today* headline news. Using these resources, faculty members can then broaden students' perspectives on various issues, regardless of the subject matter.

IN THE BEGINNING: INTRODUCING THE USE OF ELECTRONIC MAIL

Although electronic mail is now a fairly common communication method, in direct competition with "snail mail" (mail that goes through the post office), certain resources are not readily within the reach of every faculty member. Access to networks such as BITnet and Internet provide a number of benefits (Walquist, 1990). For example, it is helpful to be able to communicate and exchange information with peers from other institutions. Many a joint publication has benefited from the speed with which files can be transmitted, edited, and exchanged through electronic mail. Faculty members on the Internet can log into remote library sites throughout the United States and in many foreign countries and search book, serial, journal, and document collections, as well as large numbers of databases. For the most part, these uses of electronic mail have been on a personal level and not directly connected to what can be done in the classroom. The question then becomes: "How can electronic mail be used to its fullest potential within the classroom?"

Faculty members in departments ranging from business to political science to English have found electronic mail to be an effective means of communicating among themselves, with their students, and with colleagues outside of the institution. Communicating internationally via electronic mail was introduced by the first author in a course on Asian Government and Politics in 1990. Since then, several colleagues have benefited from the experiences gained in that experiment.

Instituting electronic mail communication on an international level has had both positive and negative effects. Students who completed the course had mixed experiences ranging from major success stories, for example, continuing friendships with original contacts from other countries, to those who experienced frustration because they were unable to make any contacts using electronic mail. Thus, some were grateful for the experience because it was positive for them, and others were resentful because it presented them with a negative experience.

Instructors who try to implement the use of electronic mail in their classrooms, especially on an international level, must be made aware of sources of possible frustration. Some conditions will not be within the instructor's control, such as the ability or willingness of individuals on the other side to respond to one's students. This initial experience, however, was valuable because it provided lessons to be learned for future implementation. For example, a second experiment with international electronic mail, building on the results of the first experience, was carried out by the second author in a Cross-Cultural Psychology course. This effort benefited from the lessons learned previously.

It should be recognized that many college students, unlike their elementary and secondary school counterparts, often get turned off by the mere thought of facing a computer. It helps when the instructor trying to introduce the computing component into a course is computer literate and relaxed and confident about its use in the curriculum (Manrique, 1990b). Thus, the instructor should make an effort to thoroughly learn how to use the e-mail system and not just send the students to the computer center for help when they have problems.

We have found that it is best to wait about three weeks into the semester to get the students into the computer lab because it becomes less threatening. In this way, students are not going to think the focus of the course is on computing. After all, computing via electronic mail is merely a component of the course, a supplementary tool for learning. Students appear to realize the value of what they are learning if they are eased into it, become immersed in it during the entire semester, and discover for themselves how interesting, enjoyable, and valuable such a component can be.

It helps to solicit support from Academic Computing Services staff, who are more than willing to provide training and documentation for faculty. In our case, the first author was able to conduct an hour-long training session within which students were allowed to engage in their own mail-sending activities, thus demonstrating to them how simple and enjoyable it could be. A written handout (a copy of a guide used by the authors can be provided on request), consisting of introductions to our VAX system and to electronic mail, and including a list of potential persons to contact, was made available to students. It helps to have a prepared list of contacts rather than ask students to look for contacts themselves. We have discovered there are a lot of people in netland who are more than willing to help in efforts such as these.

As part of our courses, students were encouraged to send messages to the authors and to each other for the first week. Our availability permitted students to become comfortable in using the e-mail facility. When this was accomplished, and they were armed with the list of contacts, students were ready to venture out into the electronic world. Students were encouraged to send messages to several people, thereby assuring that at least one person would respond.

It was helpful to get students conferring on specific topics. For example, some of the topics covered in the Asia course were: various holiday celebrations, election procedures, and veneration of the emperor. One student was going through the LSATs (Law School Admissions Test) at the time that she was corresponding with a girl from Japan. The Japanese girl, named Naoko, was also going through entrance examinations, and so the two of them discussed their own versions of "examination hell."

In summary, electronic mail has to be introduced in a training session, and documentation should be provided. Support should be available to students, who frequently struggle through the learning process. Finally, in order to make the experience worthwhile, some structure for e-mail correspondence should be provided, for example, a list of topic areas to be discussed.

LOOKING FOR ANSWERS: EVALUATING PERFORMANCE

At the end of the semester, a 1-page questionnaire was distributed to the students in the courses to assess the success of electronic mail activities. (A copy of the survey can be provided by the authors on request.) Given that these courses are upper-level and do not attract many students, throughout the four semesters that they have been offered, we have collected comments from at least 50 respondents. Feedback such as this is essential in assessing whether this type of component is worth continuing. Negative feedback provides suggestions for improvement; positive feedback encourages its use elsewhere on campus.

The first question asked how many different parties were involved in this communication effort. One person reported contacts with six different people around the world, whereas another was unable to make any contacts. Although the instructor tried to help the latter student, she did not seek additional assistance from the computer center staff as suggested. Often it is simply a matter of seeing what steps one is taking in order to diagnose a problem.

Based on survey results (see Figure 7.2), 62% of the students reported being able to make contact with at least 1-2 people. Twenty-six percent reported making contact with three or four people. For some, correspondence was limited to classmates. Others communicated with

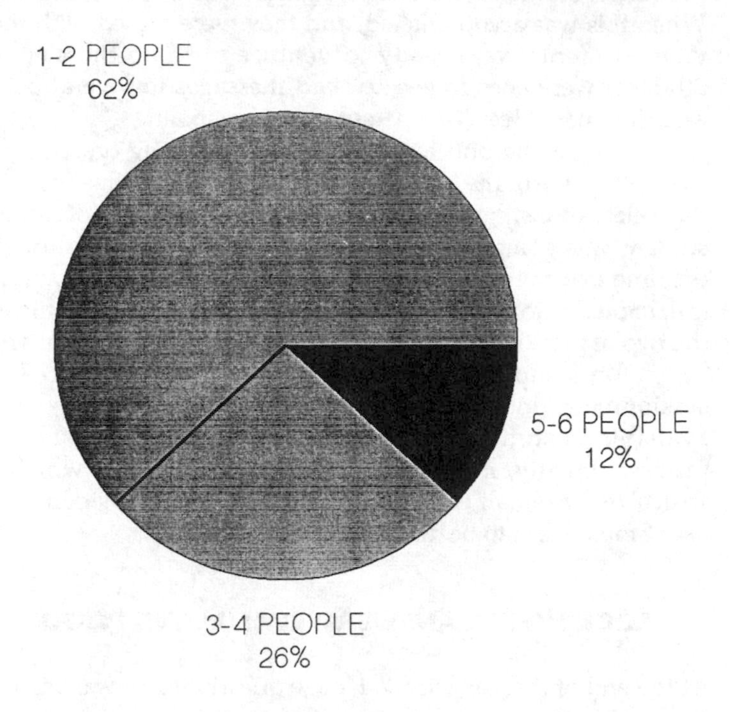

Figure 7.2. Number of contracts via electronic mail

students from St. Olaf College as a result of the interactive experience. Some made contact with people from Hawaii and Las Vegas. Still others were in contact with Holland and the Philippines. As we continued to use the e-mail approach, students were able to branch out on their own to contacts with England, Taiwan, Singapore, Egypt, China, Norway, and Ethiopia. Some of their correspondents were actually in those places, whereas others were originally from there and were pursuing studies in the United States. Most students had at least made contacts in France with the help of a professor there who wanted his students to interact with American students in order to practice and improve their English writing skills. Horizons broadened as students learned to use the e-mail component.

The success of the experiment with French students prompted the authors to pass on the results of this contact to one of our professors of the French language who expressed interest in incorporating this type of exercise into her courses. Her American students would be able to practice their French, while the French students would be able to practice their English. In this way both groups would hopefully improve their second language skills.

When asked how often they communicated with their Bitpals (see Figure 7.3), 33% answered weekly, 31% every two weeks, 31% varied, 6% answered monthly, and, of course, there was one person who answered never because she was not able to make contact at all.

We were curious to find out what was being discussed during these exchanges. Topics were quite varied and included: Christmas, dating, relationships, love lives, families, stereotypes, entertainment, school and education, cross-cultural issues, lifestyles, likes/dislikes, sports, educational and career goals, interests and hobbies, spirituality, weather, location, and habits. Thus, topics ranged from the personal (love life, dogs, and cats) to the political (views on women, politics) to current issues (the Olympics).

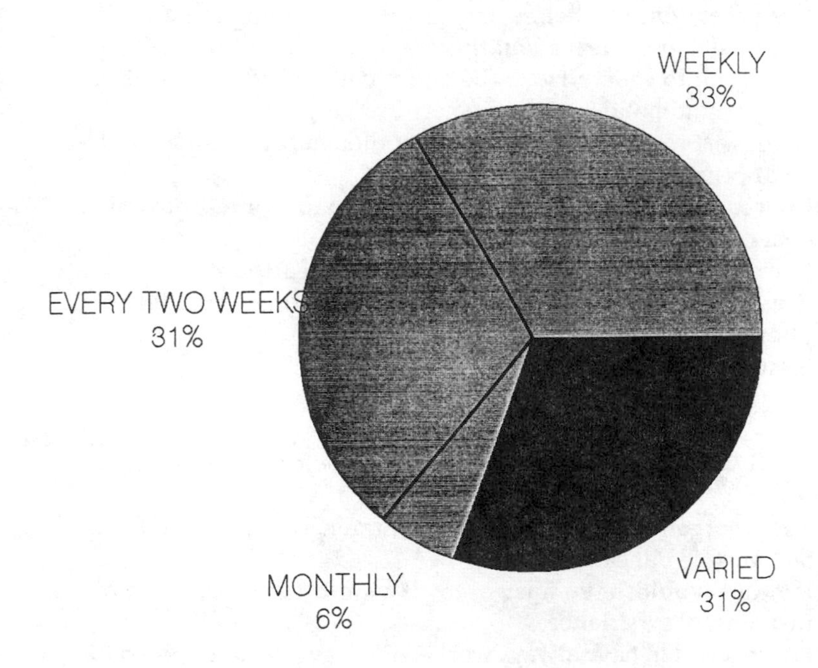

Figure 7.3. Frequency of contact

When we asked how many were willing to share the experience with others, 91.2% expressed a willingness to do so. Some even provided usernames so that we could contact them for more information. Another 8% were reluctant to do this because "no real correspondence occurred" or, when it did, the person thought letters were "too personal to share."

The next question asked whether or not students enjoyed the experience. Ninety-two percent expressed satisfaction. Although none specifically said they did not enjoy the experience, a small number answered "yes" and "no" to the question. Among reasons given for enjoying the experience were:

- This was a novel idea.
- I obtained interesting ideas about the French.
- It gave a new perspective on pen pals and served as a good motivator.
- It was fun. Eventually I want to get a home computer and Compuserve.
- It was a highlight of this class—I want to continue doing this.
- It did away with the hassles of mailing and it was more open and straight forward since these people wanted correspondence.
- I've never done this before. It's neat corresponding this quickly.
- I learned a great deal about this person in this culture. While it is difficult to generalize to the entire culture, I did learn about the area and politics.
- Nice twist to class. It brought in another culture with a hands-on approach.
- I never knew this could be done. It's the most fun I have had on a computer.
- I never heard about e-mail before. It was great!
- It is a quick way to send letters and has some qualities of a phone.
- Enabled us to visit in a unique and fast way.
- What a huge world! AND NO STAMPS!

Those who did not enjoy the experience made the following comments:

- Too unorganized. Too much extra time needed, couldn't contact anyone but classmates.
- If more would have answered, it would have been a more meaningful experience.
- I wish it would have always worked the way it was supposed to.

The overall success of this activity is reflected in the fact that many students made a request to have their accounts retained for the next semester (see Figure 7.4). On the survey, 44% said that they would like to continue their correspondence with the friends they had made over the network. Similarly, 70% informed their instructor that they would like their VAX accounts retained for the coming school year, and arrangements for those were made. Others had indicated that they could not continue correspondence because they were graduating. Some wished they had computers at home so they could still access e-mail, even if they were no longer in school. Others were just reluctant to keep their accounts because they did not know what they would be doing over the summer period.

When asked if the training session at the beginning of the semester on how to use the VAX and electronic mail was helpful, all students answered "Yes" to the question. From a user services standpoint this was encouraging because we then knew that we had been successful

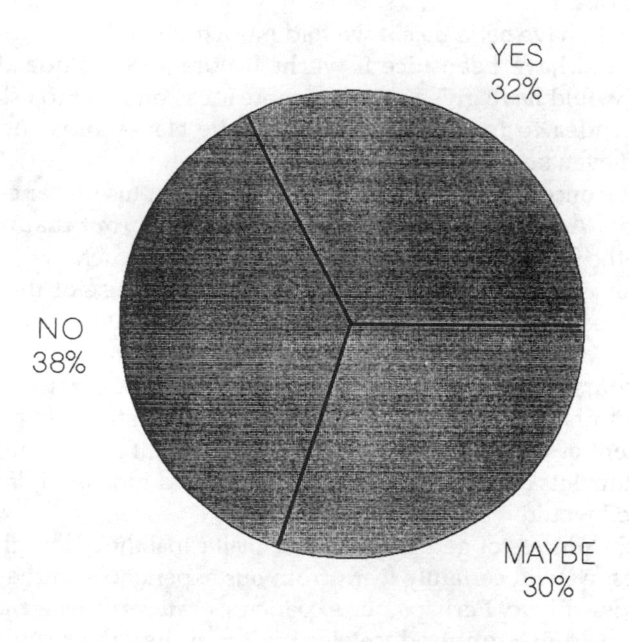

Figure 7.4. Future use of electronic mail

in reaching at least this small segment of the student body. Our task now is to make advocates of these students in order to get more of the faculty and student body to understand the value of electronic mail and to make use of it. We are hoping that some kind of "trickle down" effect will evolve as a result of this usage.

Space was provided on the questionnaire for students to write in comments, and most did share their thoughts on the exercise. These are summarized below:

- Very useful—real interaction, it made learning fun and exciting.
- If the corresponders would be set up in advance, it would eliminate the problems of not getting a response back and would help in being able to direct questions.
- Start BITnet very early in the class course because it takes a long time for individuals to get back to you.
- Make sure that the selected BITnet pals are willing to correspond.
- I thought it was interesting, but think it could use more organization.
- Excellent idea. Hope to keep my username until I graduate.
- It was very interesting, but it was too hard to contact people overseas.
- It would have been nice if we had more time.
- It would have been nice if we had more specific questions. This would have given us a few more ideas on what to ask.
- Great idea to incorporate this into the class—most people don't even know this exists!
- Maybe once a week have a student talk about his or her e-mail buddy. And give a grade on the use of e-mail (but that might take the fun out of it). I enjoyed the class very much.
- I wish a grade would be issued for e-mail because of the time involved—fun but time-consuming.

Of course, what is surprising about some of the comments is the clamor now to have their effort graded. In the past, students protested the assignment of points for the use of electronic mail in the course. But then, the comments are in retrospect and as one had indicated, if a grade were assigned would it still have been fun?

As the process of getting electronic mail capabilities into the classroom evolves, we will certainly learn from our experiences in the various courses discussed here. Perhaps our experiences can serve as a model for those who would like to introduce electronic mail into their courses. We have received many helpful suggestions from our students and, hopefully, by heeding them, we will develop better experiences for future courses.

WHERE DO WE GO FROM HERE?

Based on the generally positive feedback from students, the authors plan to continue using electronic mail in their classes. The first author will be teaching African Government and Politics, Latin American Government and Politics, and Middle Eastern Government and Politics courses in future semesters and has plans to develop the syllabus and design the course to provide similar opportunities for these students. The second author will continue to use e-mail in his Cross-Cultural Psychology course and plans to introduce it as part of a Cross-Cultural Human Development course. Students in all these courses will be allowed to gain access to various network facilities, such as the Cleveland Freenet, so they can read *USA Today* headlines.

Because we have access to various libraries on the Internet, students will also be shown how to access other sources of information for required papers. Students will be instructed in the use of listserv lists and the availability of appropriate discussion groups. During the Spring 1993, the first author taught a course in Women and Politics, and students in that course were introduced to the various resources available through the discussion group WMST-L. (For a sample listing of listserver discussion groups relevant to political topics, please refer to Manrique, 1992.)

The diversity of the groups represented in the various lists available shows fertile areas in which students can engage themselves. Thus, during the 1992 presidential election, lists like BUSH, CLINTON and PEROT (Sakkas, 1993) were valuable sources of information about the issues candidates stood for, which in turn was valuable for an American Government and Politics course.

The authors plan to continue talking with groups both on and off campus in an effort to get more faculty members involved in such endeavors. We recently received a grant that will permit us to implement the use of VAX NOTES, a conferencing system referred to elsewhere in this text, on our campus computer system. The desire to implement this at the University of Wisconsin-La Cross has been inspired by some of our readings and some of the ideas that have come out of SIGUCCS (Special Interest Group of University and College Computer Services) proceedings, electronic mail correspondences with colleagues who have been using it in various fields, and magazine and journal articles describing such efforts (Whitney, 1990). Several faculty members from disciplines as diverse as English, psychology, political science, teacher education, physical education, women's studies, foreign languages, and business have expressed an interest in joining our efforts. This began during Spring 1993.

Based on the authors' experiences, we would make a number of recommendations to those considering the introduction of an e-mail component in their courses. First, we must remember that students come into classes with different expectations. Most will not expect to do computing in a Political Science or Cross-Cultural Psychology course. They may argue that computing has no place in such courses, and they will need to be gradually eased into the acceptance of technology in courses outside of computer science. Tolerance for computers will depend on students' past experiences with computing—good or bad. Often it is not until several semesters later that students come to recognize the contributions made to their overall education by requirements in a particular course. This appears to be the case with the e-mail component requiring writing and communicating by means of computers.

Second, to overcome some of these difficulties, a successful strategy is to make this an enjoyable learning, nonthreatening experience for students. Computer activities should not be tossed at students on the first class day, but presented as a useful exercise which they can choose to engage in, if they so desire. It may be necessary to devote several class periods to helping students unravel some of the basic features of the available system.

At the same time, it helps if faculty members exhibit a level of confidence that allows students to see the same benefits that instructors see in the use of computers and electronic mail. It helps if a faculty member can answer most, if not all, students' questions so that they do not need to be sent to the computing "gurus" in the computer center. Maintaining minimal dependence on computing center staff inspires greater confidence in the abilities of both student and teacher. However, maintaining an amiable, professional, working relationship with the computing services staff is always beneficial to all parties involved, especially when technical problems beyond the instructor's capacity arise. When computing services offer free, introductory, or advanced classes in the use of e-mail, students should be encouraged, schedules permitting, to attend.

Third, faculty should be prepared with a list of potential contacts with whom students can immediately communicate. Nothing is more frustrating than to have to "look around" in the network for someone who will be willing to spend time communicating with the students. It is a commitment, and those who take the commitment seriously will have a good experience. Those who get connected with someone who communicates on an irregular basis are likely to be frustrated. Although much of this will be beyond the control of an instructor, everyone involved needs to be aware of potential difficulties.

Fourth, to encourage students to make regular and extensive use of electronic mail, an instructor can do the following:

- Send students a feed of news digests found on the network. For an Asian Government and Politics course, the *China News Digest* is a good choice.
- Have students join active listserv discussion lists. For a Cross-Cultural Psychology course, a subscription to XCULT-L, PACIFIC-L, and others might be useful.
- Have students communicate regularly with the instructor on a variety of topics so that they use their mailing skills. If they do not, they easily lose them. They can also be encouraged to communicate with each other in this manner.
- The instructor should have a lengthy list of potential BITnet pals from which to select names. A 2 or 3 to 1 ratio is suggested.
- The instructor should have a list of issues that students can discuss with their Bitpals so that there is a constant flow of information.

Finally, when all these things are accomplished, and there are many satisfied users, recognition of the value of using electronic mail and the resources available in netland becomes much easier and more satisfying for both students and instructors. Thus, we feel we have found an effective way of addressing some of the current curricular goals of higher education—using the computer to encourage students to write to peers of other societies through whom they are able to engage in a broadening of their outlook on the world around them.

REFERENCES

Manrique, C. (1990a). Walk hand-in-hand with me: Centering on efforts at internationalizing, writing, and computing across the curriculum. *Proceedings of the SIGUCCS User Services Conference XIX* (pp. 235240). New York: The Association for Computing Machinery.

Manrique, C. (1990b). Faculty in computing featuring Harry Gardiner. *ACS News, 7*(1), 7-8.

Manrique, C. (1992). Network resources for political scientists. *PS: Political Science and Politics, 25*(4), 667-690.

Raleigh, D. (1991). Writing collaborative documentation over the network or it sure beats trudging to another working session in a snowstorm! *Proceedings of the SIGUCCS User Services Conference XIX* (pp. 303-311). New York: The Association for Computing

Machinery.

Sakkas, L. (1993). *Politics on the Internet. Interpersonal computing and technology: A journal for the 21st century*, 2(2). This article is archived as SAKKAS IPCTV1N2 on Listserv@GUVM.GEORGETOWN.EDU.

Walquist, C. (1990, July-August). Internetworking and using Internet. *NCSA Data Link*, pp. 13-21.*

Whitney, R. (1990). VAX Notes—Using a computer conference to teach critical thinking. *Instructional Computing Update* (pp. 3-5). Iowa City: University of Iowa..

*This is extremely useful because of references to two classics in the literature: Doug Comer's Internetworking with TCP/IP, and Ed Krol's "Hitchhiker's Guide to the Internet: RFC 1118. (Available via anonymous ftp from mic.merit.edu as doucments/frc/frc1118.txt).

Computer-Mediated Teacher Induction

Ted J. Singletary
Holly Anderson
Boise State University

All teachers have horror stories of their first year of teaching. Teacher preparation programs do not seem to cushion the difficult transition from student to teacher. Nearly 15% of beginning teachers nationwide do not return for a second year, 26% leave after the first two years, and 60% after five years (Henry, 1986). As one of the beginning teachers in our program wrote in the network forum, "This was the most difficult and highly stressful thing I have ever done (and I am 38 years old and have been married 18 years)!"

NEEDS AND CONCERNS OF BEGINNING TEACHERS

In making the transition from teacher education to the first teaching job, beginning teachers are frequently jolted by "reality shock" (Edelwich & Brodsky, 1980; Gold, 1989; Hall, Villeme, & Phillippy, 1988). Veenman (1984) described this phenomenon as "the collapse of the missionary ideals formed during teacher training by the harsh and rude reality of everyday school life" (p. 143). Some of the most commonly expressed concerns are discipline, communicating with parents, instructional issues, managerial methods, administrative approval, and feelings of isolation (Lortie, 1975; Odell, 1986; Veenman, 1984). A beginning teacher in our program expressed feelings typical of reality shock: "The first year of teaching is the hardest because you are not certain what, how, when or why to do things. You are still learning about the intellectual ability of your students, their social development, their background knowledge, etc. All these factors affect how you teach."

Reality shock and the subsequent problems experienced by beginning teachers make them particularly vulnerable to burnout. Teacher burnout, primarily emotional in nature, may be manifested as a progressive loss of idealism, energy, and purpose as the result of stressful work conditions (Edelwich & Brodsky, 1980). Considering the overwhelming challenges faced by beginning teachers, the seeds of burnout are probably planted during this difficult period (Hall et al., 1988). Burnout leads teachers to leave the profession, and, unfortunately, those who are the strongest academically are most apt to leave (Schlechty & Vance, 1983).

Because new teachers frequently cannot always find the necessary support and information in existing school communities, induction programs have been developed. The intent of these programs is to foster a more positive initial experience and increase retention. They may, in fact, also influence teacher reform and educational restructuring in general (Cole & McNay, 1988; Griffin, 1989; Hoffman, Edwards, O'Neal, Barnes, & Paulissen, 1986; Schlechty, 1985). Hoffman et al. (1986) asserted that the "vulnerability of the beginning teacher makes induction the most accessible point of infusing change into the continuum of teacher education" (p. 16).

In order for teachers to feel free to take risks and express concerns, induction programs should provide assistance without the threat of assessment (Cole & McNay, 1988; Fox & Singletary, 1986). With the support of mentors and peers, new teachers can be helped in assimilating the norms of the profession, gaining self-confidence, and developing reflective skills of self-evaluation. Although induction must occur in school buildings and districts, university faculty can play an important role in the process.

The importance of the university's role in assisting the beginning teacher is becoming increasingly recognized. Teacher educators can enhance the induction process by extending professional preservice training into inservice classroom support. Universities can provide a forum for teachers to confer openly about problems without fear of repercussions. In addition, universities are capable of multischool networking, which is especially important when teacher isolation is compounded by rural settings (McEvoy & Morehead, 1986). A beneficial by-product of university involvement in induction is the opportunity for university faculty to study firsthand the specific daily needs of first-year teachers and to revise methods courses accordingly, thereby bringing theory and practice closer together (Hegler & Dudley, 1987; Varah, Theune, & Parker, 1986).

TELECOMMUNICATIONS SYSTEMS AND INDUCTION

Recent developments in computer technology have emerged as a means for providing support to beginning teachers. As computer technology has expanded in the last decade, telecommunications has made possible computer-mediated communication such as computer conferences and networks. A primary advantage of computer networking is the flexibility it offers. Geographical and time constraints are overcome because messages can be sent at any time of the day or night and from any place. Network participants with computers and modems use telephone lines to confer with one another publicly through discussion forums and privately through e-mail.

The status of computer networking in education was examined by a research group at Virginia Polytechnic Institute and State University (McAnge, 1990). The findings from that study indicate computer linkages are significantly affecting education through state educational computer networks, public access networks, and databases. These include BITnet, the Internet, Compuserve, and Learning Link, a national consortium that provides educators with information resources, e-mail, and gateways to educational databases. Other examples of public networks are Legi-Slate, an online service providing information on legislation of Congress, and NewsNet, a database containing business information including industry newsletters.

Computer technology has tremendous potential to facilitate teachers' learning and professional development, and the opportunities are increasing as new programs are rapidly being developed. The Office of Technology Assessment studies (as cited in Roberts, 1990) found that telecommunications has reinvigorated teaching by expanding resources for teachers and connecting teachers with colleagues and experts in the field. Computer technology can serve as a vehicle for training by providing information on educational issues and trends. In addition, communication systems provide support and assistance through the sharing of ideas and concerns and can help overcome the isolation of remote areas.

THE FIRST-YEAR TEACHER NETWORK

A grant from US WEST in August 1989 enabled Boise State University's (BSU) Department of Teacher Education to create the First-Year Teacher Network, a program inspired by a similar one instituted through Harvard University's Graduate School of Education (Merseth, 1991; Rodman, 1989). As a support network, the pilot program, to be carried out over three years, was established with the following goals: (a) to reduce the personal and professional isolation of first-year teachers by giving them the support of BSU faculty and their own peers, (b) to provide assistance to first-year teachers in rural parts of the BSU service area, (c) to assist beginning teachers in applying their university preparation to their classrooms, (d) to assist school personnel in the induction of new teachers, and (e) to increase the retention of qualified teachers in the profession.

The participants in the First-Year Teacher Network are linked by computers and modems to each other and to Boise State University faculty. Each year the 25 teachers are each lent a Macintosh SE computer with an Image Writer II dot-matrix printer and a 1200 baud Packard-Bell, Hayes-compatible modem. During the first two years of the program, the Macintosh SE computers used only two internal disk drives, capable of using single-sided, double-sided, and high-density disks in Pro-DOS, MS DOS, and Macintosh formats. A 40-megabyte internal hard drive was added to each of the systems at the start of the third year, and many of the modems have been upgraded to 2400 baud. The systems are accompanied by Microsoft Works software, an integrated program including word processing, spreadsheet, database, telecommunications, and limited graphics capabilities. Additional shareware or public domain programs, primarily games and utilities, are also available to participants.

POPULATION SERVED

We identify potential participants by soliciting lists of newly hired teachers from approximately 35 school districts within the service area, shortly after school starts each fall. The first-year teachers listed are sent a brief description of the program and asked to call if they are interested in participating. Presentations to Boise State University student teachers have increased interest among the graduates. Many of them call and ask to be considered as soon as they sign a teaching contract. From those requesting consideration, a group of 25 teachers is created representing a mix of large and small districts, males and females, elementary and secondary teachers across a broad range of subject specialties, and Boise State

University graduates as well as graduates from other institutions. The teachers' computer expertise is not a factor in the selection process, and thus, the group members vary greatly in their technological backgrounds.

Participants in the program attend two training workshops on the Boise State University campus. At the first workshop, held in September, participants are introduced to the program and its purposes, equipment is distributed, and brief instruction in the use of computers and the telecommunications system is presented. Network participants, who register for two graduate credits, are briefed on the course requirements (e.g., using the network twice weekly, attending workshops, completing the final questionnaire, preparing a brief final report on the value of the computer and the network connections). We attempt to have all teachers set up their equipment and complete an initial log-in to the Learning Link network. The initial log-in requires entering some descriptive information. Because of the large number of participants and low number of available phone lines, we have never achieved our goal.

The second workshop, held in late September or early October, responds to specific participant questions about the available software. We also show participants more about the capabilities of Microsoft Works, such as spreadsheets and databases, and demonstrate more advanced telecommunications techniques, such as downloading files. At another workshop in February the participants meet for further training and to share ideas about using the computer and helpful resources in the network.

THE LEARNING LINK NETWORK

Most of the resources available to participants are accessed through the Learning Link Network. Learning Link networks, which operate in several states throughout the United States, are partially funded by the Corporation for Public Broadcasting. Idaho Learning Link is sponsored by Idaho Public Television. The Network offers a variety of services and forums. Learning Link is available to any teacher or administrator in the state of Idaho. A toll-free telephone number allows free access throughout the state. Learning Link offers an electronic mail option and general discussion forums (bulletin boards) in subjects such as environmental education, school restructuring, and interactive media. More specialized services provide schedules and teaching materials for educational television programs on PBS or a special cable news program. Schools who enroll in CNN Newsroom are licensed to videotape a 15-minute daily newscast for students and to download lesson plans via computer for classroom use. Another portion of the network, Public Link, is available to any person in the state. Recently, Learning Link has been connected with the Internet, which gives participants the opportunity to communicate with people throughout the world.

THE FIRST-YEAR TEACHER FORUM

The First-Year Teacher forum is a part of the larger Learning Link system, but it is available only to the participants in the BSU program. A special password controls access to the forum, but participants in the project have access to all other parts of the Learning Link Network. Within the forum are a resource area, a general discussion area, and access to the network e-mail system. The resource area is rarely used, but teachers can upload lengthy documents for access by peers. E-mail is also used, but because we guarantee privacy, we cannot access records to examine the frequency or content of messages. E-mail messages to BSU faculty members are generally requests for specific answers to questions, frequently about hardware and software operation. We suspect that e-mail among participating teachers is limited to more personal communication among friends. The general discussion area is the center of much of the first-year teachers' activity. All of the quotes from participants appearing in this chapter are taken from discussion forum messages.

The discussion forum is organized around topics. For example, a teacher might post a message asking for suggestions for field trips or methods of incorporating cooperative learning in the classroom. Other teachers respond, and each suggestion often seems to trigger even more ideas. The resulting information and interaction is rich and valuable. This is also the area in which participants frequently vent frustration or share other feelings. These messages typically elicit an outpouring of support and suggestions. The responses often contain only empathic comfort, but sometimes there are suggestions for constructively dealing with the problem situation, whether it be a bossy teacher's aide or a disruptive student. Although the discussion may start on one topic, often the discussion rambles around to something completely different. Humorous comments are common and sometimes sidetrack a discussion but still seem valuable, often functioning as a tension release.

PROBLEMS

During the three years the First-Year Teacher Network has operated, there have been relatively few problems. The hardware and software have functioned well, despite the vagaries of rural telephone service in some communities in the service area. Most of the computers and modems are still operating, except for one that was destroyed when a participant's home burned. Replacement of that computer was covered by insurance.

The main problem area has been the lack of computer literacy among the participants, especially familiarity with telecommunications. Macintosh systems were chosen in the hope that the relatively intuitive interface would ease training difficulties. Although this has tended to be true, significant portions of each training session must be devoted to the set-up and operation of the hardware and software. Many of our participants seem to have never operated a computer, let alone a Macintosh, before entering the program. They also lack familiarity with integrated software packages and applications such as spreadsheets and databases.

The majority of the participants have had no experience with telecommunications, and many seem to have never heard of it. This is true even of Boise State University graduates because, until this year. there were no phone lines available in our computer lab. A recent survey indicated that few introductory courses in the educational applications of computers include instruction in telecommunications (Lintner, Moor, Friske, Mlynarczyk, Thomas, & Wiebe, 1991). Teacher preparation programs nationwide will need to address this difficulty. The lack of technological and telecommunications knowledge is significant.

Every year participants in the First-Year Teacher program ask how they will know the phone numbers of the other teachers so that they can call their computers, rather than wanting to know their e-mail addresses. The idea of a central system server is foreign to them. When we mention that the CNN news program for students can be videotaped and the program description downloaded from the Learning Link system the following morning, we always get questions about how to connect the computer to the VCR. When we demonstrate logging-on to the system at the first workshop, we use a local number. One participant continued to use this number, rather than the toll-free number provided, even though he lived beyond the local area. He had difficulty understanding why his phone bill was so high after a month of telecommunicating at long-distance phone rates.

Despite a relatively low level of initial knowledge and practice, most participants quickly become comfortable with the operation of the system. Their understanding may not be complete, but it is sufficiently functional. We have adjusted our training seminars over the years to meet participant needs. We attempt to have every teacher log-onto the system during the first training session. We schedule the second session within a few weeks of the first so that we can directly respond to questions that arise from initial experiences. We also try to group participants with similar needs and concerns in the sessions. For example, some may be struggling with setting margins in word processing, whereas others may be ready to explore using the spreadsheet as a grade book. Whenever possible we try to use participants as instructors in these small groups.

OUTCOMES

Participants' comments in the discussion forum and responses to a questionnaire at the end of each year suggest that access to a computer network can provide beginning teachers with valuable resources. Contrary to expectations stated in the grant, participants do not consider access to University faculty members a major benefit of the program. In the early stages of network use, participants frequently sought faculty input on how to operate the hardware or software. When other topics, such as classroom discipline or use of cooperative learning, were discussed in the forum, faculty input tended to stop further discussion. This could be due to the fact that many of the participants were not Boise State University graduates and had little personal contact with participating faculty, or that the faculty suggestions were so good that nothing was left to be said. Although the network is a source of information, the connection with other beginning teachers seems to be the major benefit of participation.

The comments of three participants note the value of network participation:

> Thanks for allowing me to participate in the FYT project this year. It has been a lifeline, a laughline, and above all, a PERSPECTIVE-MAKER. . . . Letting me learn and grow with several teachers all experiencing the pain and joy of this confusing and wonderful profession has been a tremendous gift.

> How do FYTs without this network survive? It is truly my "lifeline" to sanity when things pile up, my comic relief, and my complaint department when things go wrong. I always know no matter what I write, someone out there understands. Advice is nonjudgmental and given with sincere concern.

> The best part of this system has been the socialization. I enjoy the banter. Being recognized for something as inconsequential as not going to the post office as a child made me feel like part of the group. Knowing that others have struggled with the same things I have has been a great comfort. So many times during student teaching I felt I was the only one to ever have had problems like mine. Everyone on the system was struggling with similar problems. We found support without judgment.

Preliminary results of the first two years of the First-Year Teacher Network also seem to indicate some positive effects of participation on retention. These findings should be interpreted cautiously at this time. The true test of the value of participation will be shown in ensuing years. It should also be noted that participants were volunteers. There may be some connection between choosing to participate in such a program and commitment to the teaching profession. This is one of many questions to be studied further.

Although participation in the First-Year Teacher Network seems to be of value, access to a microcomputer system and any telecommunication system may also have some benefits. Participants reported that having their own computers allowed them to easily accomplish tasks such as preparing instructional materials and calculating grades. There may even be a benefit to being a part of a technologically sophisticated enterprise. It has been suggested that using computers and technology may be a way to improve perceptions of the competence and status of teachers (Singletary, 1987). This is difficult to determine conclusively, but three participants were convinced of the value of instructional technology and felt confident enough to write grant proposals for a statewide initiative to increase the availability of technology in schools. One of these proposals received funding. Our experience suggests that few first-year teachers typically write grant proposals, and fewer still have proposals funded. Information about the grant process and support from peers was available through the Learning Link Network.

As the initial grant concludes, we have also been assessing costs. Although the major costs of the First-Year Teacher Network have been supported through a grant, the program seems to be cost-effective. Hardware has been the largest single cost. If participants could use school districts' or their own computers, costs would be less than $1,000 per participant per year. This amount may not be unreasonable. Mentoring programs, especially those providing access to college or university personnel, can be expensive. Development of state or regional computer networks to support beginning teachers could be cost-effective, especially in places where public networks, such as Learning Link, already exist. This is likely to be less costly than paying for travel and personnel costs, especially in areas where schools and teachers are widely dispersed. A telecommunications network also provides access to a greater range of resources than would be possible with a single mentor.

The quality and type of interaction fostered by telecommunications has raised another question. The process of posting a question or describing a difficult situation in a discussion forum and then waiting and reading, and perhaps responding to, the comments of other participants over a period of days or weeks seems to produce significant analysis, reflection on the teaching process, and problem solving. Merseth (1990) has noted similar effects among participants in other computer networks for first-year teachers. For example, the following messages were posted in the First-Year Teacher discussion forum in January and February 1992. The peer support and the variety of suggestions offered have obvious value. The value of the multiple perspectives provided and time devoted to reflection on a problem may be initially less evident, but of equal or greater value in the long run.

Kay, a sixth-grade teacher, started one morning:

> AAArgh! One of my greatest frustrations as a teacher is kids who just don't do the work. The only kids who are failing in my classes are the ones who don't turn in their assignments, and it drives me crazy. I put out a weekly computer printout that lists the assignments across the top and their grades under the assignments. They can see their average and any missing assignments. I also have them come in on Monday's lunch if they have any missing. I give candy (bald-faced bribery . . . it works with my own children!) periodically to everyone who has all their work turned in. I also do a homework lotto where I give a prize to the name drawn. I know there will always be kids who choose not to work, but if any of you have any suggestions or ideas that have helped you, I would really appreciate hearing about them.

Pat, a male high school teacher, responded later in the day. He adds a perspective often typical of secondary teachers and provides input from his mentor:

> This problem is not limited to young kids. I teach high school and have the same problem with a number of the kids. After worrying and sweating about some of these kids, I talked to one of the "with it" experienced teachers about the problem. She said that she used to feel the same way but finally came to the conclusion that it was up to the kids to decide to do the work. She encourages them and notifies parents of problems, but if they simply won't do the work, she fails them. Some of them need to find out that they cannot coast through life with others always making excuses for them.

Linda, a third-grade teacher, responded to Kay later the same evening:

> I think your ideas are good ones, especially the lotto. Have you ever tried to give them points for completed homework? Kids having so many points at the end of a given period get to participate in a classroom party. The kids who don't have the points, have to stay in the

> room, see what they are missing and complete their missing work. Just an idea.

Kay replied the next week:

> Thanks for the great idea, Linda. Sometimes the obvious ones are the easiest to overlook. I'll try it.

Other teachers participated in the discussion shortly after the initial message. John, a middle school teacher, posted the following note the next day. He offered support and another suggestion:

> Kay, it sounds to me like you are doing about everything possible to get the students to do their homework. The extra effort you are putting in is commendable. Have you tried talking to the students one-on-one to see what their reasons for not completing assignments might be? Some of the reasons might amaze you. (I had a student whose mother would not allow her to do homework because she had to babysit her younger sister, and the mother did not feel she could do both.) You may also try pairing these "non-doers" with a "doer" in class. Peer pressure can do wonders sometimes."

Kay considered the suggestion and replied the following week:

> John, the "doer, non-doer" idea sounds like it might work. Maybe have them work together as a "team" on certain assignments or for a week, and receive a team reward. Thanks!

In the interim, Ruth, a third-grade teacher in another district, echoed the initial problem:

> I agree wholeheartedly. I spend the whole day trying to get in missing assignments and all that jazz. Now I am spending time trying to figure out how to provide incentive also. I anxiously await any suggestions for Kay.

Gill, an elementary special education teacher, added his perspective and his insights from other teachers in his building three days after the first message:

> Kay, these are my people. I would clearly be raised to the status of hero were I merely able to stimulate my special education students to turn in assignments regularly, let alone the rest of the class. I have

> students on various "point" systems and monitoring systems to increase assignment turning in behavior (What?) . . . and many are improving, but it takes a lot of maintenance—meaning me on their backs. The teachers that do get the best responses from students seem to have elaborate and varied reward systems to encourage individual, parental and peer pressure. I would keep the candy, "free time," class parties, raffles, etc., rolling on just because they work. The big, tough problem is how to "thin" all this reinforcement out into "natural" rewards, as in grades, praise, etc.

Sara, a third-grade teacher, offered her ideas later that day:

> I print out a spreadsheet with their names double-spaced in alphabetical order down the left side. When an assignment is given, I write it above one of the columns. When they turn in that assignment into the "math basket," they are responsible for checking that column off in the row next to their name. When the bell rings for recess, I can make a quick check to see who will have homework, or whatever. I usually announce, "So-and-so have not turned in their math assignments . . . if it is not brought in to me completed by tomorrow morning, you will get a zero." Say the latter only if you need to resort to such "threats." I usually dock their grade one letter if it is late. This seems to keep all my students completing their work. I hope this has helped.

Kay replied a few days later, offering another explanation:

> Sara, thanks for the suggestion. I dock their grades 50% if they're late. Of course, I make exceptions, but that's the rule. I think there's a big difference between 3rd and 6th, because I don't think a lot of my kids would even check off their assignment when they finished it. I don't have recess to hold over their heads, and 50% obviously doesn't faze the ones who don't really care. My kids are so social. They're SO concerned with who's going out with whom and who's going skiing and who will call whom that night. They're good kids. It's just that they have so much other stuff they're dealing with emotionally. But, I appreciate the suggestion. Have I rationalized away my failure to motivate sufficiently?

Sara responded in two days:

> Kay, YES, you've rationalized away your failure to motivate—but you aren't a failure. There's only so much you can do. Even at third grade the kids are into passing notes and don't understand what a D or F really means.

Bob, a secondary teacher, raised a related issue and offered his experience on the fourth day of the discussion:

> Kay, how much homework are you giving? And, does all of it have to be "homework," or could some class time be used by the students to complete the assignments? I had a class at the junior high (I teach at the senior high as well) in which many students were not doing their homework. Rather than "fight" this situation, I decided to cut back on the homework and give the students additional class time to complete the work. I realize this may have some negative consequences, but feel the benefits outweigh these—the students are learning and succeeding.

Laura, another sixth-grade teacher in another school district, responded to Bob:

> I give lots of class time to get work done. I give rewards (tokens, since I have a token economy in the classroom). If the kids used their classtime wisely, they might have homework once or twice a week. I still cannot get them motivated to do homework. I will keep up the rewards, but I also have them stay in for recess if I am not on duty. I give 70s for late work and 0 if I never get it. This still doesn't faze them. Obviously, some could care less about grades.

The dialogue continued over seven weeks and eventually included 35 messages from 14 different teachers and one BSU staff member. Other suggestions included calling parents or sending them lists of incomplete assignments. This led to a discussion of phone messaging systems that allow teachers to provide parents with information about assignments and student performance. The participants model reflection and critical thinking about a difficult teaching situation. The problem is viewed from several perspectives, and a variety of solutions are proposed and, presumably, tried. Will engaging in such discourse in a group enable teachers to become more reflective by themselves? How the telecommunications medium affects and shapes discourse and reflection is an area of inquiry worth further study.

The First-Year Teacher Network appears to be a valuable asset for participating teachers. One indication of this is increasing interest in the program as it becomes better known in the service area. Our research suggests the benefits available through participation in a supportive network may help beginning teachers survive the first year of teaching. From analyzing the computer messages and from the responses to questionnaire items about the usefulness of the network, it can be concluded that the most significant advantage of a telecommunication network is peer support. First-year teachers find the ability to reach out and touch someone in a similar situation to be comforting and informative.

REFERENCES

Cole, A., & McNay, M. (1988). Induction programs in Ontario schools: Issues and possibilities. *Education Canada, 28*(4), 5-11, 44-45.

Edelwich, J., & Brodsky, A. (1980). *Burnout: Stages of disillusionment in the helping professions.* New York: Human Services Press.

Fox, S., & Singletary,T. (1986). Deductions about supportive induction. *Journal of Teacher Education, 37*(1), 12-15.

Gold, Y. (1989). Reducing stress and burnout through induction programs. *Action in Teacher Education, 11*(3), 66-69.

Griffin, G. (1989). A state program for the initial years of teaching. *Elementary School Journal, 89*(4), 395-403.

Hall, B., Villeme, M., & Phillippy, S. (1988). Predisposition for burnout among first year teachers. *Teacher Educator, 24*(2), 13-21.

Hegler, K., & Dudley, R. (1987). Beginning teacher induction: A progress report. *Journal of Teacher Education, 38*(1), 53-56.

Henry, M. (1986). Strengths and needs of first-year teachers. *Teacher Educator, 22*(2), 10-18.

Hoffman, J., Edwards, S., O'Neal, S., Barnes, S., & Paulissen, M. (1986) A study of state-mandated beginning teacher programs. *Journal of Teacher Education, 37*(1), 16-21.

Lintner, M., Moor, P., Friske, J., Mlynarczyk, C., Thomas, L., & Wiebe, J. (1991). The required computer course for education majors: A national perspective. *Journal of Computing in Teacher Education, 1*(3), 17-23.

Lortie, D. (1975). *Schoolteacher: A sociological study*. Chicago: University of Chicago Press.

McAnge, T. (1990). *A survey of educational computer networks.* Available from Thomas McAnge, Virginia Polytechnic Institute and State University, Blacksburg, VA 24061-0524.

McEvoy, B., & Morehead, M. (1986). Teacher induction: What can a university do best? *Action in Teacher Education, 8*(4), 45-49.

Merseth, K. (1990). *Beginning teachers and computer networks: A new form of induction support* (Report No. 90-9). East Lansing, MI: The National Center for Research on Teacher Education.

Merseth, K. (1991). Supporting beginning teachers with computer networks. *Journal of Teacher Education, 42*(2), 140-147.

Odell, S. (1986). Induction support of new teachers: A functional approach. *Journal of Teacher Education, 37*(4), 26-29.

Roberts, L. (1990). *New tools for teaching and learning: Implications for the development, recruitment and training of teachers* (prepared for the hearing on H. R. 4310, Committee on Education and Labor). Washington, DC: Office of Technology Assessment.

Rodman, B. (1989, September/October) An on-line lifeline: Harvard network lets new teachers exchange ideas. *Teacher Magazine*, pp. 33-35.

Schlechty, P. (1985). A framework for evaluating induction into teaching. *Journal of Teacher Education, 36*(1), 37-41.

Schlechty, P., & Vance, V. (1983). Recruitment, selection and retention: The shape of the teaching force. *Elementary School Journal, 83*(4), 469-487.

Singletary, T. (1987). Programming for leadership. *Journal of Teacher Education, 38*(3), 26-30.

Varah, L., Theune, W., & Parker, L. (1986). Beginning teachers: Sink or swim? *Journal of Teacher Education, 37*(1), 30-34.

Veenman, S. (1984). Perceived problems of beginning teachers. *Review of Educational Research, 54*(2), 143-178.

Chapter
Nine

Computer-Mediated Communication in Medical Education

Karen E. Bruce
Family Medicine Residency Program of Topeka

Social, economic, and technologic progress has and is continuing to influence medical practice and education. Information technology has changed the practice of medicine in the last decade in a number of ways. Approximately 20,000 articles are added to the Index Medicus monthly (Toups, 1985). Medical information is regularly passed on to the public in newspaper, television/radio, and lay health journals, resulting in more broad exposure of health issues in the lay and scientific communities (Phillips, Kanter, Bednarczyk, & Tastad, 1991). Additionally, economics and the rapid advance in medical technology have raised increasing concerns regarding the quality and availability of medical care in the United States. Finally, it is becoming apparent that the U.S. health care system continues to require more generalist physicians and health care providers (e.g., nurse practitioners, physicians assistants, etc.) to meet general health care needs (Council on Long Range Planning and Development in Cooperation with the American Academy of Family Physicians, 1988). These health care professionals, as a whole, must be able to manage 85-

90% of medical problems and thus must be equipped to effectively manage the bulk of medical information that is available (Noble, 1990).

As medical informatics has developed, the question of what information is needed by various users has arisen. A survey of physicians and physicians-in-training at a major medical center indicated textbooks, colleagues, journal browsing, and MEDLINE searching were the four primary methods of obtaining information (in order of frequency of use; Woolf & Benson, 1989). Text and colleague sources of information are valid and valuable but do not generally keep pace with changes in the knowledge base, and browsing is not efficient for knowledge gathering in the face of 20,000 articles per month. Physicians are not taking advantage of available information technology that may significantly impact patient care (Huth, 1989; Toups, 1985). This technology includes national databases of medical, nursing, and allied health information, Compact Disc-Read Only Memory (CD-ROM) versions of these and other databases and textbooks, electronic communication, computer-assisted instruction, and expert systems designed to support medical decision making. Because physicians tend to prefer consultation with colleagues, some networks have provided electronic mail (e-mail) capabilities to facilitate long distance colleague communication (Barnett & Zielstorff, 1988; Muller et al., 1984). At least one network program has had requests from physicians regarding expansion of available information to include drug interactions, epidemiological data, demographics, and medical records information (Barnett & Zielstorff, 1988). A survey of residents and physicians in pediatrics and internal medicine in a major medical center indicated treatment recommendations, differential diagnosis, diagnostic criteria and drug information were the four most frequently searched areas of information (Huth, 1989), all of which are readily obtained using a variety of computer applications.

National databases and electronic communication have been readily available for more than a decade, however, little has been done to utilize them. In recent years a number of national organizations have recommended computer training in medical education, but formal requirements have yet to be changed (Northup, Moore-West, Skipper & Teaf, 1983). Medical students who leave for postgraduate training without computer and information handling skills will find themselves professionally disenfranchised as medicine moves into the 21st century (Battistella, Russell & Doughty, 1990; Muller et al., 1984; Weed, 1981, 1985). Some examples of how computers will mediate the practice of medicine within the next decade follows.

A standardized national computerized patient record has been mandated by the government for use in all hospitals, and a similar proposal has been made for physicians' offices. Decision support programs (expert systems) are becoming more sophisticated and in limited applications, such as evaluating chest pain in the emergency room, have performed well with comparable or higher sensitivity and specificity than physicians (Baxt, 1991; Sturman & Perez, 1989). It is currently expected that a physician will choose specific preventive care practices from the recommendations given by various agencies and consistently follow these guidelines, updating their practice as the guidelines change. It may well become a standard of care to reference literature and sources when documenting preventive care plans and options offered to patients. It has already been proposed that with instant access to databases containing current medical information, it will only be a matter of time until all physicians will be expected to practice based on this standard of shared knowledge (Covell, Uman, & Manning, 1985). With expert systems technology improving rapidly this may facilitate use of such updated information in conjunction with the computerized medical record, providing a "smart" medical record that will help physicians provide routine care with less effort and greater reliability. Electronic networks are being created for patient and physician information, and e-mail consultations instead of phone tag have been suggested. Finally, more physicians are finding they do have a practical need to be able to access current information readily and are eager to do so (Barnett & Zielstorff, 1988; Covell, Uman, & Manning, 1985; Rankin, Williams & Mishelevich, 1987).

Because the structure of medical education has changed little in six decades, it can be problematic to introduce computer and information handling skills in the medical curriculum. Between 25% and 75% of entering medical students have had at least some introduction to computers during their undergraduate experience. Thus, up to 75% of medical students need to have a basic introduction to computers. Nearly all students need to be introduced to the medical applications of computer technology. Students must be encouraged to use these applications frequently in practical, clinically based exercises to overcome the inertia of applying a new "nonmedical" skill concurrent with the other demands of medical school. The use of the technology to efficiently manage medical information is new to the bulk of students and includes issues regarding choosing an appropriate information source for the setting, interpreting the information obtained, and applying general information to specific situations.

Database Sources

Databases providing online searching for medical literature sources have existed for some time. Access is now available in a number of forms including personal computers (PC), PC based Compact Disc-Read Only

Memory (CD-ROM) systems, local area network (LAN) systems, and many modem accessed national online systems. The information provided can include listings of current journal literature with abstracts of the articles, the complete text of articles for a number of the more common journals, and the searchable text of major textbooks. The cost varies depending on the system and the volume of use. However, most configurations are well within the means of small group practices for educational costs. Such systems provide monthly or quarterly updated and searchable information. They are helpful when evaluation or management of a particular problem is changing rapidly and for updating physicians on changing standards for commonly encountered medical problems. They can also serve a continuing medical education (CME) function if applied in a systematic manner for updating reading materials and reference files such as treatment of hypertension, diabetes, asthma, and so on. Additional available database functions include drug interactions programs that identify potentially dangerous combinations of medications, toxicology programs to guide treatment of poisoning and overdoses, and some preventive medicine guidelines that can be used at the patient's bedside or in the office to guide treatment choices. This type of information handling and professional learning is critical for physicians to practice quality medicine in the 21st century (Noble, 1990).

Electronic Communication

Electronic communication is generally applied to billing functions in medical practices that use this function. In spite of its clear cash flow advantages reticence to use computers is indicated by an approximate 80% use in 1993 by family physicians in Kansas (Bruce, 1993). Its potential for use in medical practice beyond billing stems from its asynchronous nature and independence of user location. Traditionally physicians call colleagues for answers to most practical questions, however, studies of this communication indicates that only 30% of calls result in successful retrieval of needed information (Covell, Uman, & Manning, 1985). An additional area of need is the retrieval of laboratory and test results. If a physician can obtain such information electronically, phone tag, delayed treatment, and extra trips to the hospital or office can be reduced. E-mail is also well suited to physician-physician communication regarding patients seen in consultation and in the rural/frontier areas where physicians and practitioners have few local colleagues to call on or to whom to send patients. Few of these potentials have been well explored to date. However, they can be successfully demonstrated, and the skills in using electronic communication can be successfully taught in a practical setting in medical school by using faculty as colleague consultants.

Expert Systems

Computer-assisted instruction and expert systems provide a sort of second-hand computer-mediated function. Expert systems provide "expert consultation" using sophisticated data manipulation and presentation of information including epidemiology, statistics on historical and physical exam information for many diagnoses, the quality and costs of tests for diagnosis, and current medical information. Although this technology is in its infancy, the appropriate use of static "intelligence" in the medical practice setting is a crucial issue with which medical students must grapple. It is clear that at least for the foreseeable future, the use of these systems requires well-trained judgment and familiarity with the limitations of this "intelligence." Students often feel threatened by these programs due to their large knowledge base, their rigidity in decision making, and their own discomfort with the decision-making process. Therefore, they need to be able to apply these programs in well-planned simulated or actual clinical situations and to discuss their use with physician faculty who are knowledgeable in the use of such programs. In medical practice these programs are generally used to help cue physicians regarding unusual considerations that may need to be made in a specific case.

Computer-Assisted Instruction

Computer-Assisted Instruction (CAI) programs vary in their content, detail, and sophistication. Some are produced specifically for student use, whereas others are produced for CME purposes. The content varies from full clinical scenarios to specific diagnostic or treatment skills for emergent situations such as cardiac arrhythmias. Some are interactive and grade performance or give feedback regarding efficiency, cost-effectiveness, and so on. This type of concept has been used to grade clinical performance using a paper model for some time, and it is predicted that use of computer versions may appear in the national testing program for physician licensing and specialty certification. The interactive types of programs are well suited to independent learning by students. Additionally, with the advent of multimedia programs, these types of educational programs will continue to become more sophisticated and will be able to simulate real situations to a greater degree, thus providing a previously unavailable form of "hands-on" experience for students.

A LONGITUDINAL COMPUTER CURRICULUM FOR MEDICAL STUDENTS

Training students in computer use for medical practice is suitable for a longitudinal curriculum. This allows basic computer skills to be introduced, followed by the introduction of different types of applications as students mature in their training. The repetition and application to clinical situations has been cited as critically important for training physicians in the use of computer applications in medicine (Haynes et al., 1990; Poisson, 1986). Several other key issues include starting early, starting with the basics, doing small group and hands on training, pairing students up on machines, using clinical situations in training sessions, making assignments frequently enough to break down barriers to the use of the applications, continuing training and assignments into the clinical years, having faculty demonstrate use of the applications, and presenting the applications realistically but enthusiastically.

The breadth and depth of medical information is overwhelming compared to any undergraduate discipline and experience. Few of our students enter medical school with a good grasp of basic, nonelectronic methods of information seeking and management. They tend to be used to their role as cerebral sponges, rather than as active participants and self-learners in the learning process. This hurdle must be cleared before they have any appreciation for the innovation and utility of computer applications for information seeking and management. During the first year the Department of Family Medicine of East Carolina University runs a Primary Care Course that concentrates on practical clinical aspects of preventive medicine and chronic disease. We use actors as patients to simulate actual clinical situations and to form the basis for discussion and identification of learning needs. These sessions are all carried out in groups of 10 or fewer students. Because our first-year course starts the first week of classes, we introduce students early to the expectation that they are responsible for their own learning and that of their fellow students. They are taught how to ask basic questions to solve clinical problems. The outline for the first-year course is detailed in Table 9.1.

The second-year course runs nearly the whole year (see Table 9.2). This primary care course focuses on patient interviewing, communicating the information gathered to colleagues, and some basic decision-making skills in formulating diagnoses. Like the first-year course it is run in small groups with standardized patients.

The Department of Family Medicine runs an 8-week required clerkship during the third year (see Table 9.3). A clerkship is a hands-on learning experience in which students work day and night with an assigned physician faculty member to learn and improve basic clinical

Table 9.1. First-year Primary Care Conference—Information Handling Basics

A. Information resources—Students receive the essentials of navigating medical texts and journal articles that are reviews of clinical information during the first didactic session.
B. Use of clinical review literature—Computer literature searching is discussed, and the library reference support does individual training for students who request help.

1. Characteristics of clinical review literature and key journals that are critically reviewed are discussed.
2. Searching for review literature
   a. literature indexing, key words, and nomenclature defining Medical Subject Headings for electronic database literature searches

C. Course assignments—During the remainder of the course students have weekly assignments based on questions they are guided to develop by their faculty leader. They are encouraged to use the library CD-ROM-based literature searching. They then report their findings weekly to the small group and turn in the printout that promotes interest on the part of the rest of the small group in terms of not letting anyone "get one up."

Table 9.2. Second-year Primary Care Conference—Computer Applications in Medicine

A. Literature searching

1. Review literature is discussed briefly in context of work of prior year and continued utility for basic practical clinical information.
2. Clinical trials and research literature are introduced with concepts of epidemiology, statistical significance, sensitivity, specificity, and predictive value used in judging quality of information from tests, and choosing therapy.
3. Finding clinically important information in the literature,or how to ask the right questions to get useful information for evaluation or management of a patient's problem when using an electronic database. Various strategies are demonstrated, and the results of the searches are compared for completeness and relevance to original topic of interest. A comparison of MeSH heading use (the cataloged terms used in the database) and key words or common terminology use is made as well. These demonstrations show students that consistent methodology in formulating a search is important in order for this tool to be an effective learning and clinical aid.
   a. searching by symptoms and findings

b. searching by suspected diagnoses

c. searching by organ systems such as cardiac, etc., and pathologic categories such as bacterial infection, infarction, etc.

d. specifying information content such as diagnostic tests, treat ment, epidemiology of a disease, surgical vs. medical treatment, etc.

4. Tutorial in pairs presented by Health Sciences Library (HSL) staff. In this session students choose their own topics and perform searches to practice the skills demonstrated above and to become familiar with the software used for database searching, and printing information obtained.
5. Assignments

a. presentation of information found in literature searching for standardized patient scenarios

b. information for patient write-ups must be documented as to source with a computer printout

B. Drug interactions

1. Significance of drug interactions and medication errors in clinical practice is reviewed with cases taken from the family practice department and with summarized data from various studies of drug interactions.
2. A tutorial in pairs presented by HSL library staff for several assigned examples of common drug interactions.
3. Assigned medication review and use of drug interactions program for actual patients whose physicians request a medication review consultation. Students supervised by faculty who have pharmacology doctorates and do clinical consultation for physicians, interview the patient, obtain a current medication list and use history, then review the pharmacology characteristics of the medications and run the list through the drug program. Students look for potential interactions and determine if the patient is having any symptoms suggestive of an identified potential interaction. Further use is encouraged to assist students with clinical applications for their pharmacology course.

C. Computer-Assisted Instruction (CAI)

1. Several small group sessions using self-explanatory CAI programs are provided to introduce students to the variety of CAI programs including case studies, specific medical problems, interpretation of laboratory results, interpretation of heart rhythms, and lung and heart sounds. These programs are available throughout the year, and independent use is encouraged.

D. Diagnostic Decision Aids

1. A clinical case assignment is given 1 week prior to computer sessions. Students investigate potential diagnoses and the key symp-

toms and define each diagnosis independently using traditional information sources to then compare their findings with suggestions from the computer program for the same clinical case.

2. Small group sessions with a student at the keyboard entering data from the clinical case as recommended by the remainder of students with a discussion of the computer's diagnoses list and the students' lists. This demonstrates the breadth of information obtained rapidly by utilizing the computer program rather than pouring over textbooks or journal articles. It also tends to demonstrate the lack of specificity that can be generated by the computer program due to a lack of specificity of information provided to it or by virtue of its limitations in its algorithms.
3. Required use for simulated patient cases (implemented 1992-1993). The diagnostic aid program will be used to assist one pair of students in each group with their differential diagnosis formulation of a patient case. This result will be presented and contrasted with information obtained by the remainder of the small group. Discussion of the strengths and weaknesses of each method will be discussed.

E. Personal reference files—We also present some instruction on setting up personal library files for the literature collected during the year.

---

skills and to learn how physicians work in practice, manage their lifestyle, and perform their various roles in the community. Approximately 60-70% of the students do their clerkship with a rural physician practicing an hour or more away from the University. They all receive laptop computers to use during the clerkship. Those who do their rotation locally have access to computers at the site where they work. Before starting the clerkship they receive a 4-hour orientation to the computer applications they must use during the clerkship and review statistical concepts important for applying research information in the clinical setting. They also receive user manuals developed by the department with step-by-step commands and expected screen presentations for all programs used.

RESULTS OF IMPLEMENTING A LONGITUDINAL COMPUTER CURRICULUM

The program described above has been in place for three-years. During this past year third year students were surveyed as to their attitudes and behaviors regarding computer use in medicine before starting third-year clerkships and after completing our clerkship. Several clear patterns

Table 9.3. Third-year Clerkship in Family Medicine

A. Introduction to modem use is done in pairs with demonstration of online literature searching and bulletin board/e-mail use

B. Online literature search tutorial

1. Comparing text word and Medical Subject Heading searching. This builds on the sessions during the second year and focuses more closely on obtaining quality information to apply immediately in the patient care setting. Online databases often allow searching by text words and indexed headings. Proper use of each technique is demonstrated so that students can effectively search these databases and obtain reliable information. This skill is crucial to obtaining information from these sources due to the possibility of missing major sources of information with poor search strategies.
2. Retrieving full-text materials from journals and texts. For students who go to rural sites this service allows them to have complete information in hand within minutes, which otherwise would not be available for up to one week, depending on the service available from nearby libraries or national database services.
3. Downloading and printing is practiced so that students can use the information they obtain in their searches readily and present them to the faculty physician.

C. Medical School Bulletin Board use. Students practice posting messages and answering them and are given nicknames. This allows continued communication between students, regardless of their geographic location during the clerkship. Because the students are invariably on call with the physician at different times and run a quite busy schedule, this also demonstrates to them the value of asynchronous communication.

D. Critical appraisal of medical literature. Because they are now expected to make clinical decisions based on the information they find, we include a tutorial on the basics of critical appraisal of the medical literature and review key epidemiologic and statistical concepts.

E. Assignments

1. Ten literature searches for specific clinical questions encountered while seeing patient in the physician's office. These may relate to determining how to evaluate a certain symptom, what exam or test findings should be elicited for a symptom or disease, what therapy may be available for a disease, or any other typical clinical question. We find that after the faculty physician sees the student do this, they often will have the student do some searches for questions they have about a patient. This is an invaluable experience for the student who then realizes the reality of the need to continue learning, even out in

practice, and the reality that they will not be able to know everything. They come to appreciate the potential impact of this technology on their practice of medicine once they complete training.

2. Two CAI sessions. These sessions are printed out and turned in for credit.
3. Answer messages sent over bulletin board by faculty, and students may use the bulletin board for "consultations" with fellow students or faculty. This gives students the chance to gain "expert" opinions from colleagues who are not in close proximity, which mirrors the usual telephone "consultations" traditionally used by rural physicians, but which has the benefit of not relying on someone being there to answer the phone.

F. Diagnostic decision aids (to be implemented 1993-1994)

1. Basic use of the computer program and its limitations will have been thoroughly covered during the second-year course. Students will be required to use the program for specified common problems encountered in primary care such as headache, abdominal pain, and fever. They will discuss the diagnoses and tests suggested by the computer in relation to the diagnoses and tests suggested by the physician they work with and if possible the outcome or final diagnosis of the patient. This experience is designed to demonstrate to students the value and drawbacks of current AI programs and to help them learn to deal with the data such programs produce.

---

emerged, including a widespread lack of preparation for computer use upon entry to medical school, a variety of independent learning behaviors using computer applications, and a lack of appreciation for the potential importance of diagnostic decision aids and electronic communication.

We inquired about their level of experience in using computers when they started medical school. Only 20% of entering students did not have any computer experience. Approximately 60%, however, indicated they wére only slightly or not at all comfortable using computers when they entered medical school. Clearly further work needs to be done to improve computer skills and comfort with computers during medical school.

Changes in behavior were more consistent than changes in attitudes. Students able to complete a successful literature search in less than 20 minutes increased from 70% to 90% during the course of the third year. This change was confirmed by a decrease in the frequency with which students had to revise their search strategies. More than 50% of students did more literature searches than required to answer clinical questions during their clerkship. And 40% of students did literature searches for their own learning during the clerkship. Additionally, 20%

of students ran drug interactions programs not required by assignments, and 10% used other programs such as word processing and diagnostic decision aids for their own interest during the clerkship.

In spite of nearly 90% agreement that clinical practice would be improved by the use of computer applications, 25% of students indicated computer training was not an important criteria for choosing a post-graduate residency training program. Of those who thought residency training should include computer applications, more than 50% indicated literature searching, drug interactions, business applications, office management, word processing, and database management were important skills. The applications of electronic communications and diagnostic decision aids were felt to be important by less than 30% of students who were interested in further training.

Based on these findings, several changes are being implemented in the curriculum starting this year. First-year requirements are unchanged. Recommendations this year, however, include using a typing tutorial located in the Health Sciences Library Computer Lab for those who do not have typing skills. Additionally, students are briefly introduced to the skills and applications with which they will be expected to be proficient by the end of their medical school career.

During the second year an additional hands-on session introducing electronic mail use is planned, and the use of the diagnostic decision aid for several clinical situations will be required. The e-mail session will use BITnet/Internet as a model. Students will be given passwords for access for the remainder of medical school. They will be encouraged to make use of the medical student lists and the primary care lists. Because this addition to their skills is a cooperative venture with the Department of Medical Informatics and the Dean's Office, the students will be required to use e-mail for a variety of tasks including class assignments, seeking "expert consultation" from faculty for clinical problems, and receiving information from the Dean's Office.

The use of the diagnostic decision aid will be assigned to pairs of students within small groups who will report their findings to the group. The remaining students in the group will be assigned specific tasks involved in constructing a differential diagnosis for the same patient using literature searching. The two differential diagnoses lists, as well as recommended tests (both computer-generated and student-generated), will be compared and discussed during a separate session with a faculty member.

When the current second year students reach their Family Medicine Clerkship next year, the above applications will be integrated. Use of the diagnostic decision aid for a list of commonly encountered primary care problems will be assigned, as well as critical appraisal by the students as to the use of the application in this situation. E-mail will be used for assignments, giving feedback, and for "consulting" faculty, as well as Internet list subscriptions per individual interests.

The goals set at the implementation of computer use in the curriculum have been realized to a great degree. After three years more students express an interest in using computers for their personal learning, and a few more expect they will need this skill as practicing physicians. The continued expansion of the program since its inception, however, has created new goals, particularly as the available technology has improved. For significant achievement of these goals a number of items will need to be addressed. A curriculum that demands greater and more frequent use of computer mediated communication will improve student comfort and skill. The curriculum must continue to strive to maintain clinical relevancy of the exercises and assignments. Finally, improved role modeling by physicians in practice will go a long way toward socializing students in the use of this technology. In addition to the expected changes in the curriculum over the next two years as outlined here, an outreach program to assist practicing faculty physicians in implementing the use of computer-mediated communication in their practices has been developed. We are pleased with the results of these efforts thus far and anticipate continued success with these considerations in mind.

REFERENCES

Barnett G.O., & Zielstorff R.D. (1988). IAIMS development at Harvard Medical School. *Bulletin of the Medical Library Association, 76*(3), 226-230.

Battistella, M.S., Russell, L.R., & Doughty, B.P. (1990). Medical information for Alabama rural physicians. *Alabama Medicine, 59*(8), 21-24.

Baxt, W.C. (1991). Use of an artificial neural network for the diagnosis of myocardial infarction. *Annals of Internal Medicine, 115*(11), 843-848.

Bruce, K.E. (1993, June). Current utilization of electronic medical records by family physicians in Kansas. Faculty Development Fellowship Symposium, Department of Family Medicine, University of North Carolina, Durham, NC.

Council on Long Range Planning and Development in cooperation with the American Academy of Family Physicians. (1988). The future of family practice—implications of the changing environment of medicine. *Journal of the American Medical Association, 260*(9), 1272-1279.

Covell D.G., Uman, G.C., & Manning, P.R. (1985). Information needs in office practice: Are they being met? *Annals of Internal Medicine, 103*, 596-599.

Haynes, R.B., McKibbon, K.A., Walker, C.H., Ryan, N., Fitzgerald, D., &

Ramsden, M.F. (1990). On-line access to MEDLINE in clinical settings. *Annals of Internal Medicine, 112*(10), 78-84.

Huth, E.J. (1989). The underused medical literature. *Annals of Internal Medicine, 110*(2), 99-100.

Muller, S., et al. (1984). Physicians for the twenty-first century/Report of the project panel of the general professional education of the physician and college preparation for medicine. *Journal of Medical Education, 59*, 1-208.

Noble J. (1990). The role of the physician as a healer in the twenty-first century. *Journal of General Internal Medicine, 5*, 510-515. 5.

Northup, D.E., Moore-West, M., Skipper, B., & Teaf, S.R. (1983). Characteristics of clinical information searching: Investigation using critical incident technique. *Journal of Medical Education, 58*, 873-881.

Phillips, D.P., Kanter, E.J., Bednarczyk, B., & Tastad, P.L. (1991). Importance of the lay press in the transmission of medical knowledge to the scientific community. *New England Journal of Medicine, 325*(16), 1180-1183.

Poisson, E.H. (1986). End-user searching in medicine. *Bulletin of the Medical Library Association, 74*(4), 293-299.

Rankin, J.A., Williams, J.C., & Mishelevich, D.J. (1987). Information system linking a medical school with practitioners and hospitals. *Journal of Medical Education, 62*, 336-343.

Sturman, M.F., & Perez, M. (1989). Computer assisted diagnosis of acute abdominal pain. *Comprehensive Therapeutics, 15*(2), 26-35.

Toups, D.M. (1985). Southwestern internal medicine conference: Medical \telecommunications—fundamental changes in the art and science of medicine. *American Journal of Medical Science, 290*(5), 214-220.

Weed, L.L. (1981). Physicians of the future. *New England Journal of Medicine, 304*(15), 903-907.

Weed, L.L. (1985). The computer as a new basis for analytic clinical practice: Coupling individual problems with medical knowledge. *Mt. Sinai Journal of Medicine, 52*(2), 95-98.

Woolf, S.H., & Benson, D.A. (1989). The medical information needs of internists and pediatricians at an academic medical center. *Bulletin of the Medical Library Association, 77*(4), 372-380.

Chapter
Ten

Online Training for Online Information Retrieval Systems*

Gail S. Thomas
New School for Social Research

THE PROBLEM

Online databases like those of Dialog Information Services, Inc., provide in-person training, but, beyond help files, online training for using other online databases has been largely nonexistent. Online databases contain items of information, or records, about specific disciplines or categories of documents, collected in machine-readable form (Dialog Information Services, Inc., 1991). A need to provide online production training com-

*I wish to take this opportunity to express my thanks to the following individuals for their kind assistance and helpful suggestions in the development of these courses and the preparation of this chapter: Dr. Norman Coombs, Professor of History, Rochester Institute of Technology; George R. Plosker, Los Angeles Regional Manager, Dialog Information Services, Inc.; and Tina Vozick, Vice President, Connected Education, Inc. For more information, contact the author at Computer Wizard, KB Building, 3711 North Long Beach Blvd., Suite 808, Long Beach, CA 90807-3315, or via electronic mail (Internet: GTHOMAS@UNISON.CINCINNATI.OH.US; BITnet: TO: XB.DAS@STANFORD SUBJECT:[DCUNSN]GTHOMAS!; Unison: GTHOMAS; Dasnet: [DCUNSN]GTHOMAS; CompuServ; 76470,3307; Dialmail, 13317 or 30098).

ponents for an accredited graduate degree program motivated me to develop and teach two courses in computer skills with both lecture and laboratory components available online.

The two courses discussed in this chapter cover the use of introductory and advanced online information retrieval systems. Academic credit for the courses comes from the M. A. in Media Studies Program of the New School, located in Greenwich Village, New York City. Connected Education, Inc., a New York State not-for-profit educational corporation, since 1985 has continually presented online courses for academic credit through the Media Studies program. Paul Levinson, PhD, president of Connected Education, Inc., founded and directs the New School online program through which students can earn the MA-Media Studies degree entirely online. Besides a thesis and theory and survey courses, matriculated online students must complete production "skills" courses. Online instruction in information retrieval systems provides a hands-on production training option to fulfill this "skills" requirement (Levinson, 1989).

I used Dialog resources extensively while earning my online degree, and I noticed the ease with which I was able to switch from my online classes to the Dialog system, and back, without having to make a new phone connection. This ease in moving from one system to another formed the kernel of my idea about developing online hands-on skills training courses, complete with a database laboratory. Dr. Levinson guided the course description through the required review process at the New School. Since the first listing in the catalog, the course has proved so successful that it is regularly offered for enrollment.

Students receive three units of graduate academic credit for successful completion of each course. Undergraduate and noncredit options are also available. The general design of the courses attempts to fulfill the following two objectives:

1. To teach the elements of searching online information retrieval systems; and
2. To teach the elements of database design and construction.

Following this introductory statement of the problem, I discuss my target audience and my reasons for writing this chapter. I then expand on the methods and conduct of these courses, focusing on the example of the introductory course. Discussion of introductory course methods and conduct covers the narrative syllabus, the mode of teaching online searching, and the choice of the selected textbook.

THE TARGET AUDIENCE

These courses are designed to reach all those who have access to a modem. Connected Education has no specific hardware or software requirement—any brand personal computer and modem can be used, allowing students with a broad range of equipment to participate equally. The courses serve a broad potential student population, without regard to disability, location, or work schedule. Prospective students include persons who hold either a bachelor's degree (to obtain graduate credit) or a high school diploma (for undergraduate credit) or people interested in broadening their knowledge in a noncredit mode. Students with telephone access can live anywhere in the world, as they connect to a Sprintnet node or similar internetworking services. Because the classes take place entirely over the modem, students should know how to keyboard and feel comfortable with using computers. Additionally, each student should own or have access to a modem-equipped microcomputer with a dedicated or reasonably private telephone line. Ideally, each student would bring to the course some prior experience with modems and computers. The Connect Ed support staff works closely with students to assist them in their mastery of online skills and to intercept and resolve any technical or pedagogic problems so that their online work is not impeded, and the instructor can concentrate on a smooth flow of the course and subject matter.

Connected Education courses begin every two months except for August and September, but the electronic campus remains open for student and faculty access 365 days a year. Often, Connect Ed schedules special, short-term seminars during the summer break period for growth and enrichment rather than academic credit. I have taught such short-term noncredit seminars in online database searching skills for Connected Education, adopting a similar method as used for the credit courses, but tailored to the needs of the individual noncredit participants. Among the features of the electronic campus are topic areas that form the virtual equivalent of a university commons. The ongoing "Connect Ed Cafe" serves as a forum for discussion and debate on current issues and online concerns, thus providing a social outlet for online students and faculty who never meet face to face. The "Technical Forum" conference also remains open year round to address student questions about computer hardware and software.

Both conferences and others, including the Connect Ed online library, provide resources to the online information retrieval students. This kind of support and foundation are crucial to the comfort of the student and success of the courses. Both introductory and advanced courses fill a general need for skills training in database searching, using methods transparent to both handicapped and nonhandicapped persons. With regard to the online MA program, the courses are approved as options for the production courses required for the degree. The number of courses offered can grow directly with the number of students who wish to participate. Currently, the courses are conducted primarily as graduate-level seminars, with small classes of usually no more than 10 persons. However, because there are no chairs in the electronic classroom, theoretically any number of students can dial in and participate. The potential student body includes anyone with a modem; disabled and nondisabled persons participating on equal footing. Electronically, they move across a virtual version of the "level playing field."

THE REASON FOR WRITING

Technology provides more than a "level playing field" for these courses. Existing technological resources proved adaptable to provide online training for using online databases. By writing this chapter, I hope to suggest how existing practical resources translated from one use to another to suit the course requirements. All seminar manuals and ONTAP training passwords are used with the permission of Dialog. This chapter describes the development, scope, and conduct of the courses in online information retrieval systems. Additionally, this chapter tries to suggest what makes education over the modem unique—bringing students and faculty together across the miles, at times convenient for individual time zones and schedules.

THE COURSE DEVELOPMENT

Since 1989, I have taught online information retrieval systems courses regularly over the electronic campus through Connected Education and the New School. I teach students scattered across the United States and around the world via computer conferencing, from my office in Long Beach, CA. The electronic classroom forms part of the online campus designed by Connected Education and residing on the PARTIcipate computer conferencing portion of the Unison system, on a host computer in Cincinnati, OH. The students effectively go to the computer lab using the ONTAP databases, actually mounted on Dialog's four computers in Palo Alto, CA. The Sprintnet value-added carrier serves as the electronic corridor between the online classroom and the computer lab, enabling students and faculty to participate without leaving home or office, or while traveling with a laptop or notebook computer.

From 1986 to 1988, I completed the first MA-Media Studies degree ever granted solely through online study by the New School. At the time of my matriculation, before Dr. Levinson developed the totally online Technology and Society option, three production courses formed part of the degree requirements and such courses were taught in person at the New School. I transferred three courses from the Instructional Technology Department at California State University, Long Beach. The Technology and Society option enabled students matriculating after me to complete the entire degree online, including a requirement for online "skills" courses, especially writing, journalism, and similar courses. I sought a way to expand the scope of such online production courses to include hands-on computer-specific skills training, flexible enough to serve students with diverse backgrounds and professional interests but not requiring the use of a specific software program or a particular type of computer. The answer seemed as close as my modem.

I learned to search Dialog as part of the curriculum when I earned my MS in Library Science from the University of Southern California. Now a unit of Knight-Ridder, Dialog came online in 1972. The database provider's host computers contain nearly 400 databases on topics from electronics to philosophy and from patents to full-text regional newspapers. These databases contain over 329 million records, from directory and bibliographic entries to more than 2,000 full-text titles. The ONTAP training passwords bypass often costly current databases to allow free practice searching of about 40 representative databases. The training databases provide actual data, generally not current, but useful for searching practice. George R. Plosker, Dialog's Los Angeles Regional Manager, arranged assistance and grants-in-kind, particularly the donation of free training passwords, and instructional materials for the beta-testing period. Similar assistance also came from Vu/Text, another Knight-Ridder division.

Initially, I planned an introductory course to online retrieval systems. Given student acceptance and demand, I planned an eventual course in advanced online retrieval systems, which is also regularly offered. The fourth edition of The Independent Study Guide (1989) lists no courses equivalent to the beginning and advanced courses in online information retrieval systems for end-users. The two online classes fill several student needs. The courses provide hands-on skills training over the modem. Students receive end-user training without leaving the workplace or the home, which is equally useful to the handicapped and the nonhandicapped alike, wherever they may be located. For example, one student, a civil service librarian in upstate New York, took my introductory class in lieu of in-person system seminar training. She was in a wheelchair and preferred to attend class from her office modem rather than hassle the difficulties of traveling to New York for in-person training.

Online education does not take place in a traditional face- to-face setting. The course does not cover basic library research techniques nor focus on bibliographic instruction. The course content was not designed for dabblers. Students receive three units of graduate academic credit for completing the course, which is presented as an intensive graduate seminar. Finally, the course is not software dependent, that is, it does not focus on using a specific software database package.

After trying several books in practice, for over four years, I adopted Goldmann's *Online Information Hunting* (1992; Thomas, 1992). Goldmann developed his Subject Expert Searching Technique (SEST) from his research activities as an engineer and manager with Bell Northern Research. The clearly outlined searching procedure involves the following seven steps, recommended to the students in the online information retrieval systems courses:

1. Organize a strategy.
2. Input the first version.
3. Proceed with initial online adaptation.
4. Organize a final search version.
5. Run a final version through selected files.
6. Adapt a search to a different online service.
7. After finishing a subject search, follow-up activities offline (Goldmann, 1992).

While students use SEST with ONTAPs, the combination of the various Boolean operators are easily adapted to other online services. Appropriate for end-user or textbook purposes, the book removes the mystery from online information retrieval systems via a step-by-step consideration of planning, executing, and utilizing outcomes of cost-effective techniques of searching. He illustrates SEST with transcripts of actual searches from Dialog and other major information services. Through directed searching, students replicate many of his searches in the appropriate ONTAPs. Thus, the students learn styles of searching beyond those taught in the seminar manuals.

The course is effectively divided into thirds and concerns both electronic environments and elements of instruction.

Electronic Environments

The course utilizes three electronic environments, each located in a different state:

1. Lectures and readings reside on Connected Education's electronic campus.
2. For practice with the ONTAPs, students dial into the Dialog host computers.
3. For practice with the training databases of the Vu/Text, students dial into that division's host computers. After Vu/Text and Dialog files merged at the end of 1992, students only needed to dial into the Dialog host computers for practice searching.

Elements of the Course

1. Lectures and discussions continue throughout the period of this highly interactive course.
2. For a midterm project, each student searches for the answers to five individually assigned questions and then reports on the search results in the main course conference.
3. For the final project, each student designs and writes up a plan to utilize commercial and/or proprietary databases in his or her current or contemplated employment situation.

The timeline of the introductory course suggests the scope and content of materials covered within the eight-week period of the course:

Week 1. Introduction. The students sign on to the three electronic environments and purchase textbooks. The students enter self-introductions online. The conference participants, consisting of instructor and students, discuss the course requirements and students' individual goals in the course. Online lectures begin on the structure and content of databases. The students begin assigned readings from the online collection of files, the Connect Ed library. Students might read articles variously covering electronic data interchange (EDI) in business and the Minitel communications system used in France. Readings from texts and tutorial books continue throughout the run of the course as resource materials.

Week 2. Tutorial. The students begin working through the Dialog tutorial manual. Continuing online lectures and discussions focus on database theory and practice. Conference participants conduct preliminary discussions of final project proposals. Final projects apply database search, design, and construction to the students' respective current or contemplated working situations. Students are assigned group searching exercises to warm up for the midterm searching project. Group searching exercises might seek comparative information on the products of two companies, such as IBM and Apple Computer.

The technique of directed searching provides students with ongoing hands-on laboratory exercises throughout the course. Almost daily, I enter two or three search questions in the main course conference. The search questions are adapted from the practice questions given in the various seminar manuals. Each question posting includes the name of the appropriate ONTAP database and enough instructions to enable the students to individually replicate my search. The students are each supposed to try the search first, then check their respective results against the posted transcripts. Because the students receive no grades for the practice searches, searching first and checking results second remains an individual choice.

Students often take the beginning and advanced courses because they plan to use a technical skill in business. One student, laid off from her job, hoped to use skills learned in the course to open an information brokerage service. Another student, a magazine editor, planned to make increased use of regularly updated online databases in her daily research. Final course projects in both beginning and advanced courses focus on practical planning for utilizing online information technology on the job. For that reason, discussions of technology and society form appropriate additions to the course content. The courses were designed to fit into a technology and society curriculum.

Week 3. Midterm Search Questions Assigned. Each student is assigned five individual search questions from a bank of questions. Topics of the questions assigned to any student might run the gamut from personnel management to personal computers. The midterm search project consists of individual searches, with the results due at the end of the fourth week of the class. The midterm project emphasizes the search strategy, not just finding the correct answers. Tutorials, online lectures, and discussions on database theory and practice continue.

Week 4. Midterm Search Questions Due. Each student uploads to the main course conference the results and search strategies for each of the five individually assigned questions. The search reports and strategies form a basis for further instruction in searching techniques. Students may be asked to "re-search" a question using a different database or technique as an instructional tool, not due to deficiencies in the searching activity. For example, a student who chose a business database to research information on personnel management might be requested to look up the same topic in a full-text newspaper database. Conference participants discuss the final project proposals. For the final project proposals, each student submits a preliminary proposal for the final written project, a detailed report applying database searching, design, and construction to the individual student's current or contemplated employment situation.

Week 5. Final Project Proposals Due. The students upload to the main course conference their written proposals for their final projects. Students' proposals vary according to their employment and personal information needs. A student waitressing her way through college devised a restaurant inventory database with the table check as the basic information source. A psychologist in a residential treatment facility designed an information system to monitor patients' drug interactions. As with the midterm searching and "re-searching," the proposals form a basis for discussing refinement of searching and database construction techniques. The students continue with their individually assigned "re-searching" of the midterm questions.

Week 6. Proposals Finalized. Final Projects in Process. The students work on their final projects, which are due the next week. They actually research their chosen topics in the practice databases as much as possible, given the selective nature of the practice databases. Electronic lectures continue on the text readings and the techniques of searching. Lecture topics can range from the history of newspapers in America to pros and cons of database management in the modern business office. Students are encouraged to ask questions in the main course conference about refining their final proposals and projects.

Week 7. Final Projects Due. The students submit their final projects no later than the middle of the seventh week, uploaded to the main course conference. Each project is discussed and evaluated in the main course conference. Students are expected to react to and comment on everyone else's project in the main course conference. Students may be requested to explain the projects or to complete additional written work on the projects. The students still upload their work to the main course conference, so that all conference participants can read the proceedings. Sometimes one student's project proves unexpectedly helpful to another student. For example, a fellow student of the author of the restaurant management database proposal recommended to a restaurateur friend the techniques described by the student waitress.

Week 8. Grand Discussion of Final Projects. Wrap-Up. Conference participants continue discussing the final projects as the course ends. Students upload to the main course conference written evaluations of the content, conduct, and scope of the course. The evaluations should emphasize how they would like to see the course conducted the next time around for the next group of students. The course participants enter their final, and generally very reluctant, electronic farewells. Grades are assigned by private message from the instructor to each student.

Ingenuity, directed searching, and the right textbook all helped to solve a specific problem and develop two popular courses. Both introductory and advanced courses are scheduled regularly for public enrollment. Companies, organizations, unions, and similar affinity groups can also schedule the courses or group training on a credit or noncredit basis. (For enrollment information, contact Paul Levinson, PhD, President, Connected Education, Inc., 65 Shirley Lane, White Plains, NY 10607.)

THE SUMMARY AND CONCLUSION

Practical experience proves the feasibility of teaching online information retrieval systems online. The Sprintnet value-added carrier serves as a virtual corridor between the Connect Ed electronic classroom on Unison and the computer applications lab of ONTAP training databases. Students remain on the same phone call to their local Sprintnet node and switch from theory to practice and back again by signing off and on the appropriate system addresses. Computer skills training takes place at the respective student's convenience of time, place, and terminal for New School graduate academic credit. Physically disabled and nondisabled students participate on an equal basis, with computer technology removing access barriers to learning.

Both introductory and advanced courses in online information retrieval systems help satisfy the production course requirement for the online MA in Media Studies. Directed searching enables students to try specific searches in the ONTAP practice databases, then to check their results against transcripts of the instructor's search posted in a subtopic to the main course conference. Goldmann's book (1992) complements the course structure through the SEST and transcripts of searches capable of replication on the ONTAPs.

Brock N. Meeks, a reporter for *Communications Daily*, calls the introductory course "one of [Connected Education's] most popular courses" (Meeks, 1992, p. 21).

Adaptation of existing methods, from ONTAPs through Dialog seminar manuals to Goldmann's book, helped create an interactive online computer lab component for the hands-on study of online information retrieval systems. The two resulting practical, popular courses provide real-world transferable searching skills, while helping students fulfill production course requirements for the online degree. Actual student experience proves the feasibility of a practical solution to the problem of providing hands-on production courses online.

REFERENCES

Dialog Information Services, Inc. (1991). *Searching Dialog: The Complete Guide.*

Goldmann, N. (1992) *Online information hunting.* New York: Tab/McGraw-Hill.

Independent Study Guide, NUCEA [National University Continuing Education Association] Guide to Independent Study through Correspondence Instruction. (1989) Washington, DC: Peterson.

Levinson, P. (1989, July-August). Connected education: Progress report from the front lines of higher learning. In *Technology and Learning.* (Reprinted in *Journal of Distance Education,* Summer 1989; Boston Computer Society's, *Online Connection,* February 1990; *The Weaver,* Summer 1989; edited version published in Russian translation by G. Vaganian, Soviet Armenian Youth Newsletter, March 1989.)

Meeks, B.N. (1992, July/August). Focus: Online education, connected education is a step ahead. *Link-Up,* p. 21.

Thomas, G.S. (1992, July/August). Searcher support: Review, new edition of online searching handbook. *Database Searcher,* p. 30.

Networks and Networking

Mauri P. Collins

Pennsylvania State University

"It would be nice," I thought, "if I could just understand what they are saying!" The earnest young people at our academic computer services help desk had, from the tone of their voices, answered my question. And I heard all the words, but it sounded almost like a foreign language. I had recently bought a modem for my computer and had been told a whole new world would open up to me—but I found it to be a world with a baffling language that did not make very much sense to me. And I wondered how many of our readers had the same problems with the technical terminology and the acronyms that it seems almost impossible to avoid.

A modem is piece of equipment that turns characters into sound and back again, so that I can send messages that I have typed, or am typing, out over a phone line to communicate with other computers and other computer users. My modem processes information at 2400 baud (bits of information per second), fast enough for my needs, although the computer I use at work has a hardwired connection (a direct line from the back of my computer to the mainframe computer) that transmits information back and forth at 9600 baud.

NETWORKS AND NETWORKING

Of all the terms a new user of computer-mediated communication has to deal with, *network* may be one of the most confusing. The standard use of the word refers to the actual, physical connections between and among computers: the wires, fiber-optic cables, microwave links, phone lines, and so on, that tie computers together and allow their users to communicate with one another.

Physically connected networks come in all sizes from local area networks (LANs) of two or three machines linked together in a single room to international, composite wide-area networks (WANs) that span the globe and include satellites and microwave transmission to move the information. The physical set-up of networks can be likened to a variegated patchwork of independent telephone companies serving their own areas and yet linked together so that they can exchange the virtual equivalent of long-distance phone calls between distant locations.

THE INTERNET

The very first wide-area computer network in the United States was known as the ARPANET, and it linked research universities and military installations together so that researchers could communicate with one another and expensive resources (like computers and databases) could be shared. Over the years this initial network was joined by an ever-increasing number of regional and local networks. The Internet is made up of over 10,000 of these individual networks connecting over 20 million users worldwide.

TCP/IP

With as many different kinds of computers and operating systems and software that are in use, it has taken a great deal of cooperation to come up with a common language and set of standards that could be used to exchange information. One of the most popular standards is TCP/IP (Transmission Control Protocol/Internet Protocol), a set of instructions followed by all the Internet-linked computers for the transmission of information among them.

BITnet (Because It's Time Network) and UUCP (Unix-to-Unix Copy Program) networked computers use different sets of protocols (RSCS/NJE in the case of BITnet) and are connected to the Internet by "gateways." *Gatewaying* computers are vital to the successful transmission of data between networks because they translate alternative protocol sets into TCP/IP and allow messages to pass through the backbone and transparently between networks.

Transmission Lines–T3

The backbone of the Internet network in the United States is made up of what AT&T calls their "T3" communications lines. These T3 lines can be considered as the super highways of data transmission. They have just been upgraded from T1s (which carried 1.544 megabits a second) to the T3s, carrying 44.736 megabits a second. This has significantly increased the bandwidth, the number and complexity of messages that can be carried simultaneously. Initially all messages were just text: characters and words. Now data sent over these lines range from plain text to interactive, two-way audio/visual teleconferencing.

IP Numbers

Each computer, large or small, that can connect to any of the national networks has its own address or IP (Internet Protocol) number. Each site with a national network connection is given a specific range of numbers that it can use for its internal machine addresses. The numbers are in the format of 123.456.789.123, with the last one or two sets of numbers pointing to a specific machine, perhaps on a faculty person's desk or in a public computer lab. This is done so that mail and other traffic can be directed correctly and machines can be identified when their user logs into other computers. We rarely use the IP numbers in addressing mail or anything else, but usually prefer to use machine names in our addresses. I use a SUN Sparcstation with the friendly name of Wilbur, but it is known to the network as 128.118.058.011. *Nameservers* are computers that hold the lists that match the IP numbers to computer names and locations and make the translations transparent to the user.

Moving Traffic

When messages and files are passed through the BITnet, the message "hops" from one computer to another (store and forward) in a linear fashion, rather like a bus that stops at every bus stop on its route. If a machine is temporarily offline (broken in some way, or being fixed or upgraded), then the messages just sit patiently until the way is open again. Despite the fact that electronic communication can move at the speed of light, I have sometimes had messages take 16 hours to get from Virginia to Nevada, and 4 hours from Washington, DC to Pennsylvania, and yet, at other times, transmission appears to be instantaneous.

Some sites have Internet connections, some have BITnet connections, some have both, and some have neither. But there is an increasing number of "gateways" from one to another and to the commercial service providers. Some sites have leased telephone lines that tie them to the nearest major switching center. The lines are always open and available for traffic, and their cost is usually shared by the connected institution and various governmental organizations.

FIDONET

Some sites run software that dials the nearest switching center during the early morning hours, collects all the files and mail that are waiting, and delivers all the mail that it collects during the day. That one phone call may be the only connection with the outside, networked world. Fido is one example of this kind of software. *Fidonet* is the collective name for the thousands and thousands of individually owned, personal computers throughout the world that run Fido software. Each computer is assigned its own specific address so that messages can be routed to the correct place. The existence of Fidonet is not dependent on universities or governments and often reaches into places that other networks do not. Fidonet provides electronic mail, file sharing, and hosts a large number of discussion groups called *Conferences*.

File Transfer Protocol and Anonymous FTP

File Transfer Protocol (FTP) is a program and a protocol that allows files to be transferred from a remote computer to your own local computer. The wealth of information and public domain software (shareware) that is on many Internet sites can be copied freely because such sites allow public access via anonymous FTP. Anonymous FTP means you can log into another machine without having an account there and download archived files.

If a site has FTP available, you usually start the FTP program and connect to a remote machine by typing "FTP <address>", for example:

```
FTP nnsc.nsf.net
```

You then type "anonymous" for your login name and your e-mail address as the password. You have to type the whole of "anonymous" (without the quotes) and spell it correctly.

Directories on FTP sites are hierarchical, and you move up and down the directory tree to find the file you need. The convention for expressing hierarchies is to use a / for each level. If a location for a file on FTP.sura.net is given as "/pub/nic/network.service.guides," you use "cd" (change directory) to get to that location, either one level at a time or three levels at once:

```
cd /pub/nic/network.service.guides
```

When you are in the right directory, use "dir" to check the contents of the directory and "get <file>" (file names are case sensitive) to transfer the file from the remote machine to your local directory:

```
get how.to.ftp.guide
```

The most commonly used FTP commands are (from the perspective of your machine as "local," and the machine you FTP to as "remote":

ls	list contents of remote directory
dir (or "ls -l")	list contents of remote directory including directory information
ldir	list contents of local directory
cd <directory>	change remote working directory to <directory> (e.g. "cd pub" will take you to the directory "pub")
cdup (or "cd ..")	change remote directory to one level up
lcd	change local working directory
ascii	set to ascii mode to transfer files (default)
binary	set to binary mode to transfer files
get <file>	get file—transfer specified file from remote to local directory
mget <file> <file>	get multiple files
put <file>	put file—transfer specified file from local to remote directory
help	print help information
bye (or "quit")	terminate FTP session and exit

Files on FTP sites are stored in different formats. Text files can be copied, displayed with a text editor, and printed without any special processing. These files can be transferred in ascii mode which is the default mode. Other files, for example, compressed files and executable programs, need to be processed in different ways, and you should transfer these files with FTP set to binary mode. The format of the file is usually indicated by the extension to the file title (look for file names ending in a .zip or .z). If you are not sure of the format of the file, use the binary mode. Uncompression programs are often archived along with files at FTP sites, and your local computer systems guru can advise you on what is needed. [Netiquette hint: Anonymous FTP is a privilege, not a right, so please restrict FTPing to off-peak hours (7 p.m. to 7 a.m. local time) and, if you have a choice, use the FTP site closest to you.]

A brief description of FTP is available from:

FTP: FTP.sura.net
File: /pub/nic/network.service.guides/how.to.FTP.guide

BitFTP is a mail interface that allows BITnet/NetNorth/EARN users to FTP files from sites on the Internet. Most of the Internet FTP commands can be used with BitFTP, except the commands are typed in the body of a mail, not interactively as during an FTP session. To get a brief guide to BitFTP, send a message to BITFTP@PUCC (or BITFTP@PUCC.Princeton.edu) containing a single word "HELP."

This service is also available at no charge from Digital Electronics Corporation's Western regional mainframes. You can receive information by sending a message in the following form:

To: FTPmail@decwrl.dec.com
----
help

TELNET

Telnet is a basic Internet service that allows an interactive connection with another machine. Telnet is both a protocol (TCP/IP remote login protocol) and a program. Telnet is used for two major purposes: to remotely login to a machine to which you have access to (i.e., a userid and a password) so you can use it as if you were actually at that site; and to remotely login to machines that hold public-accessible catalogues and databases.

I usually log into my VAX account at PSU and Telnet from there to my SUN (Unix) and PSUVM accounts at Penn State and to my accounts in Nevada and Washington, DC. When I am traveling, I usually arrange for login access at a local system so I can then Telnet back to my home machine and keep up with my mail. When I am working online, I no longer reach over to the shelf for my venerable and battered dictionary. I Telnet to hangout.rutgers.edu, and following their menus, find the Short Oxford Dictionary (8th ed., 1991) that they have made available online there.

Some of the remote sites (library catalogs and computers holding public access databases) need a login name, but it is usually published with information about the service.

To Telnet to a site, type Telnet <address>", for example:

Telnet nic.ddn.mil

Watch carefully as you log into a site; it will often give you the necessary escape sequences to break the connection if you run into difficulties. ^] (control]) is an escape mechanism that often returns you to either the Telnet prompt or your system prompt. If you are at the Telnet prompt, you can end the connection by typing "close" or "quit."

A brief description of Telnet is available from:

FTP: FTP.sura.net
File: /pub/nic/network.service.guides/how.to.Telnet.guide

Electronic Mail

As soon as I had my modem set up, I immediately used it to become an e-mailer, that is, to send and receive electronic mail (e-mail). In my own case, I used my modem and home phone line to reach my account on one of Penn State's computers and to do from home what I had been doing from the public computer labs on campus. However, I could have just as easily (but for a fee) used my modem to dial the local access number of any one of a number of commercial computer communication service providers, like CompuServe, Prodigy, and Dialog. Electronic mail is referred to as "asynchronous" messaging because both parties do not have to be logged in at the same time in order to communicate.

The first thing you have to know when you want to send e-mail to someone is their address, and always the easiest way to determine that is to ask the person to whom you want to send mail. Electronic mail addresses look very different from ordinary post office addresses (called "snail mail" by e-mail users). How an address looks depends on what network the computer that has the account is connected to. I have accounts on machines that access two different networks—the Internet and BITnet.

To send mail to my home address you need to know:

my name: mauri collins
my house number and street: Calder Square, P.O. Box 10002

my city: State College
my state and zip: PA 16805-0002

To send electronic mail to my Internet address you need to know:

a login name (or userid):	mmc7	fay
a machine:	@psuvm	@archsci.arch
a location:	.psu	.su
a domain:	.edu	.edu
a country code (outside U.S.):		.au

that is, mmc7@psuvm.psu.edu or fay@archsci.arch.su.edu.au (Fay is in the architecture department at the University of Sydney, Australia)

Remember the periods or "dots" between the parts of the address (my address reads out loud as "mmc7 at psuvm dot psu dot edu"). Computers read blank spaces in e-mail addresses as delimiters ending lines, so you will see the underscore or hyphen sometimes used as a spacer, instead of a blank as in mauri_collins@machine. location.domain.

You just have to remember to copy addresses carefully, or use the "reply" feature on the mail program on your computer. It is generally sufficient to take the correct information from the "header" on the mail you have received, but it is always an excellent idea to follow-up and make sure that the message is going to your intended recipient.

Different Internet address domains you may see are .com for business or industry, .mil for military addresses, .gov for governmental addresses, .org for nonprofit organizations, and .edu for educational organizations. Addresses outside of the United States often require a country designation. Whereas Internet e-mail addresses generally go from the most specific level to the most general, mail going to the United Kingdom and onto their Jnet network needs to have the address turned around. If I were in the United Kingdom my address might look like mauri@UK.edu.psu.wilbur.

On BITnet, each computer has its own distinct name, which may or not be the same as its Internet name. My BITnet address is now MMC7@PSUVM. However, when I was at another site, my Internet address was collins@helios.nevada.edu or just collins@nevada.edu, but my BITnet address was COLLINS@NEVADA3. When sending mail from a computer that does not have a direct connection to BITnet, it is usually necessary to add additional routing information to the address as in: COLLINS@NEVADA3.BITnet.

Discussion Groups

One of the more popular uses of networks, after the exchange of electronic mail between individuals, is to join and read the incredible variety of discussion lists and news groups that are available. Discussion groups come in many forms. Some are like the bulletin boards in the local grocery store. Messages are posted and left for people to read and comment on. Some groups focus on particular topics, others are strictly for announcements, whereas others read like the transcript of a cocktail party.

Discussion groups have been likened to newspapers or talk radio. Many people read or listen or, to use the networker's term, *lurk,* and relatively few contribute. However, readership in a discussion group can bring people together from all over the world who otherwise might never have a chance to talk; it fosters the exchange of ideas and information and engenders a sense of cooperation and friendship.

LISTSERV

Many of these discussion groups are handled by a program called LISTSERV written by Eric Thomas which runs on IBM mainframe computers. The groups are often called discussion lists because essentially what the LISTSERV software holds is a subscription list of electronic mail addresses. When a message is received, LISTSERV, depending on the instructions it has been given, will send it on to the moderator/listowner, or, if the list is unmoderated, will copy the incoming message to each of the addresses on its subscription list.

If the list is moderated, then the moderator will check the message against whatever formal or informal criteria exist that govern what goes to the list's readership and either send the message on, edit it, or return it to the sender. Most moderators see their primary role as "controlling the signal-to-noise ratio." This involves making sure that the discussion is kept within the limits set forth in the group's charter and that discussion is conducted in a civil manner.

To join a discussion group, send mail to the LISTSERV at the address given for the discussion group (e.g., LISTSERV@...) with a single line in the body of the message, for example:

```
TO:LISTSERV@guvm
-----------------
SUBSCRIBE IPCT-L YOURFIRSTNAME YOURLASTNAME
```

You need to substitute your own name as in: subscribe ipct-l mauri collins.

Some common LISTSERV commands are:

SUBscribe	Listname	YourFullName	Subscribe to a list
SIGNOFF	Listname		Unsubscribe from a list
SET	Listname	Mail/NoMail	Toggle receipt of list mail
INDEX	Listname		To receive a directory of available files and archives
REV	Listname		List of subscribers
STATS	Listname		Get statistics
HELP			Get a list of these commands

A complete listing of LISTSERV groups can be obtained using anonymous FTP from FTP.nisc.sri.com, and the file is /netinfo/interest-groups. Beware before you get it, the file is Huge (over a megabyte) with over 4,000 different groups listed. A list of discussion groups in the humanities (over 800 of them) is maintained by Diane Kovacs and is available via anonymous FTP from ksuvxa.kent.edu in the directory library/acadlist.readme.

One unfortunate and often unpleasant aspect of discussion and NetNews groups is the occurrence of flaming. With no indication of tone or mood (except for the ubiquitous smilies :-); tip head to left shoulder to see the grin), it is very easy for misunderstandings to arise and to escalate with alarming rapidity. Free from the sanction of others' immediate presence (and the fear of a pop on the nose for running off at the mouth), there are those who tend to "run off at the finger tips" and whose language and interaction style becomes hostile, vulgar, and profane. And then there are those who chose to communicate in that tone all the time. If a reasoned attempt to clear up the misunderstanding is unsuccessful, a gracious exit from the communication situation is often the best remedy, as censure or argument often seems to exacerbate the problem.

USENET/NETNEWS

Usenet can be defined as computers that exchange messages with Usenet headers. It no longer refers to the physical network of UNIX-using computers as it had when it started. Much of the Usenet traffic is carried over the same computers that also handle BITnet and/or Internet traffic.

There are currently over 2,000 different Usenet newsgroups. The Usenet groups are divided into a number of major streams, for example, alt (alternative), comp (computer), soc (social), rec (recreation), and so on. There is no central authority for Usenet groups, although protocols have grown up that govern the creation of new groups. No matter what your interest you can probably find a Usenet group that discusses it; if not, you can gather some like-minded correspondents and start one. Some newsgroups are of local interest, like psu.jobs that advertises employment available on Penn States' campus, to soc.women which is carried worldwide.

A complete list of netnews groups is available via anonymous FTP from:

FTP: rtfm.mit.edu
Files: List_of_Active_Newsgroups,_Part_I
List_of_Active_Newsgroups,_Part_II
Alternative_Newsgroup_Hierarchies,_Part_I
Alternative_Newsgroup_Hierarchies,_Part_II

Differences Between LISTSERV and Netnews

There are some significant differences between Usenet Netnews and the LISTSERV discussion groups residing on BITnet and the Internet, most of which show up from the computer user's perspective. A user subscribes as an individual to LISTSERV,and similar groups and their messages are received in their personal mailbox.

In order to read the Netnews newsgroups, one's site has to receive some part of the *feed*, the stream of Netnews messages, which can be measured in tens of megabytes each day. This is stored at a central location on the site's mainframe and accessed by some kind of reader software. Sometimes Netnews messages are available on campus through the same system that handles on-campus discussion groups. Messages are held for whatever period of time the site administrators decide is appropriate, and this is often dictated by the amount of storage space available. A site may receive some, all, or none of the newsgroups.

There are now over 2,000 different Netnews groups. The first word in the name of the group is kind of a "family" name that indicates to which of the main divisions the group belongs: comp.misc is a computer-related group, soc.women is from the social science grouping, rec deals with recreational topics, talk indicates discussion groups, and bit.LISTSERV indicates groups that are mirrors of BITnet/Internet LISTSERV groups.

GUIDES TO MORE INFORMATION

The very first source of information on anything that pertains to access to the computers at your site, how they are set up, what programs are installed, and how to run them is always your very own site computer gurus. They are most knowledgeable about the idiosyncracies of their equipment and programs and can provide you with instruction, written guides, access to training classes, and so on.

There are a host of extraordinarily good guides to the use of computer-mediated communication and lists of such guides. One comprehensive beginner's guide is the work of John December at Rensselaer Polytechnic Institute, available via anonymous FTP from ftp.rpi.edu in the file pub/communications/internet-cmc. Another is Scott Yanoff's "Internet Sources Guide." This is updated bi-weekly and is posted to the NetNews group alt.internet.services, or is available by anonymous FTP from csd44.csd.uwm.edu as pub/inet.services.txt.

I have been thoroughly enjoying my wanderings in the networks and have found a wealth of knowledge and a host of friends. But I will warn you—it can become a time sink—with all your spare moments disappearing off into cyberspace.

Glossary

Compiled by Zane L. Berge, Mauri P. Collins and Michael Day

Academy One. National Public Telecomputing Network's (NPTN) Academic Projects area. It includes special areas for teachers, parents, and students, and features globally interactive projects, such as simulated space missions and an annual Teleolympics. Academy One promotes the educational use of the entire worldwide Free-Net system. For more information, contact NPTN's Director of Education, Linda Delzheit, on the Internet at aa002@nptn.org.

Address. There are two forms of machine addresses that will commonly identify any computer connected to the Internet. They are in the form or either words or IP numbers (dotted quads). For instance, GUVAX, a VAX computer at Georgetown University, is known as either 141.161.1.2 or guvax.acc.georgetown.edu.

Anonymous FTP. A form of FTP (see FTP) that allows unregistered users (those without passwords to the account) access to files. When using, one logs in as "anonymous" and uses one's e-mail address (e.g., BERGE@GUVAX) as the password.

ARPANet. A packet switched network developed in the early 1970s. The "grandfather" of today's Internet. ARPANet was decommissioned in June 1990.

Archie. An internet service that allows one to search the offerings of many FTP sites. Archie tracks the contents of over 800 anonymous FTP archive sites containing over 1 million files stored across the Internet. Two archie sites are: archie.ans.net (147.225.1.31) and archie.unl.edu (129.93.1.14). Logon as "archie".

ASCII. American Standard Code for Information Interchange, pronounced "Askee." A standard data transmission code that the computer uses to encode alphanumeric and other characters into a binary file.

Asynchronous. Transmission by individual bytes, or packets of bytes, not related to specific timing on the transmitting end. When used to describe computer-mediated communication, it indicates that communication can take place without both parties being logged on at the same time, as messages can be left for subsequent reading.

Backbone. The primary, or trunk connection, on a distributed hierarchical network system, such as the Internet. All systems connected to the backbone are assured of being connected to each other. This does not prevent systems from setting up private arrangements with each other to bypass the backbone for reasons of cost, performance, or security.

Bandwidth. Used generally to refer to the capacity or throughput of a communications link. High bandwidth implies high data throughput, which can provide a very high speed to a few users at a time, or lower data rates to many users.

BITnet. Acronym for "Because It's Time Network." Begun in 1981, BITnet is a worldwide academic and research network that connects many universities, colleges, and collaborating research centers, and is restricted to the noncommercial exchange of information. It is operated by EDUCOM. BITnet differs from the Internet in the types of services (e.g., FTP and Telnet) its users can access. BITnet uses the RSCS protocol set and provides electronic mail, file transfer, and "Tell/Send" messaging.

Boolean searching. A method of searching in some electronic databases that allows the searcher to combine terms and/or phrases by using the Boolean operators "and," "or," and "not."

Bug. A bug is a programming error that causes a program not to work or to work differently than intended.

Bulletin-Board Systems (BBS). A network-based filesharing system in which users may enter information, usually in the form of messages, for others to read or download. Many bulletin boards are set up according to general topics and are accessible throughout a network.

Campus-Wide Information System (CWIS). A tool that allows users to navigate through and retrieve data from a variety of campus sources (e.g., library, news bureau, events center, admissions and registrar, computing center).

Client. In network terminology, client can have two meanings. Sometimes it is synonymous with "user". At other times it is used to denote a relationship between two computers in which one computer is a host and is serving a client machine. In this situation, the client computer becomes a guest on the host computer in order to use the host computer's resources. The program on the client machine that provides the user interface for those resources is typically called the client software.

Client-server interface. A program, running on a host computer, that provides an interface to remote programs (called clients), most commonly across a network, in order to provide these clients with access to some service such as databases, printing, and so on. In general, the clients act on behalf of a human end user (perhaps indirectly).

Computer-Based Instruction (CBI) or Computer-Mediated Instruction. Refers to using computers to instruct human users. CBI includes Computer-Assisted Instruction (CAI) (tutorial, review and practice, simulation, etc.); computer-managed instruction (diagnostic and prescriptive testing functions); and electronic messaging, which is generally associated with networked computer classrooms.

Courseware. Software, including documentation and workbooks, that is marketed for educational purposes.

Cross-Posting. Posting a BBS message to multiple subject groups or conferences.

DEC VAX Notes. *see* **Vax Notes.**

Domain. Usually the last term in an address (q.v.). Domains are usually functional or national. Functional domains include EDU for education, GOV for government, COM for commercial, and ORG for nonprofit organizations. National domains identify a country, such as CA for Canada, MY for Malaysia, SG for Singapore, and TH for Thailand.

Download. The electronic transfer of information from a remote computer to a local one. Upload refers to the transfer from the local machine to the remote one.

Electronic Bulletin Board. *see* **Bulletin Board Systems (BBS).**

Electronic Journal (ejournal). An electronically distributed publication which, like a print journal, includes a table of contents, numerically defined issues, and an ISSN number. Recipients can reformat text as they wish and print only what they need to print.

Electronic Mail (e-mail). Transmitting textual and nontextual messages in machine readable form from one computer terminal or computer system to another. A message sent from one computer user to another is stored in the recipient's mailbox, a file on the host machine where that person receives mail.

Emoticon-(smiley). Electronic text likenesses of human faces used in mail and news to indicate a variety of emotions and reactions. You read the "face" from left to right, as if it were rotated 90 degrees counter-clockwise. The most common smiley is :-) connoting a smile or happiness. You will also often see :-(meaning sadness or disappointment, and ;-) meaning irony or sarcasm.

ENFI (Electronic Networks For Interaction). A real-time writing environment for the networked computer classroom in which synchronous communications software allows teachers and students to explore, collaborate, and expand on ideas in class in writing. They see each other in the process of for developing ideas; they write for each other and not just to "the teacher".

FAQ. *see* **Frequently Asked Question.**

Fiber optics. The technology of connecting or networking communication devices, such as computers, by means of optical fiber cable instead of copper wire.

File Transfer protocol (FTP). A TCP/IP protocol and program that one can use to transfer files over the network.

Flame. To express a strong opinion and/or to criticize someone (or something), usually in a frank, inflammatory statement couched in language often vulgar or profane, in an electronic message.

FrEdMail Network. Free Educational Electronic Mail. One of the pioneering networks of microcomputer-based BBS systems serving K-12 educators, FrEdMail was begun in 1986 by Al Rogers in San Diego, CA and has spread to include more than 150 electronic bulletin boards systems across the United States and as far away as Australia and Ireland. FrEdMail offers collaborative activities designed to help students become better writers and learners and promotes the sharing of resources and experiences among teachers. FrEdMail can now be accessed through the Internet. For more information, contact Al Rogers, FrEdMail Foundation, P.O. Box 243, Bonita, CA 91908-0243.

Frequently Asked Questions (FAQs). A document containing answers to frequently asked questions about some service, application, or function. These documents are generally updated as users gain experience with the service, application, or function.

FTP. *see* **File Transfer Protocol.**

Full Text Delivery. The ability of an information server, like Gopher, to deliver the full text of a document to a patron.

Gateway. A computer or device that acts as a connector between two logically separate networks. It has interfaces to more than one network and can translate data so that it can pass from one network to another, possibly dissimilar, network.

Gopher. An information management tool that allows users to search for specific kinds of information over a wide-area network by using a series of menus. Gopher was developed by the University of Minnesota and is freely available in client and server form. Many Gophers serve as useful front-ends to Internet databases, FTP archives, OPACs, and CWISs.

Groupware (Group Conferencing Systems). A program (often marketed for business) that permits simultaneous work on a common file by more than one networked user. All the users can see the changes made by any other person as they occur.

Host Computer. In the context of networks, a computer that provides service to a user who is typically running 'client' software that turns their computer into a "terminal" of the host.

HYTELNET. A menu-driven version of Telnet that serves as a guide to online library catalogs and other information sources, updated 2-3 times per year. It can be downloaded by Anonymous FTP and placed on a local machine. Information on Hytelnet is available from WAIS: hytelnet.src.

Informatics. A general term describing network-accessible information servers. These include data archives such as anonymous ftp sites, interactive databases such as library OPACs, and client/server systems such as Gopher and WAIS.

Internet Relay Chat (IRC). A worldwide synchronous multiuser chat protocol that allows one to converse with others in real time. IRC is structured as a network of servers, each of which accepts connections from client programs, one per user. Jarkko Oikarinen, a Finnish programmer, created Internet Relay Chat. IRC is a free program, that is, anyone with access to the Internet can get a client program and use it to talk with others.

internet. A collection of computer networks interconnected by a set of routers that allow them to function as a single, large virtual network.

Internet. (Note the capital "I") The largest network in the world consisting of national backbone nets (such as MILNET, NSFNET, and CREN) and a myriad of regional and local campus networks all over the world. The Internet uses the Internet protocol suite, including the TCP/IP protocol set that includes electronic mail, Telnet, and FTP. To be on the Internet you must have IP connectivity, that is, be able to Telnet to—or ping—other systems. Networks with only e-mail connectivity are not actually classified as being on the Internet.

Interoperability. That which allows different computer models from different manufacturers to communicate meaningfully with each other.

IP (Internet Protocol). *see* **TCP/IP.**

IP Address. The numeric address (a dotted quad) of a computer connected to the Internet; *also called* **Internet address**. It has the form 123.456.789.101. Guvax.georgetown.edu, to other computers and the network routers, is 141.161.1.2

IRC. *see* **Internet Relay Chat.**

KIDSNET. Has been renamed KIDSPHERE. See KIDSPHERE.

KIDSPHERE. The major mailing list for the discussion of K-12 computer networking. It was established in 1989 by Bob Carlitz under the name KIDSNET. In Spring 1993 it was renamed KIDSPHERE with this statement of purpose: "to stimulate the development of an international computer network for the use of children and their teachers. The first pieces of this network have already begun to take shape, and the mailing list now helps to guide its continuing evolution. Subscribers to the list include teachers, administrators, scientists, developers of software and hardware and officials of relevant funding agencies." To join the list, send your request to Bob Carlitz <joinkids@vms.cis.pitt.edu> and ask to be added to the KIDSPHERE mailing list.

LAN. *see* **Local Area Network.**

LISTSERV. LISTSERV is the software that manages electronic discussion groups or computer conference distribution lists. These discussion groups are often called "lists" because, using what is called a "mail exploder" and a subscription list of electronic mail addresses, LISTSERV sends messages directly to the electronic mailboxes of many subscribers. Participants subscribe by sending a message to the LISTSERV hosting the list of interest. Eric Thomas originally wrote the listserv software for IBM mainframes, but there is now a similar program that runs on Unix systems.

Local Area Network (LAN). A network connecting machines at one site.

Lurking. Reading or "listening" to a mailing list discussion or Usenet newsgroup without actively participating (i.e., without contributing to the discussion). Lurking is encouraged for beginners who wish to learn the history and habits of the group.

Mail Exploder. Part of an electronic mail delivery system that allows a single message to be delivered to a list of addresses. Mail exploders are used to implement mailing lists. Users send messages to a single address (e.g., mygroup-L@somehost.edu) and the mail exploder takes care of delivery to each of the individual subscribers to the list.

Modem (MOdulator/DEModulator). A device that converts the digital signals in your computer to analog signals, and vice-versa, to enable computer communication through analog telephone lines.

Moderator. The person who is "in charge" of the Listserv or a Usenet newsgroup. On a moderated list, the moderator collects the messages posted to the list, edits them, and forwards them to the list. On an unmoderated list, the moderator just steps in when things get out of control. The moderator may also subscribe and unsubscribe people on the list, if is not a public list.

National Education and Research Network (NREN). The National Research and Education Network is a proposed national computer network to be built on the foundation of the NSF backbone network, NSFnet, the current internet backbone. NREN would provide high speed interconnection between various national and regional networks.

Netiquette. A contraction of "network" and "etiquette" referring to proper behavior on a computer network.

Netweaving. When a human volunteer (netweaver) must move individual messages from network to network because there is no direct electronic connection or gateway.

Network. A group of computers connected together for the purpose of transmitting information to one another.

NIC (Network Information Center). An internet host computer designated to provide useful information services to network users.

Node. A computer that is attached to a network; also called host.

NREN. *see* **National Research and Education Network.** NSFnet-National Science Foundation Network. TCP/IP-based network that is the backbone for data transmission in the United States.

OPAC (Online Public Access Catalog). Most large academic and many public libraries have converted their card catalogs to electronic or "machine-readable" format. These online catalogs may be searched from remote locations via modem or remote login, and so they truly have become public reference sources.

Postmaster. The person responsible for answering questions about users and electronic mail addresses at a site. Can sometimes be reached by sending mail to "postmaster@host.subdomain.domain" if you are having trouble reaching someone at that host machine or subdomain.

Protocol. A formalized set of rules governing the format, timing, and error control of transmissions on a network. The protocol that networks use to communicate with each other. TCP/IP is an example of a network protocol.

Remote Access. The ability to access one computer from another, from across the room or across the world. Remote access requires communications hardware, software, and actual physical links, although this can be as simple as common carrier (telephone) lines or as complex as a Telnet login to another computer across the Internet.

RFC (Request for Comments). The document series, begun in 1969, in which the Internet's standards, proposed standards, and generally agree-upon ideas are documented and published.

Server. A dedicated computer that shares its resources, such as files and applications programs, with other computers on a network.

Shareware. Microcomputer software, distributed through public domain channels such as ftp, for which the author expects to receive compensation.

Signature (often .sig). The three or four lines at the bottom of a piece of e-mail or a Usenet article that identifies the sender. Often contains addresses, telephone numbers, e-mail addresses, and, sometimes, ingenious graphics built from keyboard characters. Long signatures (over five lines) are generally frowned on.

SMTP. Simple Mail Transfer Protocol. The Internet standard protocol for transferring electronic mail messages from one computer to another.

Snail Mail. A pejorative term referring to the postal service.

Synchronous. Data communications in which transmissions are sent at a fixed rate, with the sending and receiving devices synchronized. Synchronous communication occur in real-time, for example, with two or more users communicating online at the same time to one another.

Sysop, sysops. System operator, person in charge of maintaining a host, server, or network.

Talk. A protocol that allows two people on remote unix computer systems to communicate in real time. When you issue the "talk user@machine.place.domain" command, and the individual is logged and accepts your request, the screen display divides horizontally and you can type at each other in real time.

TELL. The interactive real-time messaging protocol for IBM mainframes running VM/CMS and with BITnet connections. (SEND is the equivalent protocol for BITnet-connected VAX/VMS systems). At the system prompt one types:

tell (or "send") user@machine a single line message

and the message will appear on user@machine's screen if they are logged in. It is unwise to send TELL or SEND messages to persons one does not know because, depending on the rank and mood of the recipient, they could result in revocation of one's access privileges.

TCP. Transmission Control Protocol. The set of transmission standards on the Internet that provides the reliable communication service on which many applications depend for accurate data transfer. It allows the transfer of data between computers that have TCP/IP, and it supports other services (protocols) such as Telnet, FTP, and

SMTP. TCP/IP is also often used for other networks, particularly local area networks that tie together numerous kinds of computers or engineering workstations.

TCP/IP. *see* **TCP**

Telecommuting. The practice of employees working partially or primarily from home, using microcomputers and modems to access information systems and perform their daily duties without regard to their actual physical location.

Telnet. A basic function provided by the TCP/IP protocol on the Internet is Telnet, or remote login, or remote terminal connection service. This allows a user to interact with another computer as if she or he were directly connected to the remote computer.

Terminal Emulation Software. Communications software that permits your personal computer or workstation to communicate with another computer or network as if your machine were a specific type of terminal directly connected to that computer or network.

Terminal Server. A computer that connects terminals to a network by providing host Telnet service.

Thread. A series of postings to an electronic bulletin board or other discussion group (e.g., Listserv) that have a common subject heading. A thread normally consists of responses to an original posting to a discussion topic, or an offshoot of another thread.

TN3270. A version of Telnet providing IBM-3270 full-screen support.

UNIX. An operating system developed by Bell Laboratories that supports several users logged into a computer or workstation at the same time, and which supports multiuser and multitasking operations. That is, this operating system allows many people to share the processing capabilities of the computer on which it is running and allows those people to use several programs at once.

Usenet (NETNEWS). A computer bulletin board system, originally distributed over computers running the unix operation system that many computer systems on and off the Internet now subscribe to. Where LISTSERV software delivers discussion group messages as mail to individual mailboxes, messages from some or all of the over 2000 Usenet newsgroups are typically stored on a site's mainframe computer. Readers can then log in to read the accumulation of messages which may amount to 15 to 20 megabytes of text a day. With the number of groups growing daily, there is truly something of interest to everyone on Usenet.

UUCP (Unix to Unix Copy Program). A protocol used for communication between unix systems, on which mail and Usenet news services were built. Internet has largely taken over the transmission of such date exchange.

VAX (pl. VAXen). Mainframe and personal computers manufactured by the Digital Equipment Corporation and in wide use on the Internet. One of the prevalent terminal emulations used on the Internet is named for the VT100, an early DEC video terminal.

VAX Notes. VAX Notes is essentially a computer bulletin board set up with a series of topics numbered 1, 2, 3 and so on. Replies to each topic are attached to each topic note. Replies to topic 3 would be numbered 3.1, 3.2, and so on. This permits users to read and respond to several different discussion topics simultaneously. It also saves and stores all topic notes and replies, permitting readers to connect at any time, even after a several day hiatus and catch up on the entire series of transactions.

Virtual Reality. Systems that transform the computing environment by immersing the user in a simulated world, which also can include movement and tactile control. Virtual reality systems permit users to interact with computer systems in a manner that more closely mimics how humans naturally operate in the real world.

VMS. A Digital Equipment Corporation operating system for VAX machines.

VT100. *see* **VAX.**

Wide-Area Network (WAN). A distributed network spanning hundreds or thousands of miles, connecting a number of Local Area Networks.

Wide-Area Information System (WAIS). An information retrieval tool developed by Thinking Machines, Inc. WAIS provides a simple-to-use interface that allows a patron to search multiple sources for information with a single natural language question.

World-Wide Web (WWW or W3). A hypertext-based, distributed information system created by researchers at CERN in Switzerland. It allows users to create, edit, or browse hypertext documents. The clients and servers are easily accessible and available.

SOURCES

Ask ERIC InfoGuide. (1993). *K-12 educators and the Internet*. Available via anonymous FTP at ericir.syr.edu.

Day, M.J. (1993). Private correspondence.

Jacobsen, O., & Lynch, D. (1991). *A glossary of networking terms*. RFC 1208.

Kehoe, B.P. (1992). *Zen and the art of the Internet*. Available via anonymous FTP on host FTP.CS.WIDENER.EDU, directory PUB/ZEN, filename ZEN-1.0.PS (Postscript file) and other formats.

Krol, E. (1991). *The whole Internet user's guide and catalog*. Sebastapol, CA: O'Reilly and Associates.

Longley, D. (1986). *Dictionary of information technology* (2nd ed). New York: Oxford University Press.

Malkin, G., & LaQuey Parker, T. (1993). *Internet users' glossary*. RFC 1392.

Mitchell, M. & Saunders, L. (1992). *Glossary*. Sent via private correspondence.

Mulliner, K. (1993). *Internet glossary*. Prepared for a workshop in Columbus, OH. Sent via private correspondence.

Other miscellaneous glossaries from unidentified sources that were sent to us as private correspondence.

Author Index

A

Adams, R.S., 50, *75*
Andrew, F. D., 54, *77*

B

Bakhtin, M.M., 94, *109*
Barnes, S., 138, *150*
Barnett, G.O., 154, 155, *165*
Barrett, E., 118, *121*
Batson, T., 32, *38*, 49, *75*
Battistella, M.S., 154, *165*
Baxt, W.C., 155, *165*
Bean, J., 67, *75*
Becker, F., 50, *75*
Bednarczyk, B., 153, *166*
Bee, J., 50, *75*
Benson, D.A., 154, *166*
Benton, J., 73, *76*
Biddle, B.J., 50, *75*
Bikson, T.K., 71, *76*
Bohrnstedt, G.W, 58, *75*
Bolter, J., 82, *92*
Boruta, M., 49, *77*
Bradburn, N.M., 58, *75*
Breed, G., 50, *75*
Briggs, L., 13, 18, 22
Brodsky, A., 137, 138, *150*
Brophy, J., 71, *76*
Brown, J., 73, *76*
Brown, K., 109, *110*
Bruce, B., 49, 51, *78*
Bruce, K.E., 156, *165*
Bruffee, K.A., 49, *76*
Bump, J., 32, 33, 34, 36, *38*

C

Cary, L., 13, 22
Cathcart, R., 82, *92*
Char, C., 49, *78*
Clark, C.M., 51, *76*
Cohen, E., 73, *76*
Cohen, M., 49, 54, *76*
Colaiuta, V., 50, *75*
Cole, A., 138, *150*
Collins, A., 72, *76*
Conner, M.H., 54, *77*
Cooper, M., 35, 38
Council on Long Range Planning
in Cooperation with the
American Academy of Family

Physicians, 153, *165*
Covell, D.G., 155, 156, *165*

D

Daly, J.A. 57, *76*
de-Haas, J., 13, 23
Dialog Information Service, 167, *177*
Dick, W., 13, 22
Dixon, J., 109, *109*
Doughty, B.P., 154, *165*
Dubrovsky, V.J., 48, *76*
Dudley, R., 139, *150*
Duguid, P., 72, *76*

E

Edelwich, J., 137, 138, *150*
Edwards, M.R., 54, *76*
Edwards, S., 138, *150*
Eilola, J., 12, *23*
Emig, J., 47, *76*
Eveland, J.D., 71, *76*

F

Faigley, L., 34, *38*
Finholt, T., 49, *76*
Fish, R.S., 54, *76*
Fitzgerald, D., 158, *165*
Fox, S., 138, *150*
Freedman, S.W., 48, *77*
Friske, J., 143, *150*

G

Gagne, R., 13, 18, *22*
Gere, A.R., 49, *77*
Gillespie, T., 54, *77*, *78*
Glass, C.R., 50, 57, *77*
Gold, Y., 137, *150*
Goldmann, N., 172, 176, *177*
Griffen, G., 138, *150*
Gumpert, G., 82, *92*

H

Hall. B., 137, 138, *150*
Harfield, D.F., 57, *77*
Hawisher, G.E., 32, 34, 35, 36, *39*
Hawkins, J., 49, *78*
Haynes, R.B., 158, *165*
Hegler, K., 139, *150*
Heinssen, R.K., 50, 57, *77*
Henry, M., 137, *150*
Hillocks, G., Jr., 50, *77*
Hiltz, S. R., 11, 22, 49, *77*
Hoffman, J., 138, *150*
Howard, J.H., 54, *77*
Huff, C., 71, *77*
Hughey, J.B., 57, *77*
Hunt, R.A., 109, *110*
Huth, E.J., 154, *166*

I

Independent Study Guide, 171, *177*

J

Jacobs, S.L., 57, *77*

K

Kanter, E.J., 153, *166*
Kaplan, N., 29, *39*
Kaufer, D.S., 54, *77*
Keim, G., 54, *77*
Kiesler, S.B., 34, 36, 39, 48, 49, 71, *76*, *77*, *78*
Kling, R., 70, *77*
Knight, L.A., 50, 57, *77*
Kraut, R.E., 54, *76*
Kuh, G., 67, *75*
Kurland, D.M., 54, *76*

L

Landow, G.P., 82, *92*
Leland, M.D.P., 54, *76*
Levin, J.A., 49, *77*
Levine, J.A., 54, *76*
Levinson, P., 168, *177*
Lintner, M., 143, *150*
Lockheed, M., *76*
Lohman, M., *76*
Lortie, D., 138, *150*

M

Manning, P.R., 155, 156, *165*
Manrique, C., 126, 133, *135*
Marcus, M.L., 70, *77*
McAnge, T., 139, *150*
McEvoy, B., 139, *150*
McGuire, T.W., 34, 36, *39*
McKibbon, K.A., 158, *165*
McLuhan, M., 82, *92*
McNay, M., 138, *150*
Meeks, B.N., 176, *177*
Meinke, R., 11, 22
Merseth, K., 140, 146, *150*
Miller, M.D., 57, *76*
Mishelevich, D.J., 155, *166*
Mlynarczyk, C., 143, *150*
Montello, D., 50, *77*
Moor, P., 143, *150*
Moore-West, M., 154, *166*
Morehead, M., 139, *150*
Morris, J.H., 54, *77*
Muller, S., 154, *166*
Murray, D., 34, *39*

N

Neuwirth, C. M., 51, 54, *77*, *78*
Noble, J., 154, 156, *166*
Northup, D.E., 154, *166*

O

O'Neal, S., 138, *150*
Odell, S., 138, *150*
Ong, W., 31, *39*, 82, *92*
Oxley, B., 50, *75*

P

Palmquist, M., 54, *77*, *78*
Parker, L., 139, *151*
Parkhill, T., 110
Paulissen, M., 138, *150*
Payne, D., 49, *78*
Perez, M., 155, *166*
Peterson, P.L., 51, *76*
Phillippy, S., 137, 138, *150*
Phillips, D.P., 153, *166*
Poisson, E.H., 158, *166*

R

Raleigh, D., 123, *135*
Ramsden, M.F., 158, *166*
Rankin, J.A., 155, *166*
Reither, J.A. 110
Riel, M., 49, 76, *77*
Roberts, L., 139, *151*
Robertson, L., 89, *92*
Rodman, B., 140, *151*
Romiszowski, A., 13, 23
Rosenthal, D.S., 54, *77*
Rowe, R., 49, *77*
Rubin, A., 49, 51, *78*
Russell, L.R., 154, *165*
Ryan, N., 158, *165*

S

Sakkas, L., 133, *136*
Satyanarayanan, J., 54, *77*
Schlechty, P, 138, *151*
Schwartz, H., 87, *92*
Schwarz, N., 72, *78*
Selfe, C.L., 12, *23*, 35, 36, 38, *39*, 82, *92*
Sethna, B.N., 48, *76*
Sheingold, K., 49, *78*
Siegel, J., 34, 36, *39*
Singletary, T., 138, 145, *150*, *151*
Skipper, B., 154, *166*
Smith, F., 109, *109*
Smith, F.D., 54, *77*
Sommer, R., 50, 75, *78*
Spitzer, M., 30, 31, 32, *39*
Sproull, L., 48, 49, 71, *76*, *77*, *78*
Stratta, L., 109, *109*
Sturman, M.F., 155, *166*

T

Tastad, P.L., 153, *166*)
Taylor, R., 87, *92*
Teaf, S.R., 154, *166*

Theune, W., 139, *151*
Thomas, G.S., 172, *177*
Thomas, L., 143, *150*
Toups, D.M., 153, 154, *166*
Turner, J.H., 50, 51, *78*

U

Uman, G.C., 155, 156, *165*

V

Vance, V., 138, *151*
Varah, L., 139, *151*
Veenman, S., 137, 138, *151*
Villeme, M., 137, 138, *150*
Vipond, D., *110*
Vygotsky, L.S., 109, *109*

W

Wager, W., 13, 18, *22*
Walker, C.H., 158, *165*
Walquist, C., 125, *136*
Weed, L.L., 154, *166*
Whitney, R., 133, *136*
Wiebe, J., 143, *150*
Williams, J.C., 155, *166*
Woolf, S.H., 154, *166*
Wormugh, D.R., 57, *77*

Z

Zielstorff, R.D., 154, 155, *165*
Zinkgraf, S.A., 57, *77*
Zuboff, S.. 118, *121*

Subject Index

B

Bitnet, 10, 83, 123, 125, 180, 181-182, 185
Boise State University, 9, 140-141
Bulletin-Board System (BBS), 8, 9, 48, 84, 87, 89, 104, 108, 190

C

Carnegie Mellon University, 52
Collaborative interaction, 5, 6, 8, 27, 33, 48-49, 53-54, 71, 90, 82, 93-109
Collaborative Writing Software
  Aspects, 39-40, 4
  Asynchronous communication, 5, 10, 48-49, 88, 112, 156, 185
  Classwriter, 40
  Comments, 54, 55, 56, 59, 67,
  Conference Writer, 40
  Daedalus, 40, 42, 87
  Forum, 41
  ICLAS, 96, 97, 102
  Interchange, 87, 88
  NEOS, 8-9, 111-121
  Open Forum, 41
  Real-Time Writer, 41
  Seen, 85, 86
  Talk, 55, 56, 59
  Team Focus, 41-42
Computer anxiety, 16, 21, 68, 70, 150, 158
Computer Conferencing, 3-4, 7, 44, 45, 82, 83, 88-89, 90
Computer Conferencing Systems
  PARTICIPATE, 170
  Vax Notes, 84, 133
Computer-Assisted Instruction (CAI), 3-4, 82, 85-90, 137
Computer-Mediated Communications
  assessment, 56-58, 127-133, 145
  computer readiness, 16-17, 143
  definition, 1, 12
  flaming, 35, 36, 37
  lurking , 22, 89
  online persona(e), 36-37
  procedural skills, 19
  shyness, 19
  social aspects, 5, 31, 48, 50-51, 70, 108, 112, 116, 129, 144, 169

synchronous communication, 46, 48-49
technical Support, 15, 134, 169, 171, 184

D

Dialog, 94, 97, 168, 170, 171, 173, 185
Discussion groups, 28-29, 133, 187-188
Reflection, 21
Distance Learning, 4, 45, 79, 85, 87, 91

E

East Carolina University School of Medicine, 9, 158, 161, 163-165
Electronic Mail (E-Mail, email), 8, 9, 19-20, 48, 54, 104, 125-127, 142, 154, 156, 185-186
Electronic Networks for Interaction (ENFI), 7, 25-46

F

Fax, 12, 84
FidoNet, 10, 182
File Transfer Protocol (FTP), 10, 182-184, 188

H

Human Interaction
many-to-many, 49, 72, 137-150
student-to-student, 97
Hypercontext, 115
Hypertext, 82

I

Indiana University-Purdue University at Indianapolis, 80, 84
Informatics, 3-4, 154
Information Retrieval Systems, 10
Inkshed, 95, 99
Instructional Design and Development
criteria for success, 7, 12, 18
formative evaluation, 20-22
instructional analysis, 14-15, 58-70
instructional design, 3, 4, 11-22, 168, 172-176
instructional goals, 13-14, 117
instructional methods, 3, 52
instructional resources, 15
instructional strategy, 18-20, 134-135
learner characteristics, 22, 34, 88
performance objectives, 17-18
summative evaluation, 21, 102

L

Learning styles, 22
Libraries, 95, 133, 172, 173
Listserv, 10, 83, 84, 88, 89, 133, 187-188, 189
Literature
18th Century, 8, 93-110
teaching, 79-92, 93-110

M

MIT, 8, 9, 111-112, 118, 120
Modem, 10, 156, 169, 179, 185
Multicultural, 3, 5-6

N

Network and Infomation Systems
Campuswide Information Systems (CWIS), 3, 54
Local-Area Network (LAN), 28, 82, 87, 96, 156, 180
Wide-Area Information System (WAIS), 3
Wide-Area Network (WAN), 3, 10, 82, 83, 89, 90, 180
Networking, 28, 30-31, 52-53, 54-56, 59-60, 64, 71, 111, 112, 113, 137-150, 154, 179-190
New School for Social Research, 10, 168

Nontraditional student, 8, 14, 16-17, 79-92, 169

O

Online Database, 9, 10, 48, 114, 119, 154, 155-156, 167-168, 171, 173-175
Online Public Access Catalog (OPAC), 3

P

Persons with disabilities, 5, 176

S

Simulations, 4, 37
St. Thomas University, 94, 96

T

Telecommunications, 15, 16, 139, 141, 143, 145
Television, 85, 91
Telnet, 10, 184-185

U

University of Maine, 15
University of Wisconsin-La Crosse, 9, 23
Usenet News, 10, 188-189

V

VAX, 126, 131, 184
Virginia Polytechnic Institute & State University, 139
Virtual Classroom, 111-113, 119, 121, 169, 170

W

Writing, 4, 25-46, 47-75, 107-108
  annotation, 114
  audience, 5, 27, 31-32, 71, 94
  peer review, 81, 118, 119-120
  practice, 32, 128, 170
  teachers of writing, 26-28, 29-30, 48
  teaching writing, 27, 47-48, 117-118
  writing anxiety, 5, 50, 58, 67-68, 69, 72